Comics and the City

Comics and the City

Urban Space in Print, Picture and Sequence

Edited by
JÖRN AHRENS AND ARNO METELING

continuum

2010

The Continuum International Publishing Group Inc
80 Maiden Lane, New York, NY 10038

The Continuum International Publishing Group Ltd
The Tower Building, 11 York Road, London SE1 7NX

www.continuumbooks.com

Copyright © 2010 by Jörn Ahrens, Arno Meteling, and contributors

ISBN: HB: 978-0-8264-0389-6
          PB: 978-0-8264-4019-8

Library of Congress Cataloging-in-Publication Data
A catalog record for this book is available from the Library of Congress.

Typeset by Pindar NZ, Auckland, New Zealand
Printed in the United States of America

Contents

IV Locations of Crime

V The City-Comic as a Mode of Reflection

Notes on the Contributors

Jörn Ahrens is Stand-In Professor in Cultural Sociology at the University of Giessen. His research focuses on cultural theory, popular media, questions of the self, violence and myth. His publications include "How to Save the Unsaved World? Visiting the Self in *12 Monkeys, Terminator 2, & The Matrix*" in A. Holba and K. Hart (eds.), *Media and the Apocalypse* (2009); and "Der Mensch als Beute. Narrationen anthropologischer Angst im Science Fiction-Film" in *Zeitschrift für Kultur- und Medienforschung* (2009).

Jason Bainbridge is Senior Lecturer in Media, Journalism and Communications at Swinburne University, Melbourne, Australia. He has published widely on a range of subjects including superheroes, media representations of law and justice, chequebook journalism, marketing newsreaders and merchandising. He is co-author of *Media and Journalism: New Approaches to Theory and Practice* (2008) and his favorite comic book of all time remains *The Micronauts*.

Jens Balzer lives in Berlin and works as cultural editor for *Berliner Zeitung*. In 1990, he co-founded the comics research centre Arbeitsstelle für Graphische Literatur (ArGL) at the University of Hamburg. He has written numerous essays on the aesthetics and history of comics and authored two comics: *Salut, Deleuze* and *Neue Abenteuer des unglaublichen Orpheus* (1998 and 2001 respectively, both with M. tom Dieck). He is the German translator of Art Spiegelman and Scott McCloud. His most recent book is *Outcault. Die Erfindung des Comic* (2009, with Lambert Wiesing).

Thomas Becker is a scholar at the "Aesthetic Experience with Regard to the Delimitation Process of the Arts" collaborative research centre at the Freie Universität, Berlin. His current research project looks at the medium of comics on its journey towards legitimate art. Recent publications include *Mann und Frau, Schwarz und Weiß: Zur wissenschaftlichen Konstruktion von Geschlecht und Rasse* (2005) and "Matrix versus the Ghost in the Shell" in *Journal Ethnologie* (2007).

Michael Cuntz works as a researcher and lecturer at the Internationales Kolleg für Kulturtechnik und Medienforschung (IKKM) at the Bauhaus-Universität Weimar. His current fields of research are: romance literature (mainly nineteenth to twenty-first century prose), visual narratives, French theories of culture and technology, agency and its distribution, and relations between humans and things. A recent publication is *Unmenge — Wie verteilt sich Handlungsmacht?* (2008, co-editor with I. Becker and A. Kusser).

Stefanie Diekmann is Visiting Associate Professor in Theater Studies at the Freie Universität, Berlin. She publishes on film, photography, theater and comics. Her fields of research include intermediality, media theory, image and text, and theory of space. She is the author of *Mythologien der Fotografie* (2003); guest editor of two issues of *Fotogeschichte* (2006 and 2007); and co-editor of *Szenarien des Comic* (2005), *Latenz* (2007) and *Poetik der Pose* (forthcoming).

Anthony Enns is Assistant Professor of Contemporary Culture in the Department of English at Dalhousie University in Halifax, Nova Scotia. His work on popular culture has appeared in such journals as *Screen*, the *Journal of Popular Film and Television*, *Popular Culture Review*, *Studies in Popular Culture*, the *Quarterly Review of Film and Video*, and *Science Fiction Studies*.

Ole Frahm is a founding member of the ArGL at the University of Hamburg. He writes about the theory, history and aesthetics of comics. His Ph.D. was published in 2006 as *Genealogie des Holocaust. Art Spiegelmans MAUS — A Survivor's Tale*. He is currently working on a book about the aesthetics of comics.

Henry Jenkins is Provost's Professor of Communication, Journalism, and Cinematic Arts University of Southern California. His publications include *Convergence Culture: Where Old and New Media Collide* (2006) and *Fans, Bloggers and Gamers: Exploring Participatory Culture* (2006). He writes regularly about the media and cultural change on his blog (http://www.henryjenkins.org) and is one of the principal investigators for Education Arcade, for the Center for Future Civic Media, for GAMBIT and for Project NML.

Anthony Lioi is Assistant Professor of Liberal Arts and English at the Juilliard School in New York City. He is an ecocritic who specializes in American literature and popular culture. His work has appeared in *Feminist Studies, Crosscurrents,* and *Interdisciplinary Studies in Literature and Environment.* He maintains a blog (http://planetaryblog.wordpress.com) which is devoted to issues of Green pedagogy.

Arno Meteling teaches literature at the Westfalian Wilhelms-University Münster. His research focuses on Romantic and modern literature, film history, media theory, and the fantastic. His publications include "Genius loci: On Memory, Media, and the Neo-Gothic in Georg Klein and Elfriede Jelinek" in E. Peeren and M. del Pílar Blanco (eds.), *Popular Spirits* (2009); *Die Unsichtbarkeit des Politischen: Theorie und Geschichte medialer Latenz* (2009, co-author); *The Parallax View: Zur Mediologie der Verschwörung* (2009, co-editor); *Monster: Zu Körperlichkeit und Medialität im modernen Horrorfilm* (2006); and *Kursbuch Kulturwissenschaft* (2000, co-editor).

Andreas Platthaus is the cultural editor for *Frankfurter Allgemeine Zeitung* and is responsible for the supplement "Bilder und Zeiten." Since 1983 he has been a member of the "German Organization of Non-Commercial Devotees of Unsophisticated Donaldism" (D.O.N.A.L.D.) and has held the position of Honorary President since 1995. In 2007 he was made a Honorary Member of D.O.N.A.L.D. His most recent book about comics is *Die 101 wichtigsten Fragen: Comics und Manga* (2008).

Björn Quiring teaches literature at the European University Viadrina in Frankfurt (Oder). His publications include "A Consuming Dish" in *Law & Literature* (2005) and *Shakespeares Fluch* (2009). His research focuses on the close but problematic relationship between law and literature.

Greg M. Smith is a professor in the Moving Image Studies program of the Department of Communication at Georgia State University. His books include *Beautiful TV: The Art and Argument of Ally McBeal* (2007); *Film Structure and the Emotion System* (2007); and *Passionate Views: Film, Cognition, and Emotion* (1999).

André Suhr is editor and team manager of the Department of Elementary Science in Primary School at Cornelsen Publishers, Berlin. His publications include *Kursbuch Kulturwissenschaft* (2000, co-editor); "Consumer Communications nach dem Ende der Zielgruppen" in *PR Magazin* (2000, with T. Düllo and O. Schieleit); and "'Would the Real Slim Shady Please Stand Up?' — Eminem und der Aufstand des White Trash" in *F.LM — Texte zum Film* (2002, with A. Meteling).

William Uricchio is Professor and Director of Comparative Media Studies at MIT and Professor of Comparative Media History at Utrecht University. He co-edited *The Many Lives of the Batman: Critical Approaches to a Superhero and his Media* (1991) and has since been exploring the alternate worlds of history and computer games. His latest book is *We Europeans? Media, Representations, Identity* (2008).

Introduction

JÖRN AHRENS AND ARNO METELING

I N RECENT YEARS COMICS HAVE received broader acknowledgment within
the context of modern culture as well as in academic debate. This
tendency has successively been underpinned by the global reception of singular achievements in comics, for example, the American
comic books *Maus — A Survivor's Tale* by Art Spiegelman, *The Dark
Knight Returns* by Frank Miller, or *Watchmen* by Alan Moore and Dave
Gibbons, all published in 1986, "our favorite year" (Jones and Jacobs
1997: 296–311).[1] But even before, one could observe an adult approach
to comics, a discourse slowly leaving the narrow confinements of comic
book culture. In Europe, especially in Franco-Belgian comics culture,
but also in Italy, with artists like Moebius, Jacques Tardi, Hugo Pratt, and
Enki Bilal, and in the U.S.A., this discourse usually conferred on certain
comic artists the status of auteur. These artists represented art and high
culture, or at least economic and political "independence," or sub- or
counter-culture (e.g. Robert Crumb or the Hernandez Brothers). Today,
the cultural and academic reception of comics has expanded and is no
longer limited to its avant-garde products. Art history, literary criticism
and cultural studies are interested in comic books as an important part
of a global popular culture, and these disciplines analyze the structure,
aesthetics and discourses of comics as well as the practices of fan culture
and the transmedial effects comic books initiate.

I

Without any doubt, comic books, their characters, and their formats are
by now deeply engraved in America's, Europe's, and Japan's cultural
memory and exert their influence on cultural communication and
dynamics. Apart from the mythical heroes of ancient Greece and Rome

1

and national popular heroes, characters like Mickey Mouse, Donald Duck, Superman, or Batman can be considered to be the most popular and most iconic fictional characters in the Western hemisphere, at least. This is supported by the fact that at the present time Hollywood's blockbuster and the independent cinema have been revived by topics and aesthetics that pertain specifically to comics. This is not only true for animated pictures, but also for real-life movies, like the superhero movies since the 1990s (*Blade 1–3, Spawn, X-Men 1–3, Spider-Man 1–3, The Hulk, The Incredible Hulk, Daredevil, Iron Man, Batman Begins, Superman Returns, The Dark Knight,* or *Watchmen*) and more or less independent comic book movies like *Road to Perdition, Constantine, Ghost World, American Splendor, From Hell, A History of Violence, Hellboy 1+2, V for Vendetta, Sin City, 300* or *Wanted.* Not only do the numerous screen adaptations of comic books emphasize the cultural influence comics have, but the specific aesthetics and narrative style of comics modify the global universe of signs.

So, the medium "comics" is not only reflected in the plethora of film adaptations or in the ever growing global fan culture, but also in the ubiquitous use of comic contents, icons and aesthetics in all aspects of modern life. Comics can be understood as one of the decisive pictorial elements of popular culture since the second half of the twentieth century. The contribution of the comic book to a cultural self-understanding of modern mass culture, its mythologies, and its perceptions of the self, thereby becomes more and more evident. Although there is a significant output of academic books on comics (see "Further Reading" below), there is still no such thing as an academic discipline called "comic book studies" within the framework of graphic art, literary, cultural, or media studies. This lack is highly conspicuous because the border between high culture and popular culture was breached long ago and other modern arts and media, such as photography, motion pictures, television series or video games are widely accepted by now and have become the subject of academic research. Yet comic books, which are already more than 100 years old, still remain only of marginal interest to the academic world. For this reason, anyone opting for the serious treatment of comics is forced to legitimate himself. This may be explained by the still-existing condescending judgment of the artistic qualities of comics or their status as ubiquitous mass media. Above all, the still prevalent academic disregard of comics seems to be motivated by two main factors: First, there is a general ignorance of the variety of the topics and subjects comic books offer, which coincides with the belief that comics are the province of children and semi-alphabetized adults. The second factor can be traced back to the specific nature of this medium, for comics are a unique hybrid media that combine words and pictures in a spatial sequence.

This combination of traditionally quite differently coded media means that, on the surface, comics appear to be simple and easily comprehensible. The merging of pictures, words and sequences evidently symbolizes an immediate nature. Therefore, comic book techniques are used for instructions, danger signs, or advertising graphics. But if a critic or researcher wants to have a closer look at comics and analyze them, as well as the interactions and mechanisms of this combination of codes, he runs into difficulties because he is in need of a comprehensive descriptive and analytical apparatus. Such an apparatus would have to contain concepts and information relating to the study of literature and of graphic art. So, on closer inspection, comics are confusing to readers of linear texts as well as to contemplative viewers of paintings and photos.

From a historical and formal point of view, the comic book perspectives used in the pictures or frames ("panels") can be described by camera positions ("zoom," "sequence shot," "pan shot," "tilt shot," or "jump cut") used in film-making. But comics remain — in stark contrast to film — a purely spatial medium. Its elements, such as panels, picture strips or pages are static. So, whereas the *mise-en-scène* can be analyzed as an arrangement of narrative space and layout of the comic book page, editing (*montage*), which marks the transition from one scene to the next and therefore indicates a lapse of time, is confined to film-making and has only a metaphorical function for the comic book. In this connection, the temporally and spatially indeterminate white borders (the "gutters") between the pictures are of special interest because they have been breached — abundantly in recent comics but even in very early comics, for example, those by Winsor McCay. To sum up: Comics are definitely part of the "Gutenberg galaxy of books" (see McLuhan 2002). The reader still has to leaf through the medium and read it, while her gaze alternates constantly between fast cursory reading and stataric viewing of pictures.

II

From an historical point of view and against the backdrop of the modern age, comics are inseparably tied to the notion of the "city." The history of comics begins — not taking into consideration the long history of combining pictures and words since Ancient times and the tradition of illustration, caricature, and picture stories in the eighteenth and nineteenth century (William Hogarth, Wilhelm Busch, Rodolphe Töpffer) — with the emergence of comic strips in American newspapers around 1900. The first contributions of cartoonists appeared in magazines such as *Puck* (1877), *Judge* (1881), or *Life* (1883), but the rivalry between the New York newspapers (or rather their publishers), between Adolph Ochs's *New York Times* (1851), Joseph Pulitzer's *New York World* (1860), and William Randolph Hearst's *New York Journal* (1895), all of which put great emphasis on illustrations and an illustrated Sunday supplement, caused a dramatic development in the importance of comic strips. On February 17, 1895, a crucial event in the history of the comic strip took place in the *New York World*: The renowned artist Richard Felton Outcault introduced the character "The Yellow Kid" in his comic strip *Hogan's Alley*. From then on, this strip, which features naturalist and partly satirical street scenes as well as background descriptions as social commentary of New York City street life, developed into one of the crucial selling points for the newspaper. Shortly afterwards, star artist Outcault switched employers, taking with him his "Buster Brown" character, the American model for all rascal comics, and started working for Hearst's newspaper the *New York Herald* (1835). Other successful comic strips that appeared in newspapers are Rudolph Dirk's *The Katzenjammer Kids* (1897), *The Captain and the Kids* (formerly *Hanz and Fritz*) (1918), and George Herriman's *Krazy Kat* (1913). Common to all these comic strips is that the characters are influenced by the incredible speed of life in the New York City metropolis and that speed determines the rhythm of the city's newspapers and comic strips. As the expansion of comic strips led to them taking up whole pages, the space reserved for the city in the comics also expanded. Winsor McCay, for example, used the whole page as the basis for his comic strip *Little Nemo in Slumberland* (1906) in order to create fantastic worlds and real cities.

Eventually, comics outgrew the newspaper world. When the new format of the comic book was established as an independent publication, new characters filled the new comic book cities with life, such as Will Eisner's *The Spirit* (1940), which started out as a comic strip in newspapers; Superman, who inhabits Metropolis (1938), and Batman, who fights crime first in Manhattan (1939) and, from 1941 on, in Gotham City. Various distinctive comic book series at the end of the 1930s thus explored the city as living space and origin of modern myths. In particular, the characters of the superhero comics and the detective comics delved deep into the aesthetic, atmospheric, and scenaristic possibilities of the city. From then on, the city acted even more as the foremost setting for comics in all genres and stylistic variants. The city functioned as an important plot element, even an atmospheric, and symbolic protagonist, and suddenly became the focus of attention in many genres.

III

There is undoubtedly a link between the medium of comics and the big city as a modern living space. This emphasizes the need to investigate how specifically urban topoi, self-portrayals, forms of cultural memorizing, and variant readings of the city (strolling, advertising, architecture, detective stories, mass phenomena, street life, etc.) are on the one hand being incorporated in comic books, and the need to investigate if comics have special competences for capturing urban space and city life and representing it aesthetically because of their hybrid nature consisting of words, pictures, and sequences on the other. Does the spatial inertia of the sequences in contrast to film, video, or television result in retardation in order to ease the saturation that has been attributed to the big city since 1900?

Since the 1930s the authors and artists of comic books have continued to incorporate urban space into their narratives again and again. In doing so, they have referenced the whole repository of iconography from other media and occasionally exceeded and expanded on that cultural history. In the U.S. the works of Frank Miller (*Daredevil, Ronin, The Dark Knight Returns, Sin City*), Alan Moore (*V for Vendetta, Watchmen, From Hell*), Warren Ellis (*Transmetropolitan*) and Dean Motter (*Mister X, Terminal City, Electropolis*) exert their influence on cinematic settings (*Blade Runner, Batman, Batman Returns, The Fifth Element, The Matrix, Sin City*). An analogous interaction between comics and cultural history can be found in the influential science fiction and fantasy comics in France and Belgium, for example, in the works of Moebius (*La cinquième essence/The Incal, Le garage hermétique*), Enki Bilal (*Nikopol*), Marc-Antoine

Mathieu (*Acquefacques*), Pierre Christin and Jean-Claude Mézières (*Valérian, agent spatio-temporel*), and François Schuiten and Benoît Peeters (*Les Cités Obscures*). In particular, the earlier Franco-Belgian École Marcinelle opened up the urban space for the so-called "semi-funnies" (André Franquin, Maurice Tillieux). Yet Japanese manga cultivated such approaches as well — still most famously in the work of Katsuhiro Otomo (*Akira, Domo*) but also in works by Jiro Taniguchi or in science fiction manga by Masamume Shirow (*Ghost in the Shell, Appleseed*).

IV

Comics employ a certain self-reflexivity. As a genuine medium of urban modernity they do not only mirror different aspects of modern life, but also adopt its formal aesthetics and cultural prerequisites. By now, every modern metropolis in the world has been made the subject of comics: Berlin, Paris, London, Tokyo and, time and again, New York City. At the same time, many fictional cities from comics have found their way into the global cultural memory: Superman's Metropolis, Batman's Gotham City, the New York City of Spider-Man, Daredevil, the Avengers or the Fantastic Four, Tokyo and the post-nuclear Neo-Tokyo of manga, or even the Duckburg of Mickey Mouse and Donald Duck. This demonstrates how important comics are to modern culture since they enduringly form people's perceptions of cultural, social, and political patterns and strongly influence what Roland Barthes has called "mythologies" (of the ordinary) (see Barthes 1972). The main premise of this book is the strong interaction between comics and the urban space as the center of modern culture and daily life in the twentieth century. The competence of comics in capturing urban space and city life can be found within the cityscape itself, for example, as combinations of words and images in the form of signage and graffiti, which are deeply influenced by the aesthetics of comics. Providing a broad range of subjects, perspectives, and interests within its focus on comics and the city, this book deals with the relationships between comic books, mass media, modern culture, and urbanity. It addresses a range of international key comic authors and works, such as Richard Felton Outcault, Winsor McCay, Walt Disney and Carl Barks, Jacques Tardi, Enki Bilal, Marc-Antoine Mathieu, François Schuiten and Benoît Peeters, Will Eisner, Alan Moore, Dean Motter, Jason Lutes, as well as crime and superhero comics.

V

The first section, "History, Comics, and the City," examines the historical background of the fundamental connection between the rise of comics and urbanity. The origins of this new kind of media are to be found in the emergence of mass societies and mass cultures at the turn of the twentieth century, especially in the context of modern newspapers. One important aspect of this relationship is the meaning of space in regard to political sovereignty and a "structuring gaze." This structuring gaze of comics implements a topographical reading of the cityscape, which is led by the point of view in frames, panels and sequences. The urban landscape is similarly structured by panel-like blocks and grids. For the purpose of individual adaptation the modern city demands certain capacities to direct and organize the gaze as modernity's central sense of perception. Also, the depiction of such a gaze always includes political implications, for example, in the division of the gaze between a pedestrian watching the sky and a superhero looking down on the city while in flight or while standing on a skyscraper. Jens Balzer's essay on the gaze and the invention of comics in New York City gives a possible answer to the question: What is it that defines the comic? By examining this question the answer comes as a tautology: The distinction between comics and pre-modern picture stories is the very modernity of comics, that is, the medium's urbanity. Comics do not demand the contemplative as well as the fixed gaze of the classic central perspective. Instead, they demand the loose and moving gaze of the urban *flâneur*. They transport the text into the vertical and therefore decentralize the image. Just how comics achieve this and what this process means are explained by Balzer using the example of Richard Felton Outcault's Yellow Kid character who first appeared 1895 in the *New York World* newspaper. Its decentralization and abstraction demonstrates the image of perception of an integral restlessness that is characteristic of the structural gaze in the metropolis of modernity.

Ole Frahm's essay on the urbanity of early comic strips discusses the "will" to see the city from a higher point, taking a panoptic and projective view that became popular in the late eighteenth century and is still popular today. This is the effect of the desire not to get in touch with the difficulties and contradictions of city life in the streets and thus to ignore the complex urbanity of the city. In contrast to this "will," the French theorist Michel de Certeau proposes that the practice of walking through the city provides a different and productive view that "reads" and "writes" the city with all of its contradictions. Frahm's essay proposes that early Sunday pages reflect these two modes of viewing and constellate these different desires in different ways. It analyzes comic book-pages by Richard Felton Outcault, Winsor McKay, and George Herriman in regard to this concept, using the central metaphor of the "window" for the comic book-panel.

Following Jared Gardner's claim that graphic narratives embody Walter Benjamin's concept of the archive as an assemblage of modern mass media that breaks down the barriers between word and image, Anthony Enns's essay on Jason Lutes' comic book series *Berlin* (1996) explores the ways in which these assemblages are also indelibly linked to the experience of the metropolis. Benjamin employed the city as an allegory for modernity and in doing so he was largely based on Charles Baudelaire's experience of nineteenth century Paris and his claim that "memories are as heavy as stone." Enns's essay explores the connections between modern media, historical memory, and the experience of the metropolis through a close reading of *Berlin: City of Stones*, the first part of an epic trilogy that traces the end of Germany's Weimar Republic from 1929 to 1933 by referring to contemporary photographs, paintings, and drawings from the period. By drawing on this repository of cultural history and iconography, Lutes constructs an intermedial text that captures both the stories and images associated with the city.

VI

The second section, "Retrofuturistic and Nostalgic Cities," examines the phenomenon of "nostalgia mode" (see Jameson 1991), which can be observed in the U.S.A. as well as in Europe. "Nostalgia" means a certain way in depicting history as being better than it really was. It is only interested in transfiguring the past into some perfect and idyllic epoch, a lost Golden Age that can never be attained again. "Retrofuturism" is a very specific variety of "nostalgia mode." Retrofuturistic literature, movies or comics create imaginations of the future that refer to futuristic designs from the past, for example, utopian and science fiction designs in the 1950s and 1960s (the "ray gun gothic" in William Gibson's words), the World Fair aesthetics of the 1930s, or the *belle époque* around 1900. In this way, the comic comes across as an interesting mode of reflection about the meaning of history and the contemporary as well as the role of the city as a life-world that takes up particular modern phantasmagorias of the future. Henry Jenkins's essay deals with retrofuturism in the comics of Dean Motter. It is about the retrofuturistic mobilization of old icons for new purposes. Comics and other forms of popular media have circled back to the pulp magazine imagery of early science fiction in search of striking new ways to represent the directions our society is taking. In some cases, they do so to regain some of the giddy excitement about the world of tomorrow which shaped the magazines of Hugo Gernsback, publisher of the science fiction magazine *Amazing Stories* (1926); the comics of Alex Raymond (*Flash Gordon*); or the rhetoric of the 1939 World's Fair. In other cases, retrofuturists do so to critique the outmoded ideologies that gave shape to those earlier utopian yearnings. Jenkins's essay focuses on some strategies for mobilizing past conceptions of the future, especially as seen in the comics *Mister X* (1983), *Terminal City* (1996), and *Electropolis* (2001) by comic writer and artist Dean Motter.

Stefanie Diekmann then focuses on François Schuiten and Benoît Peeters's graphic novels about the *Cities of the Fantastic* (*Les Cités Obscures*) (1983), a group of imaginary city-states located in a parallel universe. As an investigation of urban structures, the series constitutes a fascinating example of mock historiography, drawing on the history of art and architecture on the one hand and nineteenth century utopian designs on the other. Most noticeable about the *Cities* is the emphasis on their political, cultural, and aesthetic particularities that make them appear as models of the "Old World," or rather of Old-Worldliness. As a matter of fact, the series deals as much with the history of urban development as it mocks certain notions of urbanity and cultural diversity.

Michael Cuntz's take on the representations of Paris in Jacques Tardi's comic book writing deals with the French capital as the uncontested center of Tardi's universe, whether in his many adaptations and "illustrations" of French writers (Malet, Céline, Manchette, Vautrin, Siniac) or in his "own" invention, the *Adèle Blanc-Sec* series (1972). Cuntz's essay deals with the question of whether Paris remains the same in all comic books or whether there are significant differences, for example, the art nouveau and World Expo capital of Adèle Blanc-Sec and the rather closed universe of Nestor Burma's post-war investigations, which cannot be reduced to a mere realistic reconstruction of the settings for different historical moments. Rather than discussing the authenticity and historical accuracy of Tardi's representations of Paris, the text explores their common symbolic features, for example, Paris as a space of murder mysteries and their investigation. The differences between the versions of Paris in Tardi's comic books are not only a matter of semantics: While most comic readers will not fail to recognize Tardi's personal style in all of his works, the way in which the city itself, its buildings, monuments, streets, bistros, or apartments are drawn varies from one series to another. So, it can be argued that Tardi uses these different views on/of Paris to "imitate" or rather to translate the specific style of each adapted writer into his own his technique.

VII

The third section, "Superhero Cities," discusses the comic-based invention of superhero cities as a development particular to the U.S. In no other media or culture has a character like the superhero been invented, and he is always related to a city, either living in a real city (mostly New York City) or protecting a fictional one. William Uricchio's essay is about story, ideology and performance in Batman's Gotham City. As the super villain, the Riddler, puts it, "When is a man a city?" "When it's Batman or when it's Gotham." Batman and Gotham are as essential as the Batman origin story, which sustains the logic behind the endless iterations of the Batman-narrative with the origin story — set on the streets of Gotham — functioning as a narrative generator. Gotham City is at once utopian and dystopian, with a decided leaning towards the latter. Like the acute contrasts of Batman's or his various nemeses' character construction, the source of dramatic tension is at once visible and generative. Yet, the city represented remains ideologically skewed, locked forever by the origin story into a place of property crime, where the extraordinarily wealthy Bruce Wayne obsessively disguises himself as Batman to combat the most trivial of transgressions.

Arno Meteling's essay deals with the change in politics and superheroics between the comic book series *Starman* and *Ex Machina*. It is about two different depictions of superhero cities, before and after September 11, 2001: the fictional "Opal City" of the DC Universe in James Robinson and Tony Harris's *Starman* (1994), and the semi-fictional "New York City" in Brian K. Vaughan and Tony Harris's *Ex Machina* (2004). *Starman* discusses subjects like mythology, history, family, lineages, dynasties, and the fantastic genealogies of the DC Comics superheroes and their designated cities. In contrast to its celebration of the halcyon days of Golden Age heroes (its "nostalgia mode"), ten years later *Ex Machina* superficially shows the more or less mundane political problems of its protagonist, Mitchell Hundred, the mayor of New York City and former superhero the Great Machine. But *Ex Machina* combines superhero and mystery issues with political ones in a not-so-post-superhero city. Not only does it introduce a kind of "reality principle" (Sigmund Freud) to the superhero genre, but also questions the need for a sovereign political power in the city supported by super powers.

In his essay on Alan Moore's *Promethea,* Anthony Lioi discusses the idea of an urban ecotopia, a contradiction in terms to the mainstream of American literature and environmentalism. Drawing on the novel that founded the term — Ernest Callenbach's *Ecotopia* (1975), Lioi deals with the idea of a green city in the climax of *Promethea,* a comic book series about a heroine who is Story Incarnate and which figures Manhattan as Babylon and New Jerusalem as "the heavenly, radiant city." The protagonist Promethea is also a revision of Wonder Woman and is portrayed as a figure of Hellenistic wisdom. Her most important task is to end the world, not through physical destruction but as the vehicle of gnostic enlightenment. This enlightenment radiates from New York City itself, and engulfs the whole world in a realization that the earth is holy, a manifestation of the breath of God. The result of the enlightenment is represented visually as a city supersaturated with color, contrasting vividly with earlier images of New York from the dystopian film noir tradition or superhero comics such as *Spider-Man* or *The Fantastic Four.*

Jason Bainbridge's essay on Spider-Man and the Marvel Universe stresses the importance of New York City for comics in general and especially for superhero comics, as New York City was not only the birthplace for the comic strip in the newspapers, but also for important Marvel comics writers and artists like Stan Lee and Jack Kirby. In comics, New York City always had been a more or less generic city, adaptable to the demands of the narrative — until Marvel Comics located its superheroes, for example, the Fantastic Four, the Avengers, and Spider-Man, in this city. They are juxtaposed against the realistic and familiar backdrop of the city in order to create a cohesive Marvel Universe, consisting of extraordinary figures in front of an ordinary world. While superheroes in DC Comics, like Superman or Batman, function as archetypes in stylized and exaggerated fictitious cities, the Marvel style is about realistic compositions, locating the heroes in recognizable places in New York City, for example, with the Fantastic Four basing themselves in the Baxter Building, a Manhattan office building, Dr. Strange living in

Greenwich Village, and the Avengers living in a mansion on the Upper East Side. The Marvel Universe is predicated on the connectivity and social networks of both its titles and its individuals, and its main novelty can be called "realism." So, just as New York City makes Marvel Comics legible, Marvel Comics similarly makes New York City legible to the comic-reading community.

VIII

The fourth section, "Locations of Crime," focuses on the city as a place of crime and drama. In this case, the city can truly be called an international setting because of its stress on storytelling and the aesthetics of modernity. The imagination of crime condenses phantasms of the modern self that links to individual and socio-cultural (metaphorical and structural) yearnings, anxieties, and limitations. In Franco-Belgian comics this genre quickly developed into one of the core subjects of comic narrations. As such it continually accompanies and comments on processes of transformation within the urban environment. There is a strong tradition of detective and crime narratives (deriving from pulp literature) in comic strips too, with Chester Gould's *Dick Tracy* (1931) and *The Spirit* (1940) being the most popular ones. In his essay on Will Eisner, Greg M. Smith analyzes another aspect of *The Spirit*, namely Eisner as a "vaudevillian of the cityscape." In *The Spirit* Eisner uses urban architecture in two ways: as a naturalistic background for staging conflicts between brave heroes and menacing villains, and as a foregrounded graphic element to be textualized into highly stylized "opening credit" frames. Smith's essay examines how the cities in Eisner's comics merge both of these techniques to create cities that are themselves menacing to his immigrant characters, actively framing and constricting their struggles for immigrant assimilation and ethnic identity.

Björn Quiring's essay on urban spaces in Alan Moore's comic book *From Hell* (1991) discusses the city as a projected image of utopian order — a New Jerusalem to be attained — but also as an indomitable chaos, a repository of fragmented histories, which, in their synchronicity, produce an overload of sense and sense perception. Founded on both divine law and human violence, urban space appears both as a wilderness of incompatible, ambiguous signs and as the promise of their ordering. The comic, as an inherently modern and urban medium, situates itself within that very tension, as a juxtaposition of incompatible, mass-produced signs in which entangled images and texts both disturb and complement each other. Moore's scenarios, for example, the Jack the Ripper narrative in *From Hell*, based on Stephen Knight's famous conspiracy theory (*Jack the Ripper: The Final Solution*, 1976) and referring to the ancient and medieval mind-mapping technique of the "theater of memory," shows conspiracies that strive for a utopian synthesis of order and chaos. However, the conspiracies always fail because the new, unified sense dissociates as soon as it is produced and the need for closure remains frustrated and the eternal city elusive. Only in its representation through art, and especially through the comic form, which makes its underlying coherence as well as its insurmountable heterogeneity palpable, urbanity really seems to come into its own. Hence, Moore's comics increasingly become allegories of their own production, the narrative process drawing the city into itself.

Jörn Ahrens reads Brian Azzarello and Eduardo Risso's comic book series *100 Bullets* (1999) as a reflection on the clichés of mass culture. Closely tied to the classic narrative of the crime story, *100 Bullets*, however, gives a very new conception of the genre when it plays both aesthetically and formally with the genre's characteristics. With few exceptions, *100 Bullets* celebrates the American cityscape as the classic environment for narratives of brutality and crime. It obviously holds many references to film noir and the hardboiled detective novel and also fosters a documentary-like style by depicting a panorama of contemporary U.S.A., from the life-worlds of Hispanic immigrants up to those of millionaires. But then again, the series abstracts from these models and radicalizes and threatens its subject with irony when waving a net of meaning and symbolization in which all appearing characters are interlinked, and all commentaries and gestures are meaningful. In this way *100 Bullets* presents a fractionalized narrative that mimics the fractionalized modern cityscape, an urban landscape of postmodernity. The cities in this comic constantly seem to withdraw from the foreground, since the dense atmosphere that the city creates does not seem to be real — revealing a tendency towards alienation, which is quite en vogue in numerous U.S. crime comics today.

IX

The fifth and final section, "The City-Comic as a Mode of Reflection," examines the reflective and self-reflective aspects of comics and the modern city. It emphasizes the abilities of the medium as well as the city-scape to reflect on the conditions of their historical origin in the mass culture of urban modernity; their cultural and medial determinations; and their spatial particularities in style, content and representation. As comics and the cityscape are very much alike in terms of their semiotics and their hybrid mixing of words and pictures, it is not only historically evident that one should be regarded as part of the other, but structurally and aesthetically evident as well. André Suhr's essay reads Marc-Antoine Mathieu's comic book series on the adventures of Julius Corentin Acquefacques, civil servant for the Ministry of Humor, as a formalistic tour de force through a dystopian city. As comics and the city have always been intricately linked on a number of levels, Suhr's essay shows that this seldom becomes more obvious than in Mathieu's comics. They present a unique reflection on the conditions that define the city as the social space of modernity and bourgeois rationality. At the same time they clearly show how comics as a form of media and the specific space of the city produce similar and maybe even related modes of perception. Meta-fictional elements stress the aspect of watching a city through the frame of a comic book page or panel, for example, in Acquefacques's first adventure in *L'Origin* (1990): Acquefacques starts to receive single pages of a comic book, pages the reader soon recognizes as pages of the very comic he or she is reading at the moment. Acquefacques real-izes so too, feels the short lifespan of 42 pages rush past him, becomes the object of close scrutiny at the Ministry of Science and finally has to experience the last page of his story being burned by its author.

Andreas Platthaus's essay on Duckburg and its German counterpart, "Entenhausen," in the comics of Carl Barks deals with the enlightening similarities and differences in the portrayals of Duckburg in the original American versions and the German translations by Erika Fuchs. While working for more than 30 years as "the good artist" on Disney comics, Carl Barks developed a whole universe for his Duck family. The deep rooting of the Ducks' habits and traditions in the American way of life is contrasted by the many translations in foreign languages. The more Barks's comics gained worldwide success the less possible it was to translate them literally. So his city of Duckburg became a metropolis that every translator shaped and resettled in terms of his own nationality. The especially famous translator Erika Fuchs has changed the way the German readers regard the world of Duckburg (which she christened "Entenhausen"). In contrasting the different images of the city as it is shown in the panels by Barks and described in the balloons by Fuchs and Barks, Platthaus presents a concept of historical urbanism in comic art aesthetics.

Finally, Thomas Becker's essay on Enki Bilal's *Woman Trap* (*La Femme Piège*) (1986) deals with reflections on authorship within the shifting boundaries between order and terror in cities. Recent science fiction movies have produced negative utopias about the climactic catastrophe, eugenic practices, and the promise of security offered by a military power. This promise of risk-control seems to be gradually perverting Western democracy. However, Becker argues, one of the first models of these prophecies appeared more than 20 years ago when Enki Bilal wrote and drew his *Nikopol* trilogy. The art historian K. O. Werckmeister called this trilogy a critique of the citadel's culture because the cities in the Western world, like the London, Paris or Berlin in the *Nikopol* trilogy (remarkably it is New York City in Bilal's movie version *Immortel* [*Ad Vitam*], 2004), are shown as powerful citadels defending their standards of health and security systems against immigrants at high military costs. But, according to Bilal's trilogy, the logic of the shifting boundary between order and terror can be attacked by the production of art.

Works Cited

Barthes, Roland. *Mythologies.* London: Paladin, 1972 [1957].
Jameson, Fredric. *Postmodernism, or the Cultural Logic of Late Capitalism.* Durham: Duke University Press, 1991.
Jones, Gerard and Jacobs, Will. *The Comic Book Heroes: The First History of Modern Comic Books from the Silver Age to the Present.* Rocklin: Prima Publishing, 1997.
McLuhan, Marshall. *The Gutenberg Galaxy: The Making of Typographic Man.* Toronto, ON: University of Toronto Press, 2002 [1962].

Note

1 However, such acknowledgment is quite different in the U.S., Japan, France, or in any country, like Germany, where the legitimacy of comics is still disputed.

Further Reading

Alberghini, Andrea. *Sequenze Urbane: La metropolis nel fumetto.* Rovigo: Delta Comics, 2006.
Baetens, Jan (ed.), *The Graphic Novel.* Leuven: Leuven University Press, 2001.
Bloom, Clive and McCue, Greg S. (eds.), *Dark Knights: The New Comics in Context.* London: Pluto Press, 1993.
Brooker, Will. *Batman Unmasked: Analyzing a Cultural Icon.* New York and London: Continuum, 2000.
Carrier, David. *The Aesthetics of Comics.* University Park, PA: Pennsylvania State University Press, 2000.

Christiansen, Hans-Christian and Magnussen, Anne (eds.), *Comics & Culture: Analytical and Theoretical Approaches to Comics.* Copenhagen: University of Copenhagen, 2000.

Frahm, Ole. *Genealogie des Holocaust: Art Spiegelmanns MAUS — A Survivor's Tale.* München: Wilhelm Fink, 2006.

Gordon, Ian. *Comic Strips and Consumer Culture 1890–1945.* Washington and London: Smithsonian Institution Press, 1998.

Groensteen, Thiery. *The System of Comics.* Jackson, MS: University Press of Mississippi, 2007.

Harvey, Robert C. *The Art of the Comic Book: An Aesthetic History.* Jackson, MS: University Press of Mississippi, 1996.

Heer, Jeet and Worcester, Kent. *Arguing Comics: Literary Masters on a Popular Medium.* Jackson, MS: University Press of Mississippi, 2004.

Hein, Michael, Hüners, Michael and Michaelsen, Torsten (eds.), *Ästhetik des Comic.* Berlin: Erich Schmidt, 2002.

Inge, M. Thomas. *Comics as Culture.* Jackson, MS: University Press of Mississippi, 1990.

Klock, Geoff. *How to Read Superhero Comics and Why.* New York and London: Continuum, 2002.

McCloud, Scott. *Understanding Comics. The Invisible Art.* New York: HarperCollins, 1994.

McCloud, Scott. *Reinventing Comics.* New York: DC Comics (Imprint: Paradox Press), 2000.

Packard, Stephan. *Anatomie des Comics: Psychosemiotische Medienanalyse.* Göttingen: Wallstein, 2002.

Pearson, Roberta E. and Uricchio, William (eds.), *The Many Lives of Batman.* London: Routledge, 1991.

Platthaus, Andreas. *Im Comic vereint: Eine Geschichte der Bildergeschichte.* Berlin: Alexander Fest, 1998.

Pustz, Matthew J. *Comic Book Culture.* Jackson, MS: University Press of Mississippi, 1999.

Reynolds, Richard. *Superheroes: A Modern Mythology.* Jackson, MS: University Press of Mississippi, 1994.

Sassienie, Paul (ed.), *The Comic Book: The One Essential Guide for Comic Book Fans Everywhere.* London: Ebury Press, 1994.

Savage, William W., Jr. *Comic Books and America, 1945–1954.* Norman, OK: University of Oklahoma Press, 1990.

Schüwer, Martin. *Wie Comics erzählen.* Trier: Wissenschaftlicher Verlag Trier, 2008

I

History, Comics, and the City

1

"Hully gee, I'm a Hieroglyphe" — Mobilizing the Gaze and the Invention of Comics in New York City, 1895

JENS BALZER

WHILE COMICS ARE GENERALLY CLAIMED as an aesthetic form, there is no common denominator for their various manifestations. One hundred years of comic history has not led to the evolution of a pictorial language that could be seen as "typical" for comics — that could be used to identify a work of art unmistakably as a comic. One reason for this is that comics have always been influenced by the various publications that they appear in: newspapers and magazines, pulp magazines, and hardcover books. As a result, they come in very different styles and forms of expression, from the lavish imagery of early newspaper funnies to "literary" comics compressing the visual aspects of the form into hieroglyphic abbreviations.

What makes a comic a comic? How many panels are required to distinguish it from a cartoon? Are superheroes a must? How about recurring characters, reappearing in each episode or even panel? Is a comic without a speech bubble still a comic? Where do we draw the line between merely technical definitions and content? These questions are impossible to answer, although this impossibility might itself be seen as a constitutive aspect of comics.[1] Unlike those modern media that comics are often compared with — photography or cinema — comics cannot be linked to one single technological innovation. Though they are without doubt a part of the history of an evolving modern mass or "pop" culture, there is no single moment in time defining their arrival, no Lumière brothers showing "moving pictures" in a shop, no Daguerre fixing the image of life on copper plates.

Not to be deterred, comic historians have countered this lack by taking refuge to a kind of ersatz event as the starting point of their historiographies, an event that allows them to link the "invention" of comics with a broader field of technological and social history. It was the American comic artist Coulton Waugh who first employed, in his groundbreaking history of comics, a jug-eared boy in a nightshirt as, so to say, the beginning of everything. The first comic, maintains Waugh in *The Comics,* was an episode out of Richard Felton Outcault's cartoon *Down Hogan's Alley* that appeared on February 18, 1896 in the Sunday supplement of the *New York World* (Waugh 1974: 1–10). What interested Waugh most, of course, was the fact that this comic was also a test-run for a breakthrough in engineering.

Figure 1.1. **Richard F. Outcault. "The Great Dog Show in M'Googan Avenue."**
New York World, February 18, 1896

Taken from: Bill Blackbeard. *R.F. Outcault's the Yellow Kid. A Centennial Celebration of the Kid Who Started the Comics.* Northampton: Kitchen Sink Press, 1995.

Standing in the foreground of Outcault's cartoon is a bald little boy in a nightshirt — the testing ground, according to Waugh, for a fast-drying yellow dye, the color that had been missing in the successful implementation of four-color printing in newspapers. This step was important for tabloids. Bright colors were what caught the buyer's eye. The success of four-color printing was seen as vital for sales, and only yellow had been reluctant to stay put on the pulpy paper — seeping where it shouldn't seep, refusing to keep its tone. It was only when the printing technicians at the *World* added a tallow-based component to the dye that success was achieved — in more than one way.

The unusual, bright color turned the little boy in the nightshirt into a character that could be identified, setting the urchin apart from the masses around him and multiplying the readers' interest in *Hogan's Alley*. The series had been an unassuming presence in the paper for at least nine months. Now, the gaze and attention of the public were distracted from Outcault's main theme — genre drawings of an immigrants' slum, a popular motif in newspapers of the time — to the one thing that separated *Hogan's Alley* from every other cartoon of its kind: the recurring figure of a weird little jug-eared boy.

In Waugh's telling, the sudden and enormous popularity of the Yellow Kid was responsible for rapidly rising sales, turning the urchin into an emblem of a flourishing tabloid market that would ultimately be called the "Yellow Press." What the *World* had, every newspaper also wanted — and more, if possible, and in brighter colors. It is this undefined area that spawned what would later be called "comics" — beginning with "cartoony" panels using recurring characters, operating on jokes that relied on the repetition and variation of identical themes, and advancing to a series of separate images that made possible the narration of short and simple stories.

During the last 10 or 15 years, Waugh's elementary narrative of the evolution of comics has been drawn into doubt by several researchers. Richard Marschall was the first to observe that the color yellow, far from being the sensation that Waugh made it out to be, had actually already been in use in newspaper printing for several years before the beginning of 1896 (Marschall 1989: 19). Richard D. Olson, and after him Bill Blackbeard, showed that the dates that Waugh relies on were themselves incorrect: The jug-eared urchin was already wearing a pale yellow nightshirt on his first appearance in *Hogan's Alley* in May 1895, and the general enthusiasm for his character began at least five weeks before the date set by Waugh (see Olson 1995: 2–17; Blackbeard 1995: 31).

Still, two things cannot be disputed. The first is that the Yellow Kid really was a starting point — the starting point for the invention of comics as a genre or art form. Outcault's outrageous success led not only the *New York World*, but also its rival, the *New York Journal*, and many other tabloids to introduce supplements dedicated to comic narratives — the so-called "funny papers" — into their lists of content. It took several years for the funnies to make their way from the Sunday edition into the dailies. Newly evolving syndicates took over their distribution throughout the country. These are some of the protagonists of comic art during those first years after the Yellow Kid: Rudolphe Dirks, who translated the theme of the German picture story, or *Bildergeschichte*, *Max und Moritz*, into American comics with his *Katzenjammer Kids* (Balzer 2007: 60–6), Frederick Burr Opper with *Happy Hooligan*, Winsor McCay with *Little Nemo* and Harry "Bud" Fisher, who launched, in November 1907, the first regular comic strip, *Mutt and Jeff* (Harvey 1994: 14–25).

Second, everyone of these artists and their series profited not only from the economic success that Outcault's Yellow Kid had become, but also from the revolutionary technical experiment that Outcault, in my view at least, had undertaken. I am not speaking of printing machines, but of semiotics. Yellow Kid was the testing ground for a device that would, in an aesthetic sense, separate comics from their precursors in cultural history, the *Bildergeschichten*. This experiment consisted in the interweaving of words and images within one space, within one signifier. Its focus point was the body of the Yellow Kid.

As a recurring character or figure, the Kid stands out among the other characters not just through his positioning, at one side of the scenery, grinning directly at the reader. What makes him special is also the singular way in which the action is commented on by short sentences written on his enormous nightshirt.

With this procedure, the traditional boundaries between images and words make room for something new. *Bildergeschichten* in the nineteenth century maintained separate spaces for images and writing. In telling a story, the classical examples by Rodolphe Töpffer or Wilhelm Busch reserved one area for images, and another for writing. Writing within images was employed solely in the context of signs or posters (a possibility that was used extensively by the British cartoonists George Cruikshank and Thomas Rowlandson). If we do find spoken language in speech bubbles — there was an abundance of speech bubbles in

European political cartoons at the beginning of the nineteenth century — they seem less a part of the image than a disruptive element within its space of representation. Iconography does not incorporate language; words or sentences are not seen as an integral part of the graphic design; and writing remains outside the space of representation.

Not so with Outcault. In *Hogan's Alley*, imagined speech is introduced as part and parcel of the aesthetic procedure. Writing within images becomes the rule. Letters take on an iconographic quality, and the area of images is also a canvas for words. This development is singular and unusual, in the beginning perhaps even for Outcault himself. A close look at the early cartoons reveals a tentative, even apologetic attitude to the attempts in this direction, while later works seem to rejoice in unleashing writing on the iconographic space of representation.

When Outcault first uses the yellow nightshirt of his jug-eared urchin as a space for writing, this comes as no big deal: The whole cartoon is filled with writing on objects. The scenery shows the inhabitants of Hogan's Alley preparing for the convention to elect the Republican nominee for President. On wooden signs and boxes proponents proclaim their political views and preferences. Because of the obvious political-satirical content of the drawing, the essence of this cartoon lies less in an iconographic manifestation than in the content of the slogans themselves — in their "unusual" relationship to the iconographic scenery as a whole and their parodistic attitude towards the originals they refer to: real slogans on real banners.

In this sense, the words on the Yellow Kid's nightshirt come across as more of the same. However, unlike the posters of the marchers, there is no symbolically packaged "excuse" for this written fact, or at least, none that seems wholly satisfactory. The writing does not refer to an existing original. It has nothing to do with a voice that could be associated with the character. The "I" in the text does seem to refer to the Yellow Kid's voice — what is written can be seen as the transcription of two spoken sentences. But this becomes apparent only to those who have read them — there is no iconographic framework transporting the writing as the circumscription of something that cannot be portrayed outside the framework, into some kind of virtual area of representation.

The Kid is wearing a nightshirt with writing on it. This unremarkable fact is all that appears to the viewer at first glance: The words are objects on an object in the picture, differing in no way from all the other objects with writing on them. This changes only in their being read, in setting the sentences in relation to the imaginary voice of the Yellow Kid. And interestingly enough, this initial low-key subversion of a cultural convention concerning words and images in an iconographic context will soon lead to a massive explosion of writing all over the iconographic sceneries — and to a playful differentiation in the relationship between signifier and signified.

These beginnings show writing bound to the obvious objects of representation — slogans on posters in our first example, placards wittily announcing the merits of dogs for sale in the "Great Dog Show in M'Googan Avenue," or fantastically worded signs outside vaudeville show booths on Coney Island in a cartoon portraying a day trip of the inhabitants of Hogan's Alley.

But, after only a short while, we find a large part of the humor in the cartoons shifting towards the way in which writing appears in them. Soon there are signs hanging, lying, or standing everywhere, every one of them intent on proclaiming, proscribing, or prohibiting something. There is a proliferation of notes commenting, satirizing or ridiculing the object they are affixed to. During a trip to the North Pole, the inhabitants of Hogan's Alley chisel messages into the ice; during a summer's stay at the beach a little boy scratches observations onto the waves frozen in the picture. And, during a "Hot Political Convention in Hogan's Alley," even the clouds over the city project themselves as a

Figure 1.2.   **Richard F. Outcault. "Hogan's Alley Folk in the Surf." *New York World*, June 14, 1896**

Taken from: Bill Blackbeard. *R.F. Outcault's the Yellow Kid. A Centennial Celebration of the Kid Who Started the Comics.* Northampton: Kitchen Sink Press, 1995.

space for advertisements: "HAVE YOUR NAME ON THE CLOUDS —
THE ENTERPRISE ADVERTISING SIGN CO."

This mingling of images and words reflects a semiotic shift occurring
in the urban living space at the turn of the century. In his retrospective
"Einbahnstraße" from 1928, Walter Benjamin describes the way writing
is omnipresent, "dragged unrelentingly from billboards onto the street,"
a constant and insistent intrusion into the consciousness of the urban
observer, a "flurry of changing, colourful, rivalling letters" forcing the
observer to look and read at the same time, at least if he plans to take
account of the ensemble of urban pleasures "as a whole" and "fittingly"

Figure 1.3. **Richard F. Outcault. "A Hot Political Convention in Hogan's Alley."** *New
York World*, **July 12, 1896**

Taken from: Bill Blackbeard. *R.F. Outcault's the Yellow Kid. A Centennial Celebration of the Kid Who
Started the Comics*. Northampton: Kitchen Sink Press, 1995.

(Benjamin 1972–89: 103). Letters on the street arrange themselves as a "dictatorial vertical," in Benjamin's words, challenging the gaze of the observer, forcing it to shift constantly between different modes of perception. This gaze in motion is defined by Benjamin as a historically new way of seeing, one that forecloses the stillness of "composure." The aesthetic pseudo-peace of contemplation is gone.

"Perception arising from distraction (Zerstreuung)," writes Benjamin in his essay on the work of art in the age of mechanical reproduction, "can be registered with growing emphasis in all areas of art" and is "the symptom of far reaching changes in the way we see the world," affecting, for example, the pedestrian in big-city traffic who must learn to process and contextualize different stimulations of his senses in order to avoid being run over (Benjamin 1972–89: 505). Benjamin adds that the newspaper reader reading the ads will experience a similar sensation. The interweaving of images and words and the continuous aesthetic "chocs" to the reader's nervous system makes reading newspaper ads comparable to the challenge to one's senses in big-city traffic. The gaze of the observer trying to view a newspaper page as a whole is irritated by the seemingly incompatible expectations it finds itself confronted with. Confronted with the graphic presentation of newspaper ads, the gaze must, per force, lose its center, becoming "distracted (zerstreut)" — an extremely useful term coined by Benjamin.

Distraction, for Benjamin, is not one of many possible attitudes in aesthetic perception — a form of looking at an ambiguous aesthetic whole that can be chosen and controlled. The distraction of the gaze is a historical category. Benjamin refers to it as a specifically modern disposition of perception. The observer must be able to achieve two things: He must simultaneously process different views and stimulations to the senses — listening and seeing, watching and reading — and he must also move past or through the objects of his perception in order to be able to see them as a whole.

It is important to understand that these two movements — of the gaze and of the observer as such — are interdependent: Together, they achieve the "distracted perception" that Benjamin places opposite the "contemplative reflection" of classical art theory. The gaze of the modern *flâneur* is no longer able to concentrate, immovably, on an image that is, of course, itself in motion. For the *flâneur*, "losing oneself" in contemplation is not an option. "The basic state of mind in still contemplation," Benjamin jots down for his *Passagen-Werk*, "is waiting. With the flaneur, this state of mind is replaced by doubt" (Benjamin 1972–89: 535). Doubt, as an attribute of the gaze, is a state of mind in which the viewer cannot be sure if what he sees is really all that there is to see — or if he is looking at it in the right way. In this sense, the *flâneur* becomes the agent of a perception bereft of territory, in which the stable subject-object relationship of contemplation — which is measured by duration, by "waiting" — has ceded to a double motion, the observer moving through the city and the unstoppable flood of images and impressions moving past the observer.

In his study *Techniques of the Observer*, the American art historian Jonathan Crary stresses the relationship between Benjamin's "distracted perception" and his use of the character of the *flâneur*. Benjamin's exemplary modern observer is, according to Crary, "ambulatory", "shaped by a convergence of new urban spaces, technologies and new economic and symbolic functions of images and products — forms of artificial lighting, new use of mirrors, glass and steel architecture, railroads, museums, gardens, photography, fashion, crowds" (Crary 1992: 20). This exemplary motion in a real observer also means, according to Crary, that an aesthetic "realism" centering on the classical central perspective has become untrustworthy. Gone is the might of the gaze simulating a reality in which time stands still, where the observer is able to see everything at once, to stay in control of all he sees as a whole and objectively definable visual impression. "[Modern] perception for Benjamin [is] acutely temporal and kinetic; he makes clear how modernity subverts even the possibility of a contemplative beholder. There is never a pure access to a single object; vision is always multiple, adjacent and overlapping with other objects, desires and vectors" (Crary 1992: 20).

The intermingling of words and images that Outcault pioneers is a marked example of the growing transparency of illusion, not only because the gaze of the observer is denied the illusion of simultaneity. The unbridled relations between image and text contain a variety of possibilities for differentiation, the "realistically" plausible variety is, as we have seen, one of many. The writing on the nightshirt of the Yellow Kid means that the link between object and representation has weakened, and Outcault the artist will further this development in later episodes of the series, playing with it, sharpening it, and eventually submitting it to parody.

In a formal sense this is achieved by distributing writings not only over the whole iconographic scenery, but also on material, foundations, and surfaces. The relationship between text and texture, between writings and the materiality of the objects that carry them, is turned upside down in a strange and revelatory way. Everything can be written on, even if the reason for this often becomes apparent only with hindsight. Clouds above the "Hot Political Convention," for example, are not only icons of the invisible, but also a visible writing space with "impossible" material qualities. Even the physical states of things are drawn into the whirling indifference of iconographic and written sign definitions.

After Outcault's (and the Yellow Kid's) switch to the rival newspaper, the *New York Journal,* the *Hogan's Alley* stories in the *New York World* were continued by artist George B. Luks. His contribution was to promote the indifference that Outcault flirted with into a state of distraction: of the writing on the space of representation, of the relationship between writing and content. This is already obvious in the *World*'s first episode introducing Luks as the new artist responsible for the Yellow Kid and *Hogan's Alley*: a cartoon with the title "The Open-Air School in Hogan's Alley."

Here, the image is covered with scribbles. The commentary on the nightshirt of the Yellow Kid is the first thing we see. The urchin is standing in front of a blackboard, posing as a teacher. The blackboard is, of course, covered with writing, not with lessons but with the kind of commentaries that would be expected on a blackboard (and that could have been written by the boy or somebody else). In the general context they are devoid of meaning.

This distinguishes them from the three text areas that can be seen above the blackboard. Directly over the head of the Yellow Kid a posting on a fence is a demand to the "BOARD UV EDUKASHUN" to build adequate schools for the city's children so they don't have to be taught outdoors. A scrawl on the house behind the fence blames the Republican party for the dire situation of education, while another posting, "BORED UV EDDICASHUN," calls for a new teacher — three, it states, have already been used up on this day alone (without hurting them).

This last text especially unbalances the relationship between the modes of writing and their content. What is so obviously a commentary on the scene acted out is incompatible with its being written in giant letters on the wall of a house. What we see, similar to the nightshirt of the Yellow Kid, is an impossible materialization, a flimsy voice — this time, however, there is no reference to any kind of speaker.

In order to stay within the analogy, we would have to say that either the house "speaks" or the writing is written directly into the image. The semblance of something being written into the picture disappears only when the gaze returns to the unreadable vision of the whole. For the integrity of the images, this is what counts. In other "graffiti" in "The Open-Air School in Hogan's Alley," like that on books proclaiming "DIS IS A BUK" and "THIS IS A DANDY BUK," or the pseudo-spoken "WE'RE LURNIN TWO" on a miniaturized desk, every single instance of writing has a carrier that is material, that can be seen in the image and that gives the gaze observing the whole the illusion of a holistic representation and one common reference point.

THE OPEN-AIR SCHOOL IN HOGAN'S ALLEY.

Figure 1.4. **George B. Luks. "The Open-Air School in Hogan's Alley."** *New York World,* **October 18, 1896**

Taken from: Richard Marschall. *America's Great Comic Strip Artists*. New York: Abbeville Press, 1989.

There is one exception, however. In the lower left-hand corner, at the end of the virtual circle drawn by the gaze of the beholder on the scene (it begins with the placatory Yellow Kid, rises over the large blocks of writing, reaches the parrot's cage and returns to the floor with the content being spilled), we find some battered accessories — suspenders, glasses, a crumpled top hat. We also find the comment that "THESE" are the "CLOES" of the teacher "HE LEFT SUDDENT AND HADN'T TIME TO TAKE 'EM."

This text is the only one not written on anything that can be seen as an object within the image. Its relationship to the scenery portrayed is no longer transmitted through a visual nexus, but through the de-referential "THESE" — the reference of the sentence to its object. Here, writing is placed within the representation minus an iconographic framework, the image itself is nothing more than canvas for text — dissolving its essence as a picture.

Just as the content of writing "on the street" is no longer seen with reference to a narrative unity, the text overwrites the unified image of the city and transforms it into a heterogeneous space of representation before — or, more specifically, within — which the necessarily overtaxed observer is forced into motion with his body and his gaze; a space in which writing also refers to things surrounding it in ever new ways and functions.

This means that the unity of representation no longer belongs to images *or* words. What we have here is not a space of writing or an iconographic space, but instead, literally, the space of the distracted gaze, to be read as well as viewed. The representation is unified only through the distracted gaze of the beholder, though not in the sense that a unified signifier can be made out through the act of observation. On the contrary: With regard to the totally eccentric pleasure of writing on images and the imagery of words, the gaze of the beholder must arrive at a mode of distraction. The unity that his gaze can find depends itself on the regularity of movement.

What makes a comic a comic? We have now come full circle, back to the question that I started with, and I will answer it with a tautology. Comics differ from pre-modern pictorial narratives or *Bildergeschichten* in their modernity, meaning their urbanity. Comics are in a league apart from the contemplative, frozen gaze of landscape paintings in classical central perspective. They demand the distracted gaze of the *flâneur* in the city. Constantly in motion, they set writing in verticals and decentralize the image. Their distraction is the mirror image of the endless restlessness confronting the gaze in modern cities. Comics are part of an aesthetics that can consume the image of the "whole" only in its disharmony.

Works Cited

Balzer, Jens. "Hemd voller Hieroglyphen. Zur Revision der Bild-Text-Beziehungen im frühen Comic." In: Dirck Linck and Stefanie Rentsch (eds.), *Bildtext — Textbild. Probleme der Rede über Text-Bild-Hybride.* Freiburg: Rombach Verlag, 2007. 117–54.

Balzer, Jens. "Rüpel Mäuse Superhelden. Wie Max und Moritz zu Urgestalten des Comics wurden." In: *Die Zeit Geschichte* 4 (2007). 60–6.

Benjamin, Walter. "Das Kunstwerk im Zeitalter seiner technischen Reproduzierbarkeit (dritte Fassung) (1936)." In: *Gesammelte Schriften*, Vol. I. 2. Frankfurt am Main: Suhrkamp, 1972–89.

Benjamin, Walter. "Das Passagen-Werk." In: *Gesammelte Schriften*, Vol. V. Frankfurt am Main: Suhrkamp, 1972–89.

Benjamin, Walter. "Einbahnstraße (1928)." In: *Gesammelte Schriften*, Vol. IV. 1. Frankfurt am Main: Suhrkamp, 1972–89.

Blackbeard, Bill. *R. F. Outcault's The Yellow Kid. A Centennial Celebration of the Kid Who Started the Comics.* Northampton, MA: Kitchen Sink Press, 1995.

Crary, Jonathan. *Techniques of the Observer: On Vision and Modernity in the Nineteenth Century.* Cambridge: MIT Press, 1992.

Harvey, Robert C. "Bud Fisher and the Daily Comic Strip." In: *Inks*, Vol. 1, No. 1 (1994). 14–25.

Marschall, Richard. *America's Great Comic Strip Artists.* New York: Abbeville Press, 1989.

Olson, Richard D. "Richard Felton Outcault's Yellow Kid." In: *Inks*, Vol. 2, No. 3 (1995). 2–17.

Waugh, Coulton. *The Comics.* New York: Luna Press, 1974 [1947].

Note

1 For an historical overview on the various definitions of "comics" and the accordingly different starting points for comics historiography see Balzer (2007: 117–54).

2

Every Window Tells a Story: Remarks on the Urbanity of Early Comic Strips

OLE FRAHM

> May no window in the panel be transparent, since the
> panel itself is a window? — a window to look through in
> a space, where images form and densify themselves?
>
> (Langbein and Theweleit 1980)

I N *L'INVENTION DU QUOTIDIEN* (*The Practice of Everyday Life*), Michel de Certeau reports a past experience. He describes how he is looking down on the New York metropolis from the observation platform on the 110th floor of the World Trade Center and seeing there "a swell of verticals," that for him represents a "texturology" of "the largest characters in the world" (de Certeau 1988: 179). At a distance, the city appears as a unit that has also eluded time: That which moves there moves at the borders of the visible. When looking down into spatial depths, judging distances is very difficult; the distance becomes a surface on which the city is literally ossified. Freed of all "physical, mental, and political impurities" (de Certeau 1988: 183), it appears clean, unified, and thereby transparent. Thus it actually becomes a *city* and therefore a subject, universal and anonymous.

In light of this visual experience, de Certeau asks, "where does this desire come from — to 'look out over' this most extreme of all human texts, to tower above it and grasp it as a whole?" (de Certeau 1988: 180)

The panoramic view of the city is simultaneously a panoptic projection, which "has long (attempted) to overcome the contradictions that arise from urban conglomeration" (de Certeau 1988: 183). In the era of industrialization and the formation of the bourgeoisie as a mainly urban-based political class, it became a common necessity to see the city and its surroundings from an elevated viewpoint: "In the nineteenth century no traveler missed . . . the opportunity to climb up a high tower or a mountain to enjoy the panorama . . . of a city . . ., the peaceful total picture of the city" (Hauser 1990: 107–8). Remote from urban life, snatched from the powerful clutches of the city yet simultaneously close to it or even in its center, as a panoptic fiction the panoramic view promises control over the city and what goes on inside it.

But this control is limited, argues de Certeau. It is not all-encompassing: The "lust to see the city" (de Certeau 1988: 181) diverges from the "strangeness of everyday life, the surface of which is a border pushed forward, an edge that looms on the backdrop of the visible" (de Certeau 1988: 182). The looking-over turns into overlooking; the eye that hovers above things is blind to small changes and movements in time and space, to the coincidences of brief encounters, uncomfortable detours, the witnessing of providence at work; in short, to the irrevocable tensions that are inherent in urbanity which cause a constant renewal of the strangeness. In that light, the city appears impure, discontinuous, diverse, and uncontrollable. It articulates itself in the "spatial practice" of the pedestrians, in their ambiguous "rhetoric of walking" (de Certeau 1988: 182). This practice is neither visible nor legible, it cannot be "captured in images . . . or rewritten into a text" (de Certeau 1988: 196) because it is itself writing the "urban text" based on its movement, "multiple diverse stories without author or audience" (de Certeau 1988: 182).

The walking-writing of the passersby is thus set in opposition to the seeing-reading of the panoptic gaze. While the panoptic gaze is seeing-reading the swell of verticals as a unified surface, the spatial practice of walking transforms this order to a perforated surface. While the panoptic gaze is transparent to itself, walking is opaque to itself, nearly blind, always irritated by the entangled coexistence of heterogeneous elements in the city. There are a lot of representations of the panoptic gaze but, as de Certeau argues, there is no representation of the practice of walking, since it is singular and diverse at the same time.

With Michel de Certeau's observations one could say that there is a kind of struggle between these two perspectives on the city. One tries to control the city by the gaze, the other tries to escape this very control. De Certeau searches for practices that enable the subversion of the dominant discourse of the city and if one could say that the desire for the panoramic gaze established itself at the time when the bourgeois class started to establish its power, one has to ask what kind of power the rhetoric of walking tries to establish. Instead of answering this question directly, I would like to discuss three Sunday pages of the first 25 years of the medium we nowadays call comics. My choice of series is not very exceptional: the Yellow Kid cartoons by George B. Luks; *Little Nemo* by Winsor McCay; and *Krazy Kat* by George Herriman. The thesis that should lead the reader is rather simple: These early Sunday pages reflect the conflict Michel de Certeau analyzes in the structure of their material. They enable another optical knowledge of the city that is not opposed to the panoramic view like walking is and instead puts both ways of perceiving in genuine play.

"TO THE BORED UV EDDICASHUN": How to Learn to See and to Read in the "Open School of Hogan's Alley"

The popularity of comics and their rise as a form of parodic reflection on everyday life could not be understood without the experience of urbanity as a heterogeneous one. That is one of several reasons why the Yellow Kid could be recognized retroactively as an epistemological breach that opens the space to a new form with its own rules of perception. The Yellow Kid appeared in several strips between 1895 and 1897. Designed to be seen and read by immigrants who were a growing audience, it was published in the Sunday pages, which were recognized as entertainment. This kid from an immigrant ghetto in urban surroundings was so popular as a subject that its producer, Richard Felton Outcault, was lured from Joseph Pulitzer's *New York World* by William Randolph Hearst for his *New York Journal.* But the *New York World* still held the rights for the series in which the Yellow Kid was then the lead character of, *Hogan's Alley,* and so the Yellow Kid was for some time published in two series. "The Open-Air School in Hogan's Alley" is the first page that George B. Luks drew for the *World,* published on October 18, 1896 (Marschall 1997: 30). It is notable that Luks' work is not included in Bill Blackbeard's *R. F. Outcault's The Yellow Kid. A Centennial Celebration of the Kid Who Started the Comics* (Blackbeard 1995). By considering Outcault as the only artist of the Yellow Kid, Blackbeard reestablishes notions of an aesthetic that comics ridiculed for economic reasons. Thus we can read on the shirt of the Yellow Kid in "The Open-Air School in Hogan's Alley": "They're imitating me all around town! I'm the Sunday world's kid and have been fur a year and a half! All others are fakes." That is the first thing we have to learn in "The Open-Air School in Hogan's Alley": that the original drawing (in this case Outcault's Yellow Kid) is an imitation. This — the fact that originals are imitations — is true for all commodities.

The speech act "all others are fakes" is at the same time totally true (the original was published in the *World*) and a lie, since this Yellow Kid is also a fake, being imitated by the little yellow twins in front of it. Luks reproduces the logic of the commodity to announce that it is not only the best but also the most original, and parodies this logic at the same time — just to sell more copies.

THE OPEN-AIR SCHOOL IN HOGAN'S ALLEY.

Figure 2.1. *The Yellow Kid*

Taken from: Richard Marschall. *America's Great Comic-Strip Artists. From the Yellow Kid to Peanuts.* New York: Stewart, Tabori & Chang, 1997 [1989], 30.

The page cannot be taken in with one gaze. It does not give a panoramic view of the ghetto. Even if the church in the background marks the geometric center of the page, we have to admit that there is no graphic center of the many unrelated performances that seem to happen at the same time. A boy with a fool's cap parodies the shape of the church, sitting on a lantern. A reading boy is falling down while a cat is rising — supported by a kite that says "GOODBYE"; some children hold a book, others are joking or hitting each other while some are really sitting on a bench in front of the blackboard. There we could read the programmatic sentence: "16 TO 1 . . . WE LOVE OUR TEECHER . . . NIT." Mark the children's drawing of the figure, another comment regarding the fake kid. Obviously, it is drawn by the Yellow Kid that holds the chalk in its hand. The Yellow Kid points to the writing and for sure, reading is the main topic of the page, or to be more precise, *how to learn* reading and thus seeing.

Actually writing is dispersed in several forms all over the page: There is the ad "FLATS TO LET" next to the door (stressing the commercial character of the page itself), on a hat we can read that the girl would like to become "A SKULE TEECHER" (so she is the one, the one could count the other 16 of the poll . . .), and a cat learns to spell the word "RST — R-A-T — RAT," which we can see in a speech balloon.

While we see on the left half of the page some speechless violence (three open mouths crying without sound and for different reasons), we are addressed on the right half of the page by several "SAY!"s, a kind of chain commenting on the violence: first on the nightgown of the Yellow Kid, next on the poster above the blackboard that asks us to recognize the misery that the page makes undeniable, and third next to the cat, where the "SAY! TAMMANY SEZ THEIR AINT NO SKULES BECOS THE REPUBLICANS DIDN'T BILD THEM! AINT THAT RICH!" The Tammany Society was quite influential on Democratic politics in New York City and the page is part of the preparation for the presidential election that was held on November 3 of the same year, one of the most competitive in the history of the U.S. which the Democrats lost. It is not the first page in the *World* in favor of the Democrats, Pulitzer himself was a member of this party. In May, for example, *Hogan's Alley* marched to the convention of the "Grand Old Party" (a traditional nickname of the Republican party) to support the "Free Silver" minority. By the way, "16 TO 1" is not a meaningless number, but repeats one of the main slogans of that time, signifying that 16 ounces of silver should be equivalent to one ounce of gold. This would have made the dollar cheaper, which would have been good for the poor. In May, *Hogan's Alley* was in favor of the Free Silver movement, a minority in the Republican party — "16 TO 1 . . . WE LOVE OUR TEECHER . . . NIT" is thus also an ambivalent political statement, asking who the teacher is. The political references are as dispersed as everything else on this page.

Back to its theme of reading — dispersion is not the only principle that organizes this page. Just above the speech act on Tammany we can see and read — in the words of Jens Balzer — another "impossible materialization of a voice without reference to a speaking person" (Balzer 1996) which is not addressing the reader but the "bored uv eddicashun." The writing reminds us of ads on the walls of houses, but in this case it promotes nothing, it just asks for another teacher: "WEEVE WORE OUT THREE TEECHERS TO-DAY!" This speech act refers not to something beyond the image (this is its difference from the other two speech acts), but talks about the image itself and especially about the opposite corner of the image, where we can recognize the relics of one of the teachers. Another writing as a post scriptum explains what we see: "THE TEECHER'S CLOSE." It is no coincidence that we see his glasses — it is just another self-referential joke. And at the same time these traces and their explanation are questionable. It is said, "WE DIDN'T HURT THEM," but next to the glasses lie two bricks and if we take a closer look we can see that one of the glasses is broken. Just what we see is never certain; our gaze has to walk all over the page and must read the traces, and in a way rewrite them. Beyond the visible violence that is speechless, there is a violence that is even not really visible.

I would like to argue that there is a tension produced by this ambivalent self-referential constellation that asks us what we see when we read "BORED UV EDDICASHUN." As with everything on this page, this message has to be read at least twice and we shouldn't get bored with this education in ambivalence. A second axis of this specific constellation that extends over the page consists of the two babies in the box, which I have already mentioned ("WE'RE LURNIN' TWO") and the reading parrot who imitates speaking (and thus parodies again the imitations of the Yellow Kid): "OH! DON'T MIND A LITTLE THING LIKE THAT MR. HOGAN." The animals are the only ones whose spelling is correct. Obviously, the privilege of the humans is to use language in an ambivalent way.

Another interpretation is possible: While the animals are the only ones talking in speech balloons, the pupils read books that explain the most simple referential relation: "DIS IS A BUK" and "DOG" (another pun, since this page is connecting two dogs and the drawing). By only learning referentiality, the pupils in the Open-Air School have not learned to speak.

At the same time we could read the writing as speech acts. And the two axes of these four impossible speech acts meet more or less in an empty black square in the center of the page: "HOGAN'S EXPRESS" expresses nothing but the question of reference itself and where it lead us to. The political implication of this empty center is that the signs matter in their materiality. It would be no problem to reduce all signs to a single political meaning, but this is not the politics of the page's signs, since such a meaning wouldn't find an answer to the question of imitation. Every single meaning can be imitated by another one. By imitating a window Hogan's Express is carrying the single meaning away, in order to open the dispersed space of the city, where the question of reading itself is at stake.

Thus we have to see and to read the urban life: No one controls the writing because the image cannot be controlled by a panoramic gaze. The gaze has to move between the dispersed signs, reading them once and then again, at least twice to get their double meaning. The vertical houses are not becoming characters but the characters are — as Walter Benjamin put it — forced by "film and advertisement in the dicta-torial perpendicular" (Walter Benjamin 1991: 103) and thus become houses.

The windows of these houses are as blind as the walking gaze if it tried to find out what is behind the signs. There is nothing hidden on this page. But the signs are all producing more meaning than one can see at once. There are too many references and parodies to be read in only one viewing.

The gaze has to enjoy this heterogeneity, which can't be united by, for example, a simple political meaning. The gaze has to learn how to walk between reading and seeing. The gaze has to learn how to lose control between characters that are never the same. At the same time, one could argue, that the Yellow Kid itself is the figure that reassures the gaze by addressing us. As a recognizable figure it allows the gaze to rest and to gain control of all the meanings. But exactly at that point, where the original should reassure one's control, we have to realize that it is only an original imitation. On the page all the gestures of the Yellow Kid are reproduced; the writing on the nightgown is repeated by the hat and the African-American boy is also looking straight at the reader without saying anything. He reminds us of the fact that, in early 1896, the supreme court confirmed in a famous judgment that race segregation included schools. His silence escapes transparency and control, opaque like the windows of the houses, like the black square of Hogan's Express.

In the Dreams of Little Nemo

In three Sunday pages of *Little Nemo in Slumberland* the windows of the houses are also blind and opaque and the story is again told by the panels. Since *Little Nemo* was also published in New York, it is no wonder that every now and then the dreaming hero is visiting this city — in this case fleeing the red giants.

But the little dreamer from the castle of King Morpheus feels not very comfortable there: "We are lost," we read in the first panel on September 22, 1907, and "I'm lost," in the last. Between these two panels the little hero, who is comparatively big, tries to gain a panoptic gaze over the city (McCay 1997: 36). In a way — to stay with de Certeau's example — Little Nemo tries to climb on the World Trade Center, but he fails. The panels do not add up to an overview; individually and together they are not transparent. Even if we see spaces and specific perspectives of space, the gaze is limited: "I can't see a thing," says Nemo, even if he sees a lot of houses. But the higher the protagonists climb, the higher the houses seem to be and they thus disable the panoptic gaze over the city. The panoptic gaze must have a higher position than everything else — it's only at this position that it achieves its power. Nemo's hope — "we can find ourselves when we get up here" — is shattered. He finds himself only lost.

And where is he? Compared to all the other panels, the little giant seems not to be "in the image." He is alien to the background and to the foreground, like a sticker stuck on the image. This weird impression is stressed by the speech balloon. Now we recognize that there is no panel without a speech balloon on this page. In panels three and four the writing looks a little bit like the writing on the wall in the school of *Hogan's Alley*. And again the speech act is addressed to no one. Nemo is not talking to his wild companion, he is talking to himself, talking to overcome his fear of getting lost in the deep streets. Nevertheless it is a speech act, spatialized by the writing in the balloon on a surface. The speech balloon has no space, it despatializes the space (see Wiesing 2008).

Figure 2.2. **Little Nemo in Slumberland**

Taken from: Winsor McCay. *The Best of Little Nemo in Slumberland*, edited by Richard Marschall. New York: Stewart, Tabori & Chang 1997, 37.

The city with its sea of houses is a space without depth, a surface perforated by the blind windows.

Surfaces, speech balloons and houses have to be read and seen in the constellation of the page. The gaze looks and reads as if it is losing control — and becomes affected by this loss. Little Nemo dreams of a city that is not to be read by the panoptic gaze, a city where you have to walk, but at the same time his dreams express the fear of the city and repress this possible perception as much as possible. The desire for control is stronger than the lust to get lost. In the economy of the dream the desire to gain the panoptic power is quite destructive. When Nemo wishes that Flip was there helping him, the reason is revealed in the next two Sunday pages, published on September 29 and October 6, 1907 (McCay 1997: 37–8). They show how Flip, who is looking for his friend Nemo, destroys New York totally by running through it. All three can see all over the city but they can't enjoy their power and gain no control over the situation itself: They have to flee again because the navy attacks them. Little Nemo as a comic hero erects a phallogocentric desire that is dissolved between the signs of the comic strip. The dream of being a big one, who is not lost and is the subject that controls the situation, is visualized and told. At the same time it is frustrated. It could never erect itself fully. The city is too big. The many blind spots all over the page tell another story. The constellation between the panels and the uncountable associations between the signs let us get lost.

In Front of the White Wall of *Krazy Kat*

In my final example, *Krazy Kat* by George Herriman, the male figure of identification restraining the dispersion of the gaze could be the eponymous hero, but the sex of this figure is ambivalent. The Yellow Kid strips were constituted by the same figures in different situations; in *Little Nemo* a continuous story is told; but *Krazy Kat* always repeats the same constellation, which is represented in different ways — as variable as the sex of the main protagonist. This constellation is a famous one: Ignatz Mouse tries with all available means to throw bricks to hit the head of Krazy Kat. The dog Offissa Pupp tries to prohibit this crime, since he loves Krazy. Krazy Kat loves Ignatz Mouse and misunderstands the bricks as messages of love and often waits, desiring the bricks dearly. The last three panels of the page of October 20, 1920 summarize this constellation nicely (McDonnell *et al.* 1986: 161).

The page seems to be quite clearly arranged. At the same time, however, it is more complicated than the "Open-Air School" page by Luks. The gaze cannot rest between the figures and their unsolved constellation. It is not possible to see each panel with one gaze. The gaze has to wander from the bottom to the top or the other way round. Even if we read one panel after the other, the page provides a disturbing experience. It seems easier to read the panels in rows. Thus, to grasp what is going on, the gaze has to be dispersed. What looks first like a bare wall

Figure 2.3. *Krazy Kat*

Taken from Patrick McDonnell, Karen O'Connell and Georgia Riley de Havenon (eds.), *Krazy Kat. The Comic Art of George Herriman*. New York: Harry N. Abrams, 1986, 161. © King Features Syndicate.

becomes, in the act of reading, the page wall of a house. Its white wall is as opaque as the white paper. No one can see behind it. Thus we have to understand the meaning of the constellation of the figures on this surface: We get to know that the policeman can use his high position to control the little criminal Ignatz Mouse and to prohibit his deeds. But, for sure, his position allows no overview. To try to prohibit the crime in this case means to enable it. This is possible because the unmoving, panoptic gaze cannot watch the street. And it is possible, since the criminal, from his high point, is not trying to get the overview but only to observe the street. And Krazy Kat, the innocent pedestrian looking for love, becoming visually a "pine," assimilates himself — or herself — to the format of the panels just to get hit by a brick.

Offissa Pupp, if we read this page with de Certeau in mind, is reading the houses as transparent characters. But the houses stay opaque and thus white and alien, as long as you do not walk between them, as long as the gaze is frozen. But even if the gaze starts to become dispersed, wandering over the page, even if a window opens and an everyday-life story is told, the situation in the city is still alien. The windows only appear when someone says something in their frame. The speech act seems to materialize the bricks of the wall. Strangely, the gaze encounters here the speech act that de Certeau reads as walking in the city. On this white surface, perforated by lines, the gaze recognizes itself as a speech act that does not rule the city but enjoys getting lost in its ambivalence. Again the gaze has to walk and this walk — this is the difference with *Krazy Kat* — has no end.

Every Window Tells a Story

The panoptic gaze cleans the city of all contradictions. The city becomes a timeless and thus controllable subject. For sure, de Certeau's observations are 30 years old and the means of panoptic control have changed a lot, but the controlling of a city by a dispersed panoptic gaze has become even more important. The early Sunday pages remind us of another gaze, where things aren't so controlled. Images and writing become mixed, sometimes they can no longer be distinguished. But, as in the "Open-Air School of Hogan's Alley," the dispersed gaze enjoys this. It can distinguish, but not dissociate. The association of the signs produces an irreducible ambivalence. Even if the power structure seems to be clear, the stories open other perspectives by parodying that power. The pages, where this gaze is forced to move, all have dates. They were published on a certain day as part of an open series. The next appearance is always quite unclear.

The gaze is as transient as the pages. The ambivalence that contours the gaze's journey is not arbitrary. The meaning competes in the constellations of the signs. The dispersed gaze cannot get rid of the questions that are posed by the ambivalence but takes another walk to see and read more. Thus, like in the dreams of Little Nemo, this gaze gains no control over the city. The same is true for the comic page. The gaze is forced to move and develops its own rhetoric of ambivalence between control and the loss of control. This is the struggle of power in the modern city that comics reveal. They are not exercises in understanding the city but they do provide material for this struggle. Comics are able to tell about this struggle not least because their windows stay uncontrollably opaque. In all the examples I have discussed, the panels always show the everyday-life border of visibility that is alien and anonymous, like the materiality of signs itself. Comic pages are perforated surfaces in the sense Michel de Certeau proposed. This is the reason why even the white wall of *Krazy Kat* can tell a story in every window. You can move from window to window but you'll never get an overview. This reflection of the gaze without consciousness but as a practice of reading and seeing is the reason for the urbanity of comics. Every window tells a story: It is the story of the little ones that escape representation, a story that is still in some ways untold.

Works Cited

Balzer, Jens. "Welches Bild? Welche Bewegung? Über einige Bezüge zwischen Chronophotographie und frühen Comics." In: Harro Segeberg (ed.), *Die Mobilisierung des Sehens. Zur Vor — und Frühgeschichte des Films in Literatur und Kunst.* München: Wilhelm Fink, 1996. 279–93.

Benjamin, Walter. "Einbahnstraße." In: *Gesammelte Schriften,* Vol. IV. 1. Frankfurt am Main: Suhrkamp, 1991. 83–148.

Blackbeard, Bill. *R. F. Outcault's The Yellow Kid. A Centennial Celebration of the Kid Who Started the Comics.* Northampton, MA: Kitchen Sink, 1995.

De Certeau, Michel. *Die Kunst des Handelns* [The practice of everyday life], translated by Ronald Voullié. Berlin: Merve, 1988. Originally published as *L'Invention du quotidien, Vol. 1, Arts de faire.* Paris: Gallimard, 1980. Published in English as *The Practice of Everday Life,* trans. Steven Rendall. Berkeley, CA: University of California Press, 1984.

Hauser, Susanne. *Der Blick auf die Stadt.* Berlin: Reimer, 1990.

Langbein, Martin and Theweleit, Klaus. *Bruch.* Frankfurt am Main: Stroemfeld, 1980.

McCay, Winsor. *The Best of Little Nemo in Slumberland,* ed. Richard Marschall. New York: Stewart, Tabori & Chang, 1997.

McDonnell, Patrick, O'Connell, Karen and de Havenon, Georgia Riley (eds.), *Krazy Kat. The Comic Art of George Herriman.* New York: Harry N. Abrams, 1986.

Marschall, Richard. *America's Great Comic-Strip Artists. From the Yellow Kid to Peanuts.* New York: Stewart, Tabori & Chang, 1997 [1989].

Wiesing, Lambert. "Die Sprechblase. Reale Schrift im Bild." In: Alexandra Kleihus (ed.), *Realitätseffekte. Ästhetische Repräsentation des Alltäglichen im 20. Jahrhundert.* Paderborn: Wilhelm Fink, 2008. 25–46.

3

The City as Archive in Jason Lutes's *Berlin*

ANTHONY ENNS

N HIS 1934 ESSAY "The Author as Producer," Walter Benjamin urges writers to "transcend . . . the barrier between writing and image" by incorporating photographs and captions into their work (Benjamin 1978: 230). Because the comic form is fundamentally based on such a juxtaposition of text and image, Jared Gardner claims that it is "ideally suited to carrying on the vital work Benjamin called for generations earlier: making the present aware of its own 'archive,' the past that it is always in the process of becoming" (Gardner 2002: 803). Gardner thus concludes that the comic form represents the ultimate realization of Benjamin's hybrid medium, which potentially reconfigures the relationship between the past and the present. What Gardner fails to mention, however, is that Benjamin's description of this new textual form also mirrors his description of the city. As Graeme Gilloch points out, Benjamin also sought to produce texts that embody aspects of the urban experience: "The dominance of the visual, the predilection for the fragmented and the concern with the immediate and with 'shock' are both definitive characters of modern urban life and central formal properties of Benjamin's texts" (Gilloch 1996: 19). In other words, the comic form allows the present to become aware of its own archive not only because it juxtaposes words and images, but also because it reflects the experience of the modern city, which is itself also an archive.

This chapter will examine the connections between comics, history, memory, and the urban experience by looking at how the comic form is uniquely suited to representing the city as an archive. Following Gardner's claim that the comic form represents the ultimate realization of Benjamin's hybrid medium, which has the potential to reconfigure the relationship between the past and the present, this chapter will explore how Jason Lutes's *Berlin* similarly represents the city as a montage of texts and images that has the potential to radically alter the reader's perception of time and space.

Dialectical Images, Montages and City Plans

Historians frequently note that the rise of the comic strip was inspired by nineteenth-century attempts to break motion down into successive phases. Scott Bukatman points out, for example, that early comic strips incorporated aspects of Eadweard Muybridge's chronophotographs, which were similarly arranged in pictorial sequences that captured the linear movement of time. Bukatman adds, however, that Muybridge's static grid structures also ruptured this sense of linearity by providing alternative ways of conceptualizing the movement of time:

> The organization and display of recorded moments projected the sense of temporal continuity and its relentless rationality, but it also incontrovertibly showed that time could be fractured, our awareness of it newly dispersed along a series or array of demonstrably incomplete images.
>
> (Bukatman 2006: 89)

Like Muybridge's chronophotographs, the comic form also spatializes time by presenting sequences of images in the form of a static grid, which suggests the possibility that time can be fractured and reconfigured along multiple pathways: "Comics (generally) map time onto a linear sequence, but that sequence does not preclude other ways of apprehending time" (Bukatman 2006: 89). Although the comic form may have been inspired by early film experiments, Bukatman argues that it more closely resembles chronophotographs, which spatialize time rather than temporalizing space.

The static grid-like structure of the comic form thus allows for alternative ways of apprehending time, which potentially subverts the very notion of narrative succession. In a similar way, Benjamin's concept of "materialist historiography" also attempts to question historical narratives by focusing on the unitary or "monadological" structure of history. According to Benjamin, historians traditionally extract histori-cal events from their original context and arrange them in a narrative sequence, but materialist historians attempt to undermine such narra-tives by recognizing the monadological structure of history:

> If the object of history is to be blasted out of the continuum of histori-cal succession, that is because its monadological structure demands it
> . . . It is owing to this monadological structure that the historical object finds represented in its interior its own fore-history and after-history.
>
> (Benjamin 1999: 475)

Instead of isolating these historical events and arranging them in a coherent narrative sequence, in other words, materialist historiography reaffirms the possibility that every historical event retains its own imma-nent past and future, and its goal is not to provide an account of the past but rather to rekindle a sense of hope. The practice of materialist historiography also involves the construction of "dialectical images," in which an image of "what has been comes together in a flash with the now to form a constellation" (Benjamin 1999: 462). Images thus enable the materialist historian to fragment and disrupt narratives of historical succession, as these frozen moments emphasize the contrast between what-has-been and what-is-now. Because historical events are essentially dialectical images, Benjamin even argues that it would be more effective to represent history in the form of a montage rather than a narrative: "The first stage in this undertaking will be to carry over the principle of montage into history" (Benjamin 1999: 461).

Benjamin also compares the practice of materialist historiography to the mapping of urban space, and he explicitly contrasts two opposing methods of representing the city: the photograph and the city plan. In his essay "Paris, the City in the Mirror," for example, Benjamin writes:

> [There exists] an ultraviolet and an ultra-red knowledge of this city, neither of which allow themselves to be confined to the book form: the photo and the city plan, — the most accurate knowledge of the individual element and of the totality.
>
> (Benjamin 1972: 357)

Photographs thus depict the individual elements of the city or its monadological structure, while city plans employ a narrative structure to provide a coherent schematic of the entire city as a whole. By juxtaposing photographs of individual elements of the city from both the past and the present, photomontages represent the city as a dialectical image, which disrupts the unified plan or historical narrative of the city, as Gilloch explains:

> Benjamin's concern with the depiction of the urban is interwoven with a conscious refusal of or resistance to the presentation of an overarching, integrated, coherent view of the city as a whole. The imagistic approach highlights the fleeting, fluid character of modern metropolitan existence. It denies a systematic, stable perspective.
>
> (Gilloch 1996: 18)

Benjamin's approach to reading the city thus parallels his approach to reading history: In both cases he resists the construction of coherent narratives and privileges instead a fragmented form that denies a systematic, stable perspective. By representing the city as a montage that weaves together fragments of the past and the present, Benjamin essentially conceives of the city as an archive of historical information.

David Frisby points out that Benjamin's imagistic approach also blurs the lines between the actual city and its mythological topography: "Benjamin intended constructing a topography of Paris, not merely of its monuments and ruins but of its mythology" (Frisby 1986: 225). In his essay "Paris, Capital of the Nineteenth Century," for example, Benjamin describes dialectical thinking as the experience of awakening, when dream and reality overlap, and he argues that this experience also serves as a metaphor for materialist historiography:

> The realization of dream elements in waking is the textbook example of dialectical thinking. For this reason dialectical thinking is the organ of historical awakening. Each epoch not only dreams the next, but also, in dream, strives toward the moment of waking.
>
> (Benjamin 1978: 162)

Like dreams, in other words, the remains of the past represent fantasies of a future that has not been realized, and Benjamin's examples focus specifically on aspects of the urban environment, such as "the arcades and interiors, the exhibitions and panoramas" of Paris, which he calls "the residues of a dream world" (Benjamin 1978: 162). The practice of dialectical thinking is thus indelibly linked to the experience of the modern city, where the past constantly collides with the present and the real constantly merges with the mythological.

Mapping the Mythological Topography of Berlin

Jason Lutes's comic *Berlin* is an ongoing series that recounts the history of this city during the era of the Weimar Republic — the same period, not coincidentally, when Benjamin was writing. Lutes sometimes represents actual historical events and personages, but most of the characters and situations depicted in the comic are purely fictional. Rather than attempting to provide a coherent historical narrative, therefore, *Berlin* effectively blurs the distinctions between fiction and non-fiction or fantasy and reality. By referencing a wide range of photographs, paintings and films of Berlin, Lutes also incorporates a vast archive of historical and fictional material. For example, the first issue opens with the arrival of a train, which recalls the opening of Walter Ruttmann's 1927 documentary *Berlin: Die Sinfonie der Großstadt*. Many of the panels are similarly derived from famous photographs of locations such as Potsdamer Platz and the Romanisches Café, which were destroyed in World War II. Some of the characters are also based on August Sander's photographs of the citizens of the Weimar Republic, which initially appeared in his 1929 collection *Antlitz der Zeit* (Face of Our Time). A student at the Academy of Art, for example, bears a striking resemblance to Sander's photograph of the painter Heinrich Hoerle.

Lutes also refers to numerous paintings associated with the Neue Sachlichkeit (New Objectivity) art movement. The Jewish newspaper boy, for example, is taken directly from Conrad Felixmüller's 1928 painting *Zeitungsjunge,* and the tenement house where Marthe Müller lives is based on Franz Lenk's 1929 painting *Berlin Hinterhäuser.* The Neue Sachlichkeit art movement also plays a key role in the second and fourth issues, which feature several lectures and discussions concerning the value of objectivity. One of the art students, Max, provides a concise summary of the movement's fundamental principles: "Objectivity is the thing. The Expressionists had it all wrong! Emotion clouds our view of the world as it really is! That is what we must document!" (Lutes 2002: 37–8). This statement might be interpreted as the guiding principle of Lutes's project, as he also appears to be constructing an archive of the history of Berlin, yet the absence of any distinction between historical and artistic source material suggests that Lutes is more interested in the iconic status of these images rather than their documentary function. Instead of providing an objective portrait of Berlin, in other words, Lutes appears to be more interested in the mythological topography of the city or the ways in which the city has historically been imagined. The fact that these images are not exclusively based on historical evidence is further emphasized by the fact that he also references Hanns Kralik's 1930 painting *Aus meinem Fenster*, which actually depicts a street corner in the city of Düsseldorf rather than Berlin. By blurring the distinctions between fact and fiction or reality and myth, Lutes's strategy of visual citation effectively foregrounds the representational nature of the comic form and denies any claim to historical authenticity. *Berlin* thus represents the city as a collage or montage of intertextual references.

When viewed in this light, Lutes's comic appears to contradict the basic tenets of the Neue Sachlichkeit movement, and this is emphasized within the narrative through Marthe Müller's increasing dissatisfaction with the Academy of Art. After attending a lecture on perspective and the scientific principles of art, for example, Marthe complains: "That way of seeing the world doesn't really appeal to me" (Lutes 2002: 104). This comment anticipates her subsequent decision to drop out of school, which she explains as follows: "I don't want to see the world converging towards a vanishing point! I don't want to understand people in terms of their skeletal structure or the muscle group that controls their ability to smile. I can't reconcile those things with what I see" (Lutes 2002: 124). In her journal Marthe describes her actual experiences in Berlin as follows:

> . . . it's as if the city enfolds me. My fear of setting out in the morning has given way to a sense of relief. Gradually, the sense of being overwhelmed has become more like that of being absorbed, and instead of losing myself, I feel a part of something larger, my life like a thread, unspooling and intertwining with those I pass on the street. Immigrant housewives, beggars, and Jews; they could not be more different from me, but I imagine a higher force that binds us into a greater, unified whole.
>
> (Lutes 2002: 100)

Marthe cannot reconcile her lessons on objectivity with her own experience, in other words, because the city inspires a sense of disorientation and interconnectedness that remains missing from the Neue Sachlichkeit paintings.

Marthe's claim that Berlin is composed of many different groups of people is also established at the beginning of the comic when journalist Kurt Severing describes the city as a place where rival factions clash in the streets, including "Communists, socialists, nationalists, democrats, republicans, criminals, beggars, thieves, and everything in between" (Lutes 2002: 10). This notion is repeatedly emphasized in subsequent issues, as the reader is given the opportunity to experience the city from all of these various perspectives. The diversity of the city is heightened even further after Marthe discovers Berlin's gay subculture:

> I already knew that the streets of Berlin connect a thousand little worlds. Every streetlamp, every alleyway, every courtyard is a gathering place for people who share a specific interest. Curbside socialists, broadcast radio addicts, unemployed card players, pilsner enthusiasts — communities comprised mostly of men. But recently, I've confirmed something long suspected: that the city holds other, secret worlds, populated by those whose interests are not encompassed by 'everyday life'.
>
> (Lutes 2008: 102)

Lutes thus reminds the reader that the city is not a single, unified whole, but rather it represents a node in a vast network where many different cultures intersect and interact.

The clashes between these various groups also represent clashes between competing versions of history. For example, the fourth issue begins with two contrasting accounts of the history of Weimar Germany. On the opening page, a communist quizzes a group of young newspaper boys who work for the *Arbeiter-Illustrierte-Zeitung* (The Workers Pictorial Newspaper). His questions concerning Rosa Luxemburg's accomplishments and the circumstances surrounding her death in 1919 are given added weight by the upcoming anniversary of her death and the fact that they are standing on the very bridge where her corpse was thrown into the canal. The location of this history lesson is clearly designed to heighten its emotional impact on the young communists, and it also helps to emphasize the notion of the city as an archive where the traces of the past can be deciphered like a text. This sequence is then immediately followed by a classroom scene, in which a group of German students are taught a far more optimistic version of the origin of the

Weimar Republic. The teacher refers to the November Revolution in 1918, for example, as a peaceful demonstration, which ensured that "all privileges of birth and rank have been abolished" (Lutes 2002: 87). Several of the students offer yet a third version of this history when they accuse the Kaiser of being a coward for abdicating the throne, and this results in an aggressive confrontation between the students and the teacher. By representing the city as a site where various competing versions of history collide and coexist, therefore, *Berlin* challenges the notion of history as a coherent narrative. And by representing the ways in which the traces of the past continue to affect the everyday lives of the city's inhabitants in the present, *Berlin* also depicts the city as an archive of historical information that constantly mediates social memory.

Lutes also disrupts any sense of historical continuity through the use of flashbacks and the juxtaposition of images from different time periods. These sudden and often disturbing breaks serve to fragment and disrupt the historical narrative, and they produce shock effects that replicate both the experience of the city and the traumatic nature of this tumultuous period in German history. In other words, rather than providing a coherent narrative Lutes, represents the history of the city as a mythological or phantasmagoric dream-life from which the city's inhabitants are constantly trying to awaken. For example, the third issue opens with a depiction of the navy revolt in November 1918. When shooting breaks out, people attempt to flee through a park. The next panel shows the same park, yet the soldiers have vanished and the previously cleared streets are now crowded with traffic. The reader is not informed until the bottom of the page that ten years have passed, and the occasion is now the arrival of President Paul von Hindenburg in October 1928. This sudden shift is not only disorienting, but it also provides a perfect example of a dialectical image. By juxtaposing two images of the same park from different historical periods, these panels form a constellation that subverts any sense of narrative continuity. Lutes makes extensive use of this technique throughout the series. Later in the same issue, for example, Kurt meets his ex-girlfriend, Margarethe, at the Romanisches Café, and the images of their conversation are spliced together with images of their initial meeting ten years earlier. Kurt even perceives these two moments as discontinuous fragments, and he has difficulty imagining the thread that connects one event to the next: "I find myself grasping vainly for the lifeline of our past, a frayed and delicate ten-year strand . . . It's not the loss itself so much as the gradual change that precedes it. The imperceptible shifting of selves" (Lutes 2002: 66–9). A similar technique is employed in the fourth issue, where the image of a homeless veteran sleeping on the street is immediately followed by a panel depicting the same man fighting in World War I. The juxtaposition of these images — and the fact that their connecting thread is never revealed — once again represents history as a series of ruptures and fissures rather than a coherent narrative.

Lutes incorporates yet another flashback within the previous flashback as Margarethe recounts the story of her cousin and two schoolmates, who went off to war and never returned. Her story is accompanied by a two-panel polyptych of the Brandenburg Gate. The left panel depicts a group of young soldiers walking out of the gate in the direction of France and the war, while the right panel depicts a group of older and far more disheveled soldiers returning home years later. This juxtaposition introduces yet another level of disorientation, as the entire war takes place in the gutter between the two panels yet the panels also constitute a unified picture of the gate itself. By disrupting the narrative and abruptly jumping back and forward through time, this technique invites the reader to imagine the flow of time in different ways. In other words, like Muybridge's chronophotographs, Lutes's pages do not present a seamless series of successive phases but rather they provide a monadological structure that subverts any sense of historical continuity by spatializing time and inviting the reader to apprehend the movement of time in new ways. The most extreme example of this technique occurs in the twelfth issue, when Lutes juxtaposes an image of a deserted city street littered with corpses following the May Day demonstration in 1929 and an image of the same street one year later, where the corpses have suddenly been replaced by regular street traffic. The juxtaposition of these two images represents yet another dialectical image that fragments or disrupts any sense of historical continuity. An anonymous pedestrian also recounts the events that occurred the previous year to a passing visitor, noting that the communists "cleared out in seconds, leavin' behind th' dead an' dyin'" (Lutes 2008: 96). This comment indicates that the traces of the past remain alive in the memory of the city's inhabitants even though they may be imperceptible to outsiders. The use of this technique thus effectively allows Lutes to perform the work of materialist historiography by revealing the traces of the past that remain imprinted on the urban landscape yet cannot be neatly contained within a historical narrative.

Lutes creates dialectical images not only through the juxtaposition of

Figure 3.1: **Jason Lutes. *Berlin: City of Stones,* Montreal: Drawn & Quarterly 2002, 67 (panels 7–8). © Jason Lutes.**

Figure 3.2: **Jason Lutes. *Berlin: City of Smoke,* Montreal: Drawn & Quarterly 2008, 96 (panel 8). © Jason Lutes.**

Figure 3.3. **Jason Lutes. *Berlin: City of Smoke,* Montreal: Drawn & Quarterly 2008, 97 (panel 7). © Jason Lutes.**

visual fragments from different time periods, but also through the juxtaposition of real and imaginary scenes. In the twelfth issue, for example, a policeman who has been traumatized by his experiences during the May Day demonstration suddenly awakens from a nightmare in which he was sinking into a pile of corpses. The precise moment when the policeman awakens from his dream occurs in the space between two panels, yet their juxtaposition serves to emphasize the disorienting experience of this liminal state in which the subject's dream-life seems to converge with reality. This technique is also employed in the seventh issue when Marthe and Kurt go on a picnic in a city park. As Marthe whispers "I love you" in Kurt's ear, the scene is suddenly interrupted by a page depicting the couple, now naked and alone, surrounded by images of nature. A similar moment occurs at the end of the eighth issue, when a woman is shot on the street during the May Day demonstration. The reader witnesses this death from the victim's perspective as she falls to the ground and her eyesight gradually fades. This image is then followed by several pages that show her sitting in a natural landscape, naked and pregnant, next to her husband as a young man. While this moment clearly disrupts the narrative and subverts any sense of historical continuity, it remains unclear whether it is a flashback or a dream. This scene may even challenge any distinction between reality and fantasy, as it appears to represent the past as a dream that is still yearning to be realized in the present.

The notion that the comic incorporates both real and imaginary representations of the city is further emphasized in Kurt's journal, where he compares the newspapers published in Berlin to the stones upon which the city is built:

> I imagine the daily output of the entire newspaper district. It makes me think of drowning, but I want to be able to see it another way. Instead: human history as a great river, finding its course along the lowest points in the landscape, and each page as a stone. Tossed in without purpose, just to see the splash, thousands of them might raise the water level until it escapes the confines of the riverbed. The water spreads out, the force of the river diminishes, before long, a marsh. But if each stone is placed carefully and with purpose, perhaps something can be built. Not to dam the current, but to divert its course.
>
> (Lutes 2002: 80)

Kurt thus employs the image of a river as a metaphor for history, and he describes the city as a structure composed of texts that has the potential to divert the course of this river and thereby alter the flow of time. There are clearly parallels between this journal entry and the writings of Benjamin, who similarly described the city as a textual construct and who envisioned the possibility of using history to reconfigure the relationship between the past and the present. Like Benjamin, Kurt is also attempting to imagine alternative ways of understanding the history of the city, which would have the potential to reconfigure not only the relationship between the past and the present, but also the relations between the city's many rival factions, which each have their own competing versions of history.

Kurt's notion of Berlin as a "city of stones" (which is also the subtitle of the first collected volume of the series) also invokes Charles Baudelaire's 1857 poem "The Swan." In this poem, the speaker is crossing the newly rebuilt Place du Carrousel when his memory is flooded with the image of Andromache, the wife of Hector who became a widow following the destruction of Troy. From the poet's perspective, this mythological figure becomes superimposed over the image of modern Paris:

> Paris changes, but nothing of my melancholy
> Gives way. Foundations, scaffoldings, tackle and blocks,
> And the old suburbs drift off into allegory,
> While my frailest memories take on the weight of rocks. (29–32)
>
> (Baudelaire 1963: 110)

Like Benjamin, Baudelaire's poem rejects the notion of historical continuity. The speaker's memories appear to be more tangible and real than modern Paris, and the superimposition of a mythological figure over the actual city serves as yet another example of a dialectical image that blurs the distinction between the real and the imaginary. Kurt's description of texts as stones also echoes Baudelaire's description of memories as possessing "the weight of rocks." Like Baudelaire, in other words, Kurt is similarly mapping the mythological topography of Berlin, and by disrupting linear narratives of historical continuity he hopes to reconfigure the relationship between the past and the present, which could potentially offer new ways of imagining the future.

Kurt returns to this metaphor at the end of the sixteenth issue, where he appears far more pessimistic:

> The world outside is filled with different sorts of words . . . The air is consumed by chanted slogans and playground songs, the sky held aloft by walls of words. Walking home, I see a copy of the paper disintegrating in the runoff from autumn's first rain. The letters slip away, one by one. And I sit here typing more of them; swimming against the tide.
>
> (Lutes 2008: 206)

This passage is juxtaposed with an image of a newspaper lying in a puddle on the street, its printed letters flowing from the page into a sewer drain. By providing yet another example of a text immersed in a stream of water, this passage seems to refer to his earlier description of history as a river. Unlike his first use of this metaphor, however, the text in this example is not able to divert the course of the stream. Therefore, instead of remaining hopeful that his writing could potentially disrupt the historical narrative, Kurt seems to imply here that his texts are simply being washed away in the current of time. Kurt thus remains committed to the notion of the city as a textual construct or archive, yet he gradually loses faith in the idea that it could potentially resist the stream-concept of history, which threatens to erase any traces of the past that are not part of the linear narrative of historical continuity.

Lutes's comic thus repeatedly addresses the ways in which the representation of history and the city are inherently linked. In order to prevent one version of history from overwhelming all of the others, Lutes repeatedly depicts the process of writing history as the process of capturing the forgotten traces of the past, which can still be deciphered in the text of the urban landscape. Like Benjamin, therefore, Lutes represents the past as a series of ruptures or fissures in order to restore the lost fragments of the past and thereby rescue the dead. Benjamin himself described Berlin as a city that "has more . . . than some others, of those places and moments when it bears witness to the dead, shows itself full of the dead" (Benjamin 1985: 316). Lutes's characters are similarly haunted by the dead, who refuse to remain silent or forgotten. Many of the characters have recurring memories of traumatic war experiences, political upheavals, and lost loved ones, and the narrative is repeatedly disrupted by references and flashbacks, which suggest that the past continues to impact and disrupt the present. Even though Rosa Luxemburg was murdered in 1919, for example, Lutes's characters are constantly reminded of her presence, and she continues to inspire political struggle in the present. On the anniversary of her death, a newspaper boy even tosses an artificial flower made of newspaper into the same canal where her corpse was thrown ten years earlier. Not only does this moment illustrate the degree to which the past remains a vital part of the everyday lives of the city's inhabitants, it also seems significant that the boy's make-shift memorial consists of a discarded text that is thrown into a stream of water. The newspaper boy's flower thus represents yet another example of the pages of text that Kurt describes as either stones capable of diverting the river of history or discarded fragments that are simply washed away by the currents of time. In other words, like Berlin itself — and I am referring here to both the city and Lutes's comic — this flower similarly represents a textual construct that attempts to capture the traces of the past in the present or the traces of the imaginary in the real. By restoring these lost traces, both the flower and Lutes's comic represent the city as an archive or montage — a collection of fragments rather than a coherent, linear narrative — and they both seek to rescue the dead from oblivion, which is, according to Benjamin, the principle task of materialist historiography.

Conclusion

In his autobiographical writings about his own childhood in Berlin, Benjamin frequently draws connections between the urban experience and the process of remembering. As Gilloch points out, for example, Benjamin explored how "the urban setting shapes, and is in turn shaped by, the work of remembrance," and he wished "to show that the past is not complete and unalterable, but rather that it is the task of the present to redeem the forgotten dead" (Gilloch 1996: 77). The comic is ideally suited to carrying on this work, as Gardner claims, but this is not only because it transcends the barrier between word and image, but also because it has the potential to transform the reader's perception of time and space. Like Muybridge's chronophotographs, the panels of a comic are laid out in sequential order, but their monadological structure also allows for the possibility of imagining new ways of apprehending time. Through the use of sudden breaks and flashbacks, the combination of words and text, the use of dialectical images, the incorporation and citation of other texts, and the use of shifting perspectives, *Berlin* effectively represents the city as an archive or montage rather than a coherent city plan, and it thus employs the unique characteristics of the comic form to construct a fragmented text that challenges linear narratives of historical continuity. In other words, *Berlin* does not attempt to provide a coherent explanation for the rise of fascism or the fall of the Weimar Republic, but rather it deconstructs the mythological topography of Berlin and offers new possibilities for imagining the future. The end result is a memorial that testifies to the experiences of the city's lost inhabitants, that recognizes the continued presence of the past in the urban landscape, and that thereby attempts to rekindle a sense of hope.

Works Cited
Comics
Lutes, Jason. *Berlin: City of Smoke.* Montreal: Drawn and Quarterly, 2008.
Lutes, Jason. *Berlin: City of Stones.* Montreal: Drawn and Quarterly, 2002.

Secondary Literature
Baudelaire, Charles. *The Flowers of Evil*, trans. Anthony Hecht, ed. Marthiel and Jackson Mathews. New York: New Directions, 1963.
Benjamin, Walter. *Gesammelte Schriften*, Vol. IV, ed. Tillman Rexroth. Frankfurt am Main: Suhrkamp Verlag, 1972.
Benjamin, Walter. *One Way Street and Other Writings*, trans. Edmund Jephcott and Kingsley Shorter. London: Verso, 1985.
Benjamin, Walter. *Reflections*, trans. Edmund Jephcott. New York: Schocken Books, 1978.
Benjamin, Walter. *The Arcades Project*, trans. Howard Eiland and Kevin McLaughlin. Cambridge, MA: Harvard University Press, 1999.
Bukatman, Scott. "Comics and the Critique of Chronophotography, or 'He Knew When It Was Coming!'" In: *Animation: An Interdisciplinary Journal* 1, No. 1 (2006). 83–103.
Frisby, David. *Fragments of Modernity: Theories of Modernity in the Work of Simmel, Kracauer and Benjamin.* Cambridge, MA: MIT Press, 1986.
Gardner, Jared. "Archives, Collectors, and the New Media Work of Comics." In: *Modern Fiction Studies* 52, No. 4 (2002). 787–806.
Gilloch, Graeme. *Myth and Metropolis: Walter Benjamin and the City.* Cambridge: Polity Press, 1996.

II

Retrofuturistic and Nostalgic Cities

4

"The Tomorrow That Never Was" — Retrofuturism in the Comics of Dean Motter

HENRY JENKINS

THE PROTAGONIST OF WILLIAM GIBSON'S "The Gernsback Continuum" is a photojournalist, collecting images for a coffee table book, *The Airstream Futuropolis: The Tomorrow That Never Was.* As he searches for ramshackle roadside attractions and other traces of the ways people in the 1930s and 1940s imagined the future, he encounters what Gibson calls "semiotic ghosts," glimpses of a parallel world where the euphoric dreams of urban boosters and technological utopians had come true: "Behind me, the illuminated city: Searchlights swept the sky for the sheer joy of it. I imagined them [the residents] thronging the plazas of white marble, orderly and alert, their bright eyes shining with enthusiasm for their floodlit avenues and silver cars" (Gibson 1981: 1–11).

Gibson's story was a bold gesture from a brash new writer, sweeping aside the technological utopian fantasies that had emerged in the pulp magazines of the 1930s and shaped the science fiction genre ever since. As his oft-time collaborator, Bruce Sterling, explains:

> Times have changed since the comfortable era of Hugo Gernsback, when science was safely enshrined — and confined — in an Ivory Tower. The careless technophilia of those days belongs to a vanished, sluggish era, when authority still had a comfortable margin of control.

> Not for us the steam snorting wonders of the past: the Hoover Dam, the Empire State Building, the nuclear power plant.
>
> (Sterling 1981: XIII)

Gibson and Sterling wanted to push science fiction in new directions and saw little use for streamlined airships.

Dean Motter's *Mister X* (1983) comics emerged from this very same context — at a transitional moment when shifts in the technological landscape and the emergence of the discourse of the digital revolution were transforming science fiction as a genre. *Mister X* appeared one year after *Blade Runner*, one year after Fredric Jameson's "Can We Imagine the Future?", one year before the year made famous by George Orwell's *1984*, three years before the *Mirrorshades* anthology, which established cyberpunk as a genre, and three years before Joseph Corn's *Imagining Tomorrow: History, Technology and the American Future*, which made yesterday's tomorrows a topic of historical and literary investigation (Corn 1986; Corn and Horrigan 1984). The expiration date had passed for many of the technological and geopolitical changes predicted at such landmark events as the 1939 World's Fair. Cyberpunk allowed us to look forward, retrofuturism invited us to look backwards.

Fredric Jameson's "Can We Imagine the Future?" captures the uncertainty gripping science fiction at this moment:

> We can no longer entertain such visions of wonder-working, properly 'science-fictional' futures of technological automation. These visions are themselves now historical and dated — streamlined cities of the future on peeling murals — while our lived experience of our greatest metropolises is one of urban decay and blight. That particular Utopian future has in other words turned out to have been merely the future of one moment of what is now our own past.
>
> (Jameson 2005: 288–9)

We might take two big ideas from Jameson's account of retrofuturism — that past imaginings of the future need to be understood as historical artifacts of older ideologies about human progress and that their remobilization in the present can be used as a means of reflecting on the failures of those dreams to become realities.

This essay will build on this idea of science fiction as a mode of historical critique, re-reading the retrofuturist project through the lens of more recent theoretical work on residual media. In doing so, I will be focusing primarily on a series of comic books written and conceived by Dean Motter over the past three decades (*Mister X, Terminal City, Terminal City: Aerial Grafitti, Electropolis*), all operating within a shared fictional world inspired by early twentieth-century representations of the "city of the future." Motter describes his books as "antique futurism," which he explained during an interview with the author:

> "Since the advent of the industrial revolution, our society has been predicting the cultural future via the machine. Whether in gigantic architectural visions such as the World Fairs, or the near-whimsical *Popular Science* covers, dreams of flying cars, household robotic servants, or jet packs. These visions, while engineering achievements of varying degrees of success and accuracy, were often oblivious as to how the culture would change. McLuhan (as well as the fictions of Orwell, Huxley and H.G. Wells) considered what would happen to humanity itself, not simply the evolution or devolution of our artifacts . . . So 'antique futurism' became my way of having some fun, while raising the questions."
>
> (Jenkins 2007)

For Motter, "antique futurism" involves the reassertion of human experiences and identities into historical imaginings of a future technological utopia.

Reconceptualizing the Residual

Retrofuturism is apt to gain new prominence and potency during moments of media transformation. Marshall McLuhan has described the ways that the introduction of a newer media often makes us more self-conscious about its predecessors (see McLuhan 1994). The current moment of media change is stimulating a retrospective perspective in science fiction and fostering new kinds of historical scholarship, both of which seek to understand the continuing place of older media forms in contemporary culture. As Charles R. Acland explains in his *Residual Media* anthology,

> Figures from the past . . . creep up to remind us of their existence and of the influence they wield in the present. For an era such as ours that

puts a premium on advancement and change above all else, declarations of the presence of the past can be confusing or alarming. There is nothing like that old party pooper "historical consciousness" to dull the gleeful celebrations of progress and the new.

(Acland 2007: 13)

If Carolyn Marvin has invited us to study "when old technologies were new" (Marvin 1990), Acland and his contributors urge us to consider old media when they are old. They argue that the continued presence of older communication forms and practices encourages a heightened awareness of the process of scheduled obsolescence and invites a questioning of the prevailing discourse of media revolutions. Residual media, according to Acland, consists of "reconfigured, renewed, recycled, neglected, abandoned and trashed media technologies and practices" which occupy a peripheral space in our culture (Acland 2007: 20). Acland speaks of these older forms as "things and sentiments that won't stay lost, dead, and buried" and references Marc Auge's comment that "history is on our heels, following us like our shadows, like death." Both analogies mirror Gibson's description of "semiotic ghosts" (Acland 2007: 14; Augé cited in Acland 2007: 15; Gibson 1981: 7).

Raymond Williams saw the residual as operating alongside more oft-cited categories of the dominant, the emergent and the archaic: "The residual, by definition, has been effectively formed in the past, but it is still active in the cultural process, not only and often not at all as an element of the past, but as an effective element of the present" (Williams cited in Acland 2007: 21). While archaic practices no longer serve any vital cultural functions, Williams sees the residual as representing "areas of human experience, aspiration, and achievement which the dominant culture neglects, undervalues, opposes, represses, or even cannot recognize" (Williams cited in Acland 2007: 21). Retrofuturism suggests the process by which ideas that once were emergent become residual as tomorrow becomes yesterday.

Will Straw agues that the introduction of digital media has altered our relationship to the residual through our collective project of collecting and recycling the "stuff" of past eras: "The Internet . . . provides the terrain on which sentimental attachments, vernacular knowledge, and a multitude of other relationships to the material culture of the past are magnified and given coherence" (Straw 2007: 4). Straw might well have been thinking about the range of digital practices that supports the growing hobbyist and collector interests in retrofuturism. Collectors can go to eBay to bid on spoons, mugs, plates, pennants, programs, and other knickknacks from the 1939 World's Fair, "the world of tomorrow" (Hillis *et al.* 2006).

Go over to YouTube to access the oft-discussed and rarely seen *Just Imagine* or old *Flash Gordon* and *Buck Rogers* serials. Wikipedia provides ample annotation on the various designers, architects, illustrators, and writers who shaped our sense of what the future looks like. Amateur archivists have assembled digital reproductions of the covers of pulp science fiction or popular science magazines, cataloging an earlier generation's predictions about the shape of things to come. Others have gathered home movies and postcards to construct virtual tours of the 1939 Fair — one of which even has a gift shop where you can buy low-cost reproductions of retro goods. Such activities blur the line between private collections and shared archives as amateur curators educate others into the lore of retro culture. As Straw explains:

> A significant effect of the Internet, I would argue, is precisely this rein-vigoration of early forms of material culture. It is not simply that the Internet, as a new medium, refashions the past within the languages of the present, so that vestiges of the past may be kept alive . . . In fact, the Internet has strengthened the cultural weight of the past, increasing its intelligibility and accessibility. On the Internet, the past is produced as a field of ever greater coherence, through the gathering together of disparate artifacts into sets or collections and through the commentary and annotation that cluster around such agglomerations, made possible in part by high-capacity storage mechanisms.
>
> (Straw 2007: 4)

Ironically, the Westinghouse Time Capsule was one of the major attractions at the 1939 World's Fair — a cache of then contemporary goods being preserved for future generations. Those attending the Fair were intrigued by the prospect of what future archeologists might make of these various memory traces of their own times. *The World of Tomorrow*, a documentary about the Fair, lovingly inventories the contents of the time capsule:

> They were putting in scientific texts and books reduced down to microfilm and messages from our time written by Thomas Mann and

Albert Einstein. There were radio programs and records and comics, daily newspapers, copies of Life and a dozen other magazines. There was a Lilly Dashiel hat, a telephone, a pack of camels. A baseball and a golf tee. There were eyeglasses, a clock, a kewpie doll, a slide rule and a light bulb, a menu from Childs and a dollar in change . . .

The time capsule is premised on a future scarcity — on preserving that which might not otherwise survive. The opposite has turned out to be the case. Even as the time capsule, presumably, remains in deep storage awaiting future generations, the junk that tourists bought at the fair survives, still circulating within an avid collector community.

One subplot in *Terminal City* centers on the aging Hollywood dance team of Fields and Boyles (modeled clearly on Fred and Ginger). B.B., a young woman, has found her way to Terminal City in search of work, unaware that the construction companies that built the city's monumental architecture have largely closed. As her aging landlady is showing her a low-rent apartment, B.B. notices the tattered posters from Fields and Boyles musicals on the walls. She remarks, "My father used to take me to the drive-in when I was a kid to watch those old films. They were great" and referring to the leading lady, she adds, "My dad . . . Gosh, he idolized her. Especially after mom died" (Motter and Lark 1997: 56). The landlady is so touched by the story that she offers B.B. a discount on the rent. Here, residual media operates as a shared reference point across generations.

Loving reproductions of residual media run through a surprising array of contemporary comics. Seth, the artist who drew much of Motter's *Mister X* issues, has devoted much of his career to exploring the allure of older forms of popular culture — whether it's the protagonist of *It's A Good Life If You Never Weaken*'s search for a forgotten comics artist; Wimbledon Green's adventures as a larger-than-life comics collector, or the old memories kicked up by the protagonist's yellowing postcard collection in *Clyde Fans*. Kim Deitch's works (such as *Alias the Cat* or *Boulevard of Broken Dreams*) are crammed with detailed reconstructions of historic animation and comics-related collectibles, often focusing on the narrator's various purchases on eBay as he tries to trace the reign of Waldo, a demonic figure modeled loosely on Felix the Cat (Deitch 2002, 2006, 2007). Ben Katchor's *Julius Knipl, Real Estate Photographer* books are organized around cheap novelties and forgotten haunts of New York City's bygone days (Katchor 1991, 1996, 2003). Alex Ross uses images of a curio shop in *U.S.* to capture Uncle Sam's confused memories of American history (Ross 1997). And Chris Ware organizes several issues of his *Jimmy Corrigan* series around memories and artifacts from the Chicago Expositions of the late nineteenth century (Ware 2004). The autobiographical turn in many contemporary independent comics encourages such writers to reflect on their lives as fans and collectors.

There are some detailed frames created by Seth for some of the *Mister X* comics, which include representations of a whole array of art deco bric-a-brac. Yet, more often, Motter and the collaborating artists design their urban landscape by raiding the image bank of mid-twentieth-century science fiction. In an interview with the author, Motter commented that he was lucky to have identified artistic collaborators who were also fascinated with older images of the future and could work from specific references to older magazine covers or etchings of New York landmarks.

Figure 4.1.   **Seth's illustration for *Mister X* lovingly recreates mid-twentieth-century bric-a-brac and residual media.**

Where Tomorrow Is Today . . .

Consider, for example, this passage from an issue of *Electropolis*:

> Electra City was built at the very beginning of the Electric Age. It was an exciting, sparkling jewel that symbolized a nation's dreams of the future. "Where Tomorrow is Today and Today's yesterday." That's

how they used to describe it. Sounds goofy now but I would envision
its scintillating skyline — the shimmering arcs of the colossal Van Der
Graff Towers and gigantic Strickfadden machines, the air traffic flit-
ting about like moths around a streetlight. I still get that impression
from time to time but when folks began abandoning the city core, the
underworld moved in and that image became obscured by grandiose,
short-lived, and usually catastrophic ambitions. It would never be
the same.

(Electropolis, No. 4: 1)

Motter wallows in what some have called the "electrical sublime" but
in doing so, he blurs the lines between historically accurate Van de
Graaff generators and the mocked-up mad scientist apparatus Kenneth
Strickfadden developed for the Universal horror films of the 1930s.

Nevertheless, these "futuristic" images form a coherent, consistent
and compelling construction of the city; we recognize buildings from
one issue to the next, even from one comic series to the next, and each
new element adds to the integrity of the whole. These elements may
be represented with varying degrees of stylization and abstraction as
they pass through the pens of artists with such different styles as Paul
Rivoche, Jaime Hernandez, Ty Templeton, Dave McKean, and Seth (just
to mention those who contributed to *Mister X*) but we still feel that they
belong in the same fictional universe. Many can be traced back specifically to the 1939 World's Fair — that shining moment when so many
of these archetypes stepped off the printed page and gained a material
reality. As the narrator of *The World of Tomorrow* explains:

> I think that there are moments where you can see the world turning
> from what it is into what it will be. For me, the New York World's Fair is
> such a moment. It is a compass rose pointing in all directions, toward
> imaginary future and real past, false future and immutable present, a
> world of tomorrow contained in the lost American yesterday.

Building on a description from the Firesign Theater's Peter Bergman,
Motter describes *Mister X*'s Radiant City as "a city being imagined in the
30s, built in the 40s and stalled somewhere in the 50s. I'd add that it was
forlornly recalled in the 80s." Each of those temporal markers sums up
a different moment in the historical evolution of our understanding of
the future. The utopian imagination has long embraced the idea of an

Figure 4.2. **The Electrical Sublime in all its glory from the opening of Dean Motter's** *Electropolis.*

"end of history," but there is something suffocating or claustrophobic about a city locked down by a single vision, unable or unwilling to adapt to changed circumstances.

If Sterling once wanted to displace the old "steam-snorting wonders," Motter wants to revisit them as the residue of a bygone era. Here, for example, is the way *Electropolis* describes one of Electra City's architectural wonders:

When erected, the Diogenes Tower was the tallest building on earth atop which was mounted the world's most powerful ozone vapor beacon. The beams from the lighthouse would be visible from hundreds of miles away, even on the foggiest night. Built as the center piece of the Brave New World's Fair, it was probably the most ambitious engineering construction effort of the century.

(*Electropolis*, No. 1: 1)

The Tower was designed to be suicide proof, anticipating its attractiveness to jumpers, but in a fate as ironic as the sinking of the unsinkable *Titanic*, a detective is found hanging from the tower before the building even opens.

Or consider the way *Mister X* characterizes its primary location:

Radiant City was built to be the Dream City, a vast and beautiful Metropolis, designed to fulfill the grandest aesthetic, and architectural ideals, it now moulders in dilapidation. Its citizens are afflicted with sleep disorders, opium addiction, and a surfeit of perversions. It is a place as corrupt as the decadent upper class that rules it, and the human parasites that prey upon them.

(*Mister X*, No. 1: n.p.)

Where Do You Fit In?

The narrator of *The World of Tomorrow* describes his boyhood self as mystified by the 1939 Fair: "Actually tomorrow scared me a little. Could I grasp the immense plan expressed in occult symbols all over the Fair? Would I be up to tomorrow?" Or as a sign in the background of a *Terminal City* panel asks us, "Where Do You Fit In?"

Motter's comics are similarly fascinated by cryptic icons of technological and scientific mastery — as represented through the images carved onto the side of key landmarks such as the *Modern Times* newspaper office (which echoes Chaplin's film) or the Herculean Arms apartment building. The offices Mister X visits are massive communication centers where powerful men control vast empires; the huge mausoleums depicted in the Duncan Cemetery, the Great Mall where robots perform theater, the vast aviary or the huge lobbies depicted in the various hotels and apartment buildings are not built on a human scale. No actual human being would be adequate to the demands this future placed upon them. These cities decline as their residents fall short of those over-inflated expectations.

More simply, though, these buildings have failed to capture their inhabitants' imaginations or inspire their ambitions. Tom Gunning has argued that earlier Fairs were memorable because they were designed to be remembered. Their epic structures sought to astonish on first impressions but were never designed for sustained exposure. Gunning maps the growing disenchantment as we become habituated to such wonders: "Astonishment is inherently an unstable and temporary experience. One finds it difficult to be continually astonished by the same thing. Astonishment gives way to familiarity" (Gunning 2003: 14). We stop seeing our environments when they become simply the backdrop for more mundane activities: "What happens in modernity to the initial wonder at a new technology or device when the novelty has faded into the banality of the everyday?" (Gunning 2003: 42).

Here we might think about Motter's recurring images of somnambulists, sleepwalking along the roofs of skyscrapers, oblivious to their engineering accomplishments or to the vistas that open out before them. Those who suffered from Escher Syndrome (named after graphic artist M.C. Escher) are benumbed to "the banality of the everyday." As a psychiatrist explains in *Terminal City*,

> "The condition really defies any satisfactory explanation. There have been a growing number of cases of somnambulism wherein the subjects are found in strange and precarious situations. They awaken on ledges or rooftops, often hundreds of stories above the street. In many cases there is no physical access to those places. Their means of getting there are completely without explanation and they seem to have no memory."

> (Motter and Lark 1997: 106)

These sleepwalkers are simply one hint of the psychological imbalances experienced by those forced to inhabit utopia. Background images of people jumping off the rooftops, flying cars crashing into buildings, or committing back-alley crimes, all suggest a city which is mentally unbalanced and socially out of sync.

The Hernandez brothers vividly capture this movement from astonishment to disenchantment in a "Tales from Somnopolis" extra: Across three pages of wordless panels we move from skyscrapers, zeppelins, and caretaking robots through increasingly darker images of social decay and urban blight, ending up an apocalyptic image of a flood which washes the city clean again. The series of panels ends with the text, "We hope this tour of our fair and radiant city answers any questions that you may have been too shy to ask. Thank You" (*Mister X*, No. 1: n.p.).

A Tale of Three Cities

Mister X, Terminal City, and *Electropolis* can be read collectively as "A Tale of Three Cities," in which each city has been designed with the best of hopes but is achieving the worst possible results:

> Radiant, Terminal and Electra — they all fell like Babel — each in its own terrible way. One drove its citizens insane. The population went from suffering from disorders like simple kinephilia and luxophrenia to full-blown omniphobia within a single year. Another succumbed to a titanic social depression caused by the termination of the fair it had been built to celebrate. And this township became overpowered by the very industry that had created it, paralyzed by electromagnetism and avarice.
>
> (*Electropolis*, No. 4: 15–16)

It's all there in the story of the "Cast Iron Beach," starting with the high hopes of its boosters: "It was a magical place back then. It was designed to be the amusement section of the fair. It actually opened two years early. Folks came from all over to see it. To enjoy it" (Motter and Lark 1997: 125). But once the city's economy lost its way, the attraction falls into disrepair: "The sand washed away, leaving only the rusting steel plates . . . One can almost hear the ghosts of the midway echoing off the metal scaffolding that once supported a wonderland more fantastic than Alice ever encounters" (Motter and Lark 1997: 77). Or consider the case of "Slant Town," an upper-class neighborhood built upon an unstable hillside property, until the bedrock collapsed, leaving the whole neighborhood dangling at a nine-degree angle (Motter and Lark 1997: 169). The inhabitants of this city now must live in and around the abandoned facilities created for the Brave New World's Fair much as residents of Queens may drive past the rusting remains of the Unisphere from the 1964 New York World's Fair on their way to their nowhere jobs. Things aren't going to get any better from here. Nothing new will be built.

Howard Seigel has traced the ways that a certain ideology of technological utopianism shaped the iconography of early science fiction:

> Technological utopianism derived from the belief in technology —
> conceived as more than tools and machines alone — as the means
> of achieving a "perfect" society in the near future. Such a society,
> moreover, would not only be the culmination of the introduction of
> new tools and machines; it would also be modeled on those tools and
> machines in its institutions, values and culture.
>
> (Seigel 1986: 119)

Early technological utopian writers sought social reform but by the time of the 1939 Fair, this discourse had been co-opted by major corporations to help sell television sets and electric dishwashers.

The original technological utopians believed a more perfect society would emerge from breakthroughs in transportation and communication technologies:

> Connecting all sectors of the technological utopia would be superbly
> efficient transportation and communication systems, powered almost
> exclusively by electricity . . . The specific means of transportation
> would include automobiles, trains, subways, ships, airplanes, even
> moving sidewalks. The means of communication would include pneu-
> matic mail tubes, telephones, telegraphs, radios, and mechanically
> composed newspapers.
>
> (Seigel 1986: 127)

Given this history, it is no accident that Motter refers to one of his cities as "Electropolis" and another as "Terminal City." As comic critic Steve Parker writes,

> Terminal City itself is named for the fact that it lies at the crossroads
> of a number of transport routes . . . But the city also earns the termi-
> nal appellation in another sense, in that becomes the end of the line for
> characters like Quinn, marooned there with his reputation in tatters, or
> BB, the construction work she's seeking having long since dried up.
>
> (Parker 2001)

Figure 4.3. **Motter's vision of the city is built from images half remembered from old popular science and science fiction magazines.**

The books lovingly detail the various transportation options — showing us what it is like to take a joy ride in a flying car, arrive in the city via airship, or walk through the lobby of the futuristic railroad station. At the same time, the books are fascinated with the various systems of communication, depicting what were once seen as futuristic breakthroughs, such as television (introduced to the public at the 1939 Fair) as obsolete and malfunctioning (depicted here in grainy black and white images). Motter's Terminal City still produces and consumes newsreels, Electropolis uses flouriscopes to search crime scenes, and Radiant City still delivers messages through pneumatic tubes.

Rather than philosopher-kings, these cities — Futurama, Radiant City, Democracity, and all of the others — were ruled by godlike engineers, city planners, architects, and designers. As Siegel explains, "in utopia, efficiency would govern government as thoroughly as it would education and industry . . . Because technicians rather than politicians would run the utopian government, it would be technical rather than political in nature" (Siegel 2003: 129).

This technocratic vision sought to perfect human nature through central planning and social engineering. As the narrator of *The World of Tomorrow* explains, "City planners and architects believed they knew what the future had to be like and what ordinary Americans needed to learn to be able to live successfully in it."

Motter's Mister X is a living embodiment of this technocratic vision, perfecting a "unified theory of civilization" he calls psychetecture. The real power in Radiant City rests not with the political leaders, corporate executives or crime bosses but with the Consortium from the Ninth Academy, a cadre of experts from a range of disciplines who pooled their knowledge to design and regulate the ideal urban environment. Mister X's planned city was designed as proof of his belief that good design could enhance the mental health of its residents, but his designs were fatally compromised in their execution. Upon visiting his city for the first time, Mister X reacts with horror as he realizes what they have done to his master plan: "They changed the original design! They cut down on the building materials, cut corners, used a lot of cheap substitutes! The psychetecture was ruined! God knows what effects the actual city is having on all our minds!" (*Mister X*, No. 4: 16). He is determined to either destroy the city or restore its balance.

In one issue, Dave McKean portrays Mister X as an all-knowing figure, whose familiarity with secret passageways allows him to come and go everywhere without being detected:

> He looked into each of the city's eyes, each of its windows and seemed to understand. Where I could see only questions, he saw answers. With each spire and corner, each curve, each cornice he studied. His shoulders became heavier with the burden of knowledge. The burden of dreams.
>
> (*Mister X*, No. 11: n.p.)

And in a dream sequence, Seth depicts Mister X as the very embodiment of the city he designed, his head a cluster of art deco skyscrapers. Like Howard Roark in Ayn Rand's *The Fountainhead*, Mister X refuses to compromise his vision even if it means destroying his own creations. Yet, the more we spend time with Mister X, the less certain we are about his own sanity. Perhaps it was all a delusion from the beginning. Perhaps he has been driven insane by "the shortage of right angles or prime ciphers," the imbalanced claustro/agoraphobic ratio, or the distorted visual ambiguity quotient. Seth's drawings become looser, more distorted, depicting this world as seen by an unhinged mind. Dave McKean's short story captures perfectly the impossibility of grasping the totality of the city through a single intellect:

The city is one huge melting pot of time. During the day, a hazy structure that we must embrace in order to remain sane. But at night, in our sleep, we glimpse the randomness of it all. A city of pauses, fast forwards, stills, cues, and plays. Or is this again the abstract logic of my dreams.

(*Mister X*, No. 11: n.p.)

In the end, the city escapes human comprehension. The only way to survive may well be to sleepwalk along the rooftops, never adopting a panoramic perspective on the whole.

Read through a contemporary lens, the cities imagined by the technological utopians can seem bloodless and antiseptic. This is part of what generates such horror for the protagonist of Gibson's "The Gernsback Continuum":

They were both in white: loose clothing, bare legs, spotless white sun shoes . . . He was saying something wise and strong, and she was nodding, and suddenly I was frightened, frightened in an entirely different way . . . They were smug, happy, and utterly content with themselves and their world. And in the Dream, it was their world . . . It had all the sinister fruitiness of Hitler Youth propaganda.

(Gibson 1981)

Unlike Gibson, Motter stops short of equating technological utopianism with fascism, melding his critique of technocracy with a collector's fascination with the objects in his portfolio.

A kind of nostalgia shapes his representations, for example, of earlier forms of popular entertainment. Images of spectacular night clubs and exotic eateries run through the books — Club Congo, the Jaded Dragon, the Zircon Club in *Mister X*; Rick's Atomic Cafe, the Elbow Room, the Science Club in *Terminal City*; and Flying Saucer Cocktails, the Color Bar, the Mermaid Lounge in *Electropolis*. Motter and his collaborators may be drawing inspiration from the amusement area of the 1939 World's Fair — an embarrassment read by the lofty idealism that shaped the "world of tomorrow," a fascination to those of another age who saw the fair as a last gasp of declining show-business traditions. Motter makes fun of these mid-twentieth-century performances in a scene late in *Electropolis* where a burned-out zeppelin pilot watches an aging and overweight mermaid swim around in her tank: *The World of*

Tomorrow shows a much younger and more attractive "mermaid" swimming topless at an actual 1939 attraction.

These popular amusements have seen better days. But these show people — the stunt fliers, human flies, down-and-out boxers, entertainment entrepreneurs, escape artists, washed-up movie stars and jaded strippers — are the most human figures in the series. As Motter explained in our interview,

> "That era of entertainment was rich with spectacle. Live public exhibition isn't much these days. With TV and the internet now doing most of the work . . . But in the early part of the 20th century, show business was big, clumsy and dangerous (in the pre-Disneyland era), and pretty 'rustic' (in terms of finish). It was exotic, and not always predictable. The industry simply makes it easier and safer today."
>
> (Jenkins 2007)

Cosmo, *Terminal City*'s human fly, describes his camaraderie with the other performers when the Fair first opened: "The competition, while fierce, was usually friendly. There was a kind of bond between those of us in the daredevil trade. We were really competing against the NEW AGE itself. We were fighting against our own obsolescence" (Motter and Lark 1997: 57). Cosmo now works as a window washer, but from time to time, the book calls him back into action and he emerges as the closest thing to a traditional superhero to be found in Motter's work. Through his eyes, we learn the fate of the other show folk: "Woody the Wingwalker's plane temporarily lost control. Little Egypt was eaten alive during her Famous Aquarium Escape when the mummy case was dropped in the wrong tank. Tom McBomb's cannon backfired" (Motter and Lark 1997: 57).

Cosmo is a human embodiment of the residual culture that engulfs the citizens of *Terminal City,* a hero who can be taken out of mothballs for one last adventure because he still holds on to older values and virtues. We might contrast him with Menlo Park, the robot detective at the center of *Electropolis:* Menlo wants desperately to be the kind of tough guy detective that Bogart played in the cinema, but no one quite accepts him as a knight of the streets. He speaks in clichés and the others roll their eyes; he sputters and sparks, but he isn't quite able to replace the human dick who was once his owner. Cosmo is the real thing; Menlo is simply a replicant.

Then there's show business entrepreneur Monty Vickery (a curious cross between Billy Rose, who helped to stage spectacles at the actual fair, Carl Denham the fictional adventurer who brought back King Kong to New York City to amaze the masses in the 1933 film, and Merian Cooper and Ernest Schoedsack, the real-world adventures and producers of the film). Vickery travels the globe collecting the inhabitants of his Evolutionary (including what he promises is the "missing link" in human evolution) and in a master stroke of showmanship, he stages a boxing match in which Kid Gloves fights his way up the evolutionary ladder. As a follow-up, Kid Gloves battles the machines, which are replacing humanity (witness the figure of the robot who manages human laborers at the Herculean Arms). When Gloves bests the machines his heart bursts, like a latterday John Henry, signaling the last gasp of a raw humanity that has not been overcome by mechanization. Here, again, we see the show folk "fighting against their own obsolescence" (Motter and Lark 1997: 57).

"Professor Motter's Hobbyhorses"

Motter surrounds his showmen protagonists with a colorful cast of secondary characters pulled from old *Dick Tracy* comics or long discarded pulp magazines. As Motter explains, "These extraordinary environs needed to be populated by familiar, likeable characters. Archetypal, even cliché" (Jenkins 2007). In Motter's comics larger-than-life characters like the mysterious Woman in Red, Li'l Big Lil (a cross between *Batman*'s The Joker and *Dick Tracy*'s Flat Top but in a plump and aging female body), the Killer Bs, Micassa and Sucassa the art thieves (who engage in constant comic patter inspired by Abbott and Costello), and a slew of other colorful characters struggle to possess the Crown Jewels of Alcazar, the Onyx Astrolab, a map buried beneath a cheap painting of horses playing cards, or some other high-sounding geegaw. These pop culture archetypes become yet another form of the residual at work here. Even though the official representations of the World of Tomorrow promised that we would have overcome crime, eradicated greed, and otherwise perfected human nature, these lowlifes seem to belong in the debased and debauched version of these utopian imaginings depicted here.

As the series moves forward, we see more and more such figures and we find more and more puns and inside jokes that appeal to those most immersed in retro culture. The mayors of Terminal City have included Orwell, Huxley and Gernsback. We meet characters with names like Tessla Coils, Menlo Park, Boris St. Elmo, Alfred MacGuffin, Johnny Picasso, or Raymond Alexander. These jokes extend into the backgrounds: Looking closely at a page set at Ralph's Used Robots, we spot Maria from *Metropolis*, R2D2 and C3PO from *Star Wars*, the Daleks from *Doctor Who*, Robbie the Robot from *Lost in Space*, Klaatu from *The Day the Earth Stood Still*, and even what looks like one of the Rock'em Sock'em Robots. These panels represent a mini-history of the place of the robot in the popular imagination across the past century. Or another panel from the same book shows Metropolis (Superman's or Fritz Lang's — we don't know), Gotham City and Opal City as potential destinations at the train terminal, again linking Motter's cities to the history of urban representation in comics.

By then Motter and his collaborators had taught us to scrutinize every frame for buried details and to search out further information on any elements we do not immediately recognize. We are operating in the space of what Umberto Eco called "the already said" or James Collins described as "the foregrounding of citations" (Eco 1984; Collins 1991).

Collins has pointed to the ways comics, such as *Watchmen* or *The Dark Knight Returns*, tap our memories of earlier moments of popular culture, encouraging us to tap informal archives of commercial artifacts and the shared expertise of the fan community. Motter places similar expectation on his reader's mastery over retro culture and residual media:

> "Of course I hope my readers are hip to my world by now. Initially the approach was to put as many of my influences on the table without the stories becoming scrapbooks for 'Professor Motter's hobbyhorses'. This was the way I gave a wink and a nod to those who were similarly inspired by the same subjects. It paid off, I think. I have met many like-minded creators as a result."
>
> (Jenkins 2007)

As a practical matter, each of these references offer a secret handshake to those already immersed in retro culture. For everyone else, it is easy enough to find a secret decoder ring somewhere on the web.

So we have come full circle, back to the relationship Straw has posited between digital media and residual culture. Motter's works tap the residual at every possible level — from the broad outlines of his city to the smallest detail in the décor, from the names of characters to the archetypes and clichés through which those characters are constructed (one advertisement for *Electropolis* reduces the story to three genre icons — "The Femme Fatale, The Detective, The Architect"). Motter and his collaborators are clearly fans and collectors of this retro culture and, at the same time, they are using these images to pose a mild critique of the ideologies that shaped these earlier images of the future. Throughout all of this, we feel a certain melancholy in our recognition that the imagined world of tomorrow never came or more accurately, in these stories, it came and never left. Either way, the result is a set of shattered dreams and broken promises.

Works Cited
Comics
Deitch, Kim. *Alias the Cat.* New York: Pantheon, 2007.
Deitch, Kim. *Shadowland.* New York: Fantagraphics, 2006.
Deitch, Kim. *The Boulevard of Broken Dreams.* New York: Pantheon, 2002.
Katchor, Ben. *Cheap Novelties: The Pleasures of Urban Decay.* New York: Penguin, 1991.
Katchor, Ben. *Julius Knipl, Real Estate Photographer.* New York: Little, Brown and Company, 1996.
Katchor, Ben. *The Beauty Supply District.* New York: Pantheon, 2003.
McKean, Dave. "Tales from the Somnopolis," *Mister X,* No. 11, n.p.
Motter, Dean. *Electropolis.* Berkeley, CA: Image Comics, 2001–2.
Motter, Dean and Lark, Michael. *Terminal City.* New York: DC Comics (Imprint: Vertigo), 1997.
Motter, Dean and Lark, Michael. *Terminal City: Aerial Graffiti.* New York: DC Comics (Imprint: Vertigo), 1997–8.
Motter, Dean *et al. Mister X.* Toronto, ON: Vortex Comics, 1983–90.
Ross, Alex. *U.S.* New York: DC Comics (Imprint: Vertigo), 1997.
Ware, Chris. *Jimmy Corrigan: The Smartest Kid on Earth.* New York: Jonathan Cape, 2004.

Secondary Literature
Acland, Charles R. "Introduction: Residual Media." In: *Residual Media.* Minneapolis, MN: University of Minnesota Press, 2007.
Acland, Charles R. (ed.). *Residual Media.* Minneapolis, MN: University of Minnesota Press, 2007.
Acland, Charles R. "The Swift View: Tachistoscopes and the Residual Modern." In: Charles R. Acland (ed.), *Residual Media.* Minneapolis, MN: University of Minnesota Press, 2007. 361–84.
Bird, Larry. World of Tomorrow. WNET New York, 1984.
Collins, Jim. "Batman: The Movie, Narrative: The Hyperconscious." In: Roberta E. Pearson and William Uricchio (eds.), *The Many Lives of the Batman.* New York: Routledge, 1991. 164–81.

Corn, Joseph J. (ed.). *Imagining Tomorrow: History, Technology, and the American Future.* Cambridge, MA: MIT Press, 1986.

Corn, Joseph J. and Horrigan, Brian. *Yesterday's Tomorrows: Past Visions of the American Future.* Baltimore, MD: John Hopkins University Press, 1984.

Eco, Umberto. *Postscript to the Name of the Rose.* New York: Harcourt Brace, 1984.

Gibson, William. "The Gernsback Continuum." In: Bruce Sterling (ed.), *Mirrorshades: A Cyberpunk Anthology.* New York: Bantam, 1981. 1–11.

Gunning, Tom. "Re-Newing Old Technologies: Astonishment, Second Nature, and the Uncanny in Technology from the Previous Turn-Of-The-Century." In: David Thorburn and Henry Jenkins (eds.), *Rethinking Media Change: The Aesthetics of Transition.* Cambridge, MA: MIT Press, 2003.

Hillis, Ken, Petit, Michael and Epley, Nathan Scott (eds.). *Everyday eBay: Culture, Collecting and Desire.* London: Routledge, 2006.

Jameson, Fredric. "Progress versus Utopia, or, Can We Imagine the Future?" In: *Archaeologies of the Future: The Desire Called Utopia and Other Science Fictions.* London: Verso, 2005. 288–9.

Jenkins, Henry. "The Future Isn't What It Used to Be: An Interview with Comics Creator Dean Motter (June 6, 2007)." Available online at: http://www.henryjenkins.org/2007/06/an_interview_with_comics_creat.html (accessed October 1, 2009.)

McLuhan, Marshall. *Understanding Media: The Extensions of Man.* Cambridge, MA: MIT Press, 1994.

Marvin, Carolyn. *When Old Technologies Were New: Thinking about Electronic Communication in the Late Nineteenth Century.* Oxford: Oxford University Press, 1990.

Parker, Steve. "The Friday Review: *Terminal City* (November 9, 2001)." Available online at http://www.ninthart.com/display.php?article=150 (accessed June 4, 2008).

Seigel, Howard. "The Technological Utopians." In: Joseph J. Corn (ed.), *Imagining Tomorrow: History, Technology and the American Future.* Cambridge, MA: MIT Press, 1986.

Sterling, Bruce. "Preface." In: Bruce Sterling (ed.). *Mirrorshades: A Cyberpunk Anthology.* New York: Bantam, 1981.

Straw, Will. "Embedded Memories." In: Charles R. Acland (ed.), *Residual Media.* Minneapolis, MN: University of Minnesota Press, 2007. 3–15.

5

Remembrance of Things to Come: François Schuiten and Benoît Peeters's *Cities of the Fantastic*

STEFANIE DIEKMANN

I N MANY WAYS, FRANÇOIS SCHUITEN and Benoît Peeters's comic book series *Cities of the Fantastic* is a perfect illustration of the concept of the "pastiche" as it has been developed by Fredric Jameson in his landmark publication on postmodernist aesthetics (Jameson 1991). In Jameson, there is, of course, no mention of comics, while painting, photography, film, video, architecture, and literature all have a place in his argument. Nevertheless, most of the much quoted remarks on "complacent eclecticism" (Jameson 1991: 18), "depersonalized visual curiosity" (Jameson 1991: 17) or "cannibalization of all the architectural styles of the past" (Jameson 1991: 19) could have been written as a comment on the world created by Schuiten and Peeters — just as that world could have been designed in response to Jameson's book. (It was not. The first three volumes appeared years before the publication of *Postmodernism, or, The Cultural Logic of Late Capitalism*.)

At a moment when some of the core concepts and key words of postmodernist theory have acquired a certain patina, it is interesting to revisit the Fantastic Continent. Conceptualized as a long-term narrative about a civilization "out of time," the series now seems to unfold within a time bubble of its own in which the principles of "imitation of dead styles" (Jameson 1991: 12) and the approach to the past "by way of our own pop images and simulacra" (Jameson 1991: 25) are still intact. The series' attitude towards the imaginary museum of architectural history has not changed much over the past three decades, and any visit to the Fantastic Cities seems to set time back to the 1980s and early 1990s when eclecticism and faux historicity were very much en vogue.

In their *Guide des Cités / Guide to the Cities* (1996) and also on the Cities' "official" website *Urbicande*, Schuiten and Peeters present their inventions as ethnographic realia (both mimicking and mocking the pretense of real existence, which is constitutive for conventional forms of storytelling). This pseudo-ethnographic, proto-encyclopedic approach will be pursued in the following observations, not so much in the spirit of homage but to convey something of the strange mixture of tongue-in-cheek attitude and meticulous rendering, which characterizes all publications on the Fantastic Continent.

The Cities

There are ten big Cities of the Fantastic: Alaxis, Armilia, Blossfeldstadt, Brüsel, Calvani, Mylos, Pâhry, Sodrovno-Voldachie (an agglomeration), Urbicande, and Xhystos.[1] It is possible that other Cities exist or will be brought into existence through tales, but for the moment these are the places and names as they are listed in the *Guide des Cités*, which serves as a handbook to the Fantastic Continent and as a guide to the Cities' main sites and characteristics.

Like that other famous account of imaginary urbanity, Thomas More's *Utopia*, the books by Schuiten and Peeters deal with a territory, not with one city state alone. However, unlike the cities of Utopia, all modeled on the same prototype (More 2003), the Cities of the Fantastic are different in appearance and often different in the challenges (topological, meteorological, institutional, political) they pose to their inhabitants. Each of them constitutes a realm of its own, and although the *Guide* lists a number of characteristics that apply to the Continent in general, it also has a separate entry for every City and gives each its own attribute: Alaxis is the "City of Pleasure," Calvani is the "City of Plants," Mylos is called "The Industrial Complex," etc.

In our world, chronicles of the Cities started exactly 25 years ago with a story about *Les murailles de Samaris / The Great Walls of Samaris* (1983).[2] Since then, the chronicles have developed into an extensive project with a core series of no less than 11 volumes,[3] and another 10 volumes published *hors série* plus supplementary works like the *Guide*. Interestingly enough, the *Guide* points out that stories about successful passages between the Cities and our world have increased in recent years, which suggests that the Fantastic Continent may become more accessible and open to exploration in the near future.[4]

Furnishing

Like other narrators of other tales about other fantastic places, Schuiten and Peeters claim to have made the passage themselves at least once, that is, to have traveled the Continent, to have visited several of the Cities, and to have received first-hand descriptions of those they have not visited.[5] From this passage, they have returned, like Marco Polo or the heroes of Jonathan Swift, Jules Verne, and Italo Calvino, to bear witness to the existence of places that would otherwise remain unheard of. (One wonders if there are any studies about the "re-" in utopian narration: the retrospective character of utopian fantasies; the return that precedes the tale; the tale that constitutes a form of return in itself; the remembrance of the utopian city in words or images; the deeply melancholic nature of the whole enterprise.)

Based on their travels and notes, the two artists report that the Cities are best described as "a distorted mirror image" (Schuiten and Peeters 1997: 6) of our world that is similar in many aspects and strikingly different in others. "The exact relation between the two worlds is still a mystery," they write, "there are certainly connections but their true nature is yet to be determined."[6] A little vague in nature, this statement places the Fantastic Continent somewhere between two definitions Umberto Eco has given: one of the utopian city in science fiction and one of "classical" Utopia. In science fiction, Eco writes, there is always an attempt to explain the existence of the parallel or mirror world through "fissures" and "fractures" in the space-time continuum.[7] By contrast, classical Utopia is usually imagined as a faraway place in a remote corner of the world which is also inhabited by the readers. Accounts of these places seem to show little interest in questions of collocation or logical possibility. Instead, they concentrate on what Eco calls "the furnishing" (Eco 1990: 215–16): infrastructure, urban planning, architecture, technological development and local facilities, and in a more abstract sense, social and political order.

A certain amount of respect has been paid to the conventions of science fiction in the stories about the Cities of the Fantastic, for example when the *Guide* hints at the existence of "connections" and "passageways" between the Fantastic Continent and our world (Schuiten and Peeters 1997: 48–58), or when a two-way passage between different realms and spheres is illustrated in *L'enfant penchée / The Tilted Child* (1995). Nevertheless, the main focus, from *Les murailles de Samaris* to *La théorie du grain de sable / Theory of the Grain of Sand* (2008), is undoubtedly on the "furnishing," and within the furnishing most closely on the whims and wonders of architectural ambition.

Architecture

Even in its more forbidding aspects, the Fantastic Continent is a picturesque world which lends itself to beautiful and very decorative illustrations, from Pâhry, the famously beautiful, to Mylos, the industrial complex with its towers, chimneys, and fearsome machines. As I have already pointed out, urban planning and architecture on the Fantastic Continent are by no means uniform. Yet they are fairly homogenous within every City in the sense that each is dominated by a specific architectural style or a specific feature. For this reason, travel on the Fantastic Continent could be described as a tour of architectural designs and prototypes: industrial buildings and Victorian styles (Mylos), iron girders, structural engineering and art deco (Xhystos), crystal palaces and greenhouses (Calvani), Orientalism (Alaxis), the high-rises of the 1920s (Pâhry), onion domes and painted roofs (Sodrovno-Voldachie).[8]

In the rare case that one of the Fantastic Cities presents different faces (façades, skylines) to the viewer, it does so programmatically like the City of Samaris, which tricks the eye of its visitors with a huge stage setting made to suggest solidity and a long architectural history, or like the City of Urbicande where the North Bank is left to uncontrolled growth and decay while the South Bank appears as an extremely ordered ensemble designed to the tastes of this City's repressive magistrate (see *Les murailles de Samaris* and *La fièvre d'Urbicande*). Of course, confinement to one style or principle may result in uniformity and monotony. From the *Guide* we learn that in Blossfeldtstadt, where all designs are modeled on the ornamental, proto-architectural photographs made by Karl Blossfeldt in the late 1920s (see Blossfeldt 1994), repetition of forms soon became the object of critical comments, finally leading to

Figure 5.1. **View of Xhystos**

From: François Schuiten and Benoît Peeters. *Les murailles de Samaris*. Brussels: Casterman, 1983, 13. © Casterman.

a liberalization of architectural laws. In Xhystos, where no such liberalization took place, several quarters and many streets are so identical in appearance that the inhabitants get lost for hours in the inner city and are unable to find their way back to their homes (Schuiten and Peeters 1997: 130).

The Cities of the Fantastic are not designed to be lived in. They are best approached in the role of an explorer, and it is not by chance that many books in the series tell their story from the point of view of the visitor (*Le murailles de Samaris*), the traveler (*La route d'Armilia*), the vagrant/stranger (*Mary, la penchée*), or the investigator (*La tour*). Sometimes, an inhabitant of the Cities (of course, there are inhabitants but they are never very comfortable) becomes an explorer of the place that he seemed to know well, like Constantin Abeels in *Brüsel* or the unfortunate "urbitect" Eugen Robick in *La fièvre d'Urbicande*, only to discover that he does in fact know very little about it, which may either cause him to leave the City or to make a new start in his approach.

Models

An unwritten rule seems to demand that in accounts about imaginary cities (More's Utopia, Tomasso de Campanella's City of the Sun, Johannes Valentinus Andreae's Republic of Christianopolis, to mention but a few), the political and the architectural should not be treated as two different aspects of urbanity. On the contrary, they usually appear closely linked (see Krau 2006: 77). The series about the Fantastic Continent is no exception to this rule, as politics and political troubles in the Cities are usually "about" architecture (*Brüsel, La tour*), and if not directly about architecture then about cartography and the maintenance of inner and outer city borders (*La frontière invisible / The Invisible Frontier*). Disturbances of the architectural order always seem to imply disturbances of the political and vice versa (*Le murailles de Samaris, La fièvre d'Urbicande*), and if a collapse occurs in a City's administration, this collapse may well become literal and translate into a breakdown of the urban setting itself.

The interdependency of architectural and political order is one link between the Fantastic Continent and older examples of utopistic urbanity. Another is the fact that the descriptions and depictions of the Cities evoke a number of topoi, which have dominated the representation of imaginary cities from the very beginning. The Sunken City, the City as Monument, the Glorious, Sinful City, the Tower, the Fortress, the Labyrinth, the New Jerusalem: They all have been resurrected and created, not just in the history of comic book literature at large (Luther 2006: 128 *et seq.*), but also in the fantastic chronicles by Schuiten and Peeters in which the Sunken City is called Armilia and the Glorious, Sinful city could be either Alaxis or Pâhry, where cities like Xhystos and Galatograd (part of the agglomeration of Sodrovno-Voldachie) were originally built as fortresses, where a labyrinth is among the main attractions of the City of Pâhry, where a tower of gigantic proportions stands at the very center of the Fantastic Continent's mythology, and where at least two of the Cities, Urbicande and Calvani, have once been wiped out by catastrophes and replaced by new structures which, like the New or Celestial Jerusalem, are erected on the ruins of the old.

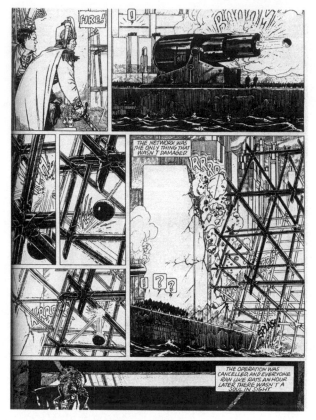

Figure 5.2. **Architectural and political disturbances**
From: François Schuiten and Benoît Peeters. *Fever in Urbicande*. New York: NBM, 1990, 57. ©
Casterman; © NBM for English translations.

Retrofuturism

Time is warped on the Continent and in the Cities. It is not experienced differently from time in our world (there are still night and day, the days do not seem longer, the nights do not seem shorter) but it is measured differently, and calculation of time starts anew every now and then, at intervals that are not transparent to the outside observer.

The *Guide des Cités* gives various explanations for the difference between our time and time on the Continent. In some aspects, these explanations are modeled on the difference between time in space and time on earth, for example, when time on the Continent is described as passing more slowly,[9] so that ten years in any of the Fantastic Cities equal more than 100 years in this world. The three centuries chronicled by the *Guide*'s fantastic timetable — from Giovanni Battista's expedition into the tower (*La tour*) to Mary von Rathen's rise as the new leader of Mylos (*L'enfant penchée*) (Schuiten and Peeters 1997: 24–33) — would add up to more than 3,000 years on the other side of the "distorted mirror," and the Continental development of art and technology would "cover" everything from the ancient polis to the internet. However, in a constellation of distorted mirrors, things tend to be turned around and twisted more than once, and the history of art, architecture and technology on the Fantastic Continent is not organized according to any concepts of linear development or to the 1:10 ratio suggested by the *Guide*. It follows its own laws which are those of eclecticism and simultaneity.

Those who search the series about the Fantastic Cities for art historical and architectural references will discover allusions to the work of Piranesi, Etienne-Louis Boullée, Hugh Ferris; to other visionary architectural drawings; to the tales of Jorge Luis Borges, Franz Kafka, Italo Calvino and Julien Gracq; to films by Fritz Lang and Terry Gilliam, and to the designs of Victor Horta or the Arts and Crafts movement (supplemented by elements of medievalism; which are most prominent in *La tour* and *L'enfant penchée*). A list of influences put together by Benoît Peeters in a contribution to an anthology about imaginary architecture is even more extensive (see Peeters 2006: 143–5) but no matter how many styles and designs are evoked by the settlements on the Fantastic Continent, the most present epoch is the long nineteenth century, era of architectural follies and accelerated urbanization.

It is also an era of technological innovations, both real and imagined. Steam engines, aircrafts, telephones, and photography all play a role, as do more prosaic inventions like vacuum cleaners and synthetics. In their rendering of these inventions, Schuiten and Peeters show a decided preference for the "retro" aesthetics of outdated forms and shapes, the ornamental aspects of machinery and vehicles, and the appeal of muted colors and fragile contours. (All this evokes the idea of the *fin-de-siècle* in much the same way as "Rome" or "China" are evoked in some of the artifacts discussed by Roland Barthes in his *Mythologies* (see Barthes 1972).) The same principle applies to the depiction of those devices which do not exactly have a counterpart in our world but are still vaguely familiar as they seem to have sprung from the books by H.G. Wells and Jules Verne:[10] zeppelins, amphibian vehicles, spacecrafts with wings and tails and a glass capsule for aeronauts; electronic brains, extensive filing systems; laboratories, observatories, giant telescopes; and, of course, an array of the most amazing skyscrapers and superstructures, all depicted with a great love for detail and with an eye for decorative effects.

In a sense, this is a series of picture books, an illustrated encyclopedia of past visions of the future. It is also a series of pastiches,[11] never completely imitative, yet never completely original, often reminiscent of projects that actually existed and always ambivalent in its depiction of early modernity. As Jens Balzer has indicated in an interesting article on retrofuturist comic book aesthetics (in his case: works by Myazaki, Moebius, and Ware), these aesthetics are never innocent as they represent a spectrum of escapist, faux-nostalgic or plainly "fake" approaches.[12] This applies also to the comic book series by Schuiten and Peeters in which the commemoration of modernist imagination goes hand in hand with narratives of failure, destruction, and a general sense of incalculability and imminent disaster.

Ambitions

Among the nineteenth-century projects that have a history on both sides of the distorted mirror are the opera house of Paris (Pâhry); the Great World Fair (again held in Pâhry, glamorous city of festivals and representative architecture); the Palace of Justice in Brussels (Brüsel); the huge conservatories of which some still survive in the botanical gardens of Europe while a far greater number cover the center of the City of Calvani; the industrial cathedrals of the Victorian age duplicated everywhere in the City of Mylos; and many more. Sometimes, the mirror world is marked by a certain banality (there is a passing mention of vacuum cleaners and of a successful marketing campaign by Brüsel magnate Henry de Vrouw), sometimes the mirror image appears a little too constructed (for example in the case of Sodrovno-Voldachie, long closed off from the rest of the Continent and based on a Cold War model of the "Eastern Bloc" (Schuiten and Peeters 1997: 116–18)) but these are exceptions to the unwritten rule which demands that the Cities of the Fantastic are best portrayed as a world of grand schemes and ambitious designs.

Size matters on the Continent. This is not a world of small scales, and no matter what plans and projects are pursued by the representatives of the Cities, they are usually carried out to maximum effect. According to the *Guide*, appraisal of Fantastic Technology is based on two main principles:

First, that all machinery should be attractive to the eye (it is, and great trouble is taken by François Schuiten to produce adequate depictions of the aircrafts of Blossfeldstadt or the chronometrical spheres of Armilia). Second, that it should be as large as possible as largeness is taken as an indicator of solidity and value (Schuiten and Peeters 1997: 45). The same seems true of architectural projects like the mythical tower, the cartographic research station on the plains of Sodrovno-Voldachie or the new municipal buildings in the City of Brüsel. All these buildings are huge in scale and very impressive (whereas, as Jameson has pointed out, "the

Figure 5.3. **Megalomanic architecture, slighty dysfunctional. The cartographic research station of Sodrovno-Voldachie**

From: François Schuiten and Benoît Peeters. *The Invisible Frontier*. New York: NBM, 2002, 9.
© Casterman; © NBM for English translations.

technology of our own moment no longer possesses this same capacity for representation" (Jameson 1991: 36). Unfortunately, they also tend to be rather dysfunctional, and the chronicles of the Fantastic Continent are full of stories about failed projects, abandoned construction sites, and other enterprises that have been left half-finished.

This, however, does not make them any less interesting to Schuiten and Peeters. On the contrary, while it is undoubtedly true that the authors of *Les murailles de Samaris*, *La fièvre d'Urbicande* or *Brüsel* celebrate the wonders of imaginary architecture (and architectural imagination), tales of hubris and excessive planning also form part of their tales. The architects, "urbitects"[13] and cartographers whose fate is tied to the Cities of the Fantastic are all forced to acknowledge their limitations when they come face to face with urban or spatial structures, which seem to metamorphose out of their own account, without any intervention from the designers and for no plausible reason.

Space organizes itself on the Fantastic Continent. The same is true of architecture, and the fact that those reorganizations and transformations take place at very irregular intervals and always unpredictably makes them all the more unsettling. In *La fièvre d'Urbicande*, the structure of the divided city and the near-perfect grid are disturbed (and literally "crossed out") by the exponential growth of a mysterious cube, discovered at one of the construction sites and deposited in the office of the chief urbitect. In *Brüsel*, the brutalist implementation of a new city structure is followed by the collapse of the buildings and later by a flood which leaves the city uninhabitable. In *Le frontier invisible*, maps become invalid and cartographic work turns into a hopeless enterprise when geographic markers of the former border start to shift, and in *Les murailles de Samaris*, two settlements, which were once solid and inhabitable, are transformed into stage settings that are maintained by an invisible force ("depth is replaced by surface, or by multiple surfaces" (Jameson 1991: 12)).

Progress

You do not want to underestimate the Cities — neither their transformative powers nor the forces at work within them. There is a strong undercurrent of cultural pessimism in the stories about the Fantastic Continent, the interest in past visions of the future notwithstanding, and it is in accordance with this pessimism that ambition turns into hubris

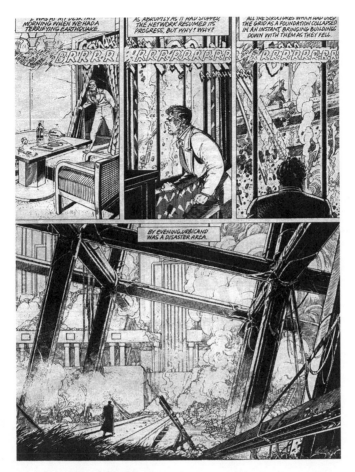

Figure 5.4. **The cube and the city**
From: François Schuiten and Benoît Peeters. *Fever in Urbicande*. New York: NBM, 1990, 84.
© Casterman; © NBM for English translations.

and that hubris is punished by failure and humiliation in the face of the Cities' unpredictability.

That tale of cultural pessimism is probably most prominent in *Brüsel*, which may account for this comic's particular popularity. As a matter of fact, *Brüsel* could well be used as a textbook on the perils of modernization and be re-named *A Lesson for Constantin Abeels* as it tells the story of this character's fall from and stand against "progress," which he experiences as a corrupt and destructive force. To fall from "progress," Constantin has to start out as a believer — in "progress" as a cause and in the necessity to remove whatever stands in the way of it (like, for example, organic plants, sickness, old buildings, and medieval squares). The characters he encounters in the course of his quest propose to take care of the removals and to introduce whatever serves the progressive cause (examples here: plastic plants, medical technology, skyscrapers, elevated highways). And it takes a long time before the protagonist begins to doubt their authority and decides to leave the City in search of a better place.

That it should take him so long is a little surprising as signs of dysfunctionality and destruction can be found in *Brüsel* from the very beginning, starting with the breakdown of phone lines and water supplies and then increasing chapter by chapter, affecting most aspects of life in the City, that is, administration, building regulations, transport and medical care. Again and again, *Brüsel* points out that "progress" as it is imagined by the Abeels and other characters goes against the laws of nature itself: the change of seasons (the inventor Axel Wappendorf and Professor Dersenval hope to do away with it), human anatomy (Professor Vincent has developed a method to "optimize" the inside of the human body in one single operation), the need for food, even the need to breathe. Therefore, belief in "progress" must seem both monstrous and ridiculous, and the final declaration "we have all been sick" — "yes, sick with progress" is as heartfelt as it seems inevitable and a little overdue (Schuiten and Peeters 1985: 119).

This is a comic book with a simple message and clear-cut oppositions. Or so it seems. At the same time, it is also the comic book in which Schuiten and Peeters's fascination with "big" construction and technology appears at its most obvious: in the city model, which prefigures the model city planned by the magistrate, in the administration's electronic brain with its many cables and massive casings, in the electrotherapeutic apparatus (reminiscent of so many Frankenstein films), in the medical instruments, in Mr. de Vrouw's zeppelin, and, finally, in the strange vehicle that is used in the protagonists' escape from Brüsel (in the direction of the City of Calvani, a "green" settlement and the appropriate destination for those who wish to recover from the evil impacts of civilization).

Gender

In these tales of order and disorder, the role of women is rather stereotyped. From Brüsel to Sodrovno, from Urbicande to Mylos, the Cities of the Fantastic are first and foremost a setting for the conflicts and confrontations of "representative men": the artist, the visionary, the builder, the entrepreneur, the politician, the bureaucrat. The search for clarity and control is theirs, as is the struggle with the unpredictable transformations of the urban scenario. Most of the tales are told from their perspective (with the exception of *L'enfant penchée* which, on closer inspection, may not be an exception at all, as Mary von Rathen's story is juxtaposed with that of the painter Augustin Desombres), and if the transformations of a City translate into the transformations of characters, it is the men who show themselves affected while the women seem largely indifferent, or at least unperturbed.

The Cities may not be men's work entirely. But they certainly are a man's world where urban development and urban rule are negotiated by male protagonists and their adversaries, where the work of town planning (*La fièvre d'Urbicande*), construction work (*Brüsel*), maintenance (*La tour*), investigation (*Les murailles de Samaris*), cartography (*La frontière invisible*), economy (*La route d'Armilia, L'enfant penchée*), and political representation is carried out by men, and where men's encounters with their limits is equated with encountering the limits of ratio and plausibility. The appearance of women usually takes place only after some disturbance in the order of things has already been noticed: Constantin Abeels meets Tina after his shop has been cut off from the water and the telephone networks, Eugen Robick meets Sophie after the miraculous cube has started to grow out of his house, Giovanni Battista meets Milena when the signs of the Great Tower's disintegration have become obvious and alarming, and so forth.

In each of these cases, the female character brings the double promise of sex and subversion. Again, this is very obvious in *Brüsel* where Tina Tonero (one of the few female characters with a surname) divides her time between seduction and sabotage, often carrying on both at the same time. Sophie in *La fièvre d'Urbicande* is a brothel owner who starts a campaign to replace the supporter of the old regime by her lover Robick.[14] In *La frontière invisible*, Skodra is also a sex worker whose subversive potentials become manifest directly on her body where the "true" frontier of Sodrovno is reproduced in the form of a mark, and in *L'enfant penchée* the link between the female body and the subversion of order is literalized even further as the protagonist's physique defies the laws of gravity itself (that is: *ordinary* gravity) and shows the influences of a "counter-sphere," which will manifest itself later in the story.

In accordance with the overall "retro" charms of the Fantastic Cities, the concept of rebellion promoted in the series is somewhat anachronistic as desire is equated with disturbance and sex is equated with unruliness while femininity is clearly associated with corporeality and emotion. No matter how much the laws of gravity may be disturbed (or the principles of order and rationality be challenged by the mysterious metamorphosis of space and surroundings), the laws of gender stereotyping remain firmly intact, and it is in their representation of gender relations that the chronicles by Schuiten and Peeters appear most repetitive.

Future

Is there a future for the Fantastic Cities? If the ongoing success of the series suggests that there is, this future lies not in any response to or reflection on "changing aesthetics," but in the series' virtuosic aptitude to develop the image of the Fantastic Continent further and further without introducing any actual development. The Cities do not adapt, nor is there any sign that the principles of decorative rendering, mysterious hints and overall eclecticism, which govern their representation, will ever be abandoned. The time capsule is closed, the Continent sealed off against outside influences but still accessible as a destination of imaginary travel — all the more so, if that travel is motivated by nostalgia, which is often the case in comic book history.

Works Cited
Comics
Schuiten, François and Peeters, Benoît. *Brüsel.* Brussels: Casterman, 1992. Published in English as *Brüsel.* New York: NBM, 2001.
Schuiten, François and Peeters, Benoît. *La fièvre d'Urbicande.* Brussels: Casterman, 1985. Published in English as *Fever in Urbicande.* New York: NBM, 1990.
Schuiten, François and Peeters, Benoît. *La frontière invisible,* Vol. 1. Brussels: Casterman, 2002. Published in English as *The Invisible Frontier.* New York: NBM, 2002.
Schuiten, François and Peeters, Benoît. *La frontière invisible,* Vol. 2. Brussels: Casterman, 2004. Published in English as *The Invisible Frontier,* Vol. 2. New York: NBM, 2004.
Schuiten, François and Peeters, Benoît. *La route d'Armilia.* Brussels: Casterman, 1988.
Schuiten, François and Peeters, Benoît. *La théorie du grain de sable,* Vol. 1. Brussels: Casterman, 2007.
Schuiten, François and Peeters, Benoît. *La théorie du grain de sable,* Vol. 2. Brussels: Casterman, 2008.

Schuiten, François and Peeters, Benoît. *La Tour.* Brussels: Casterman, 1987. Published in English as *The Tower.* New York: NBM, 1993.

Schuiten, François and Peeters, Benoît. *L'enfant penchée.* Brussels: Casterman, 1996.

Schuiten, François and Peeters, Benoît. *Les murailles de Samaris.* Brussels: Casterman, 1983. Published in English as *The Great Walls of Samaris.* New York: NBM, 1987.

Secondary Literature

Balzer, Jens. "Wer hat an der Uhr gedreht. Gefälschtes Gedächtnis, stillstehende Zeit. Über einige Motive in den Comics von Myazaki Hayao, Moebius und Chris Ware." In: Stefanie Diekmann and Matthias Schneider (eds.), *Szenarien des Comic. Helden und Historien im Medium der Schriftbildlichkeit.* Berlin: SuKuLTuR, 2005. 145–56.

Barthes, Roland. *Mythologies,* translated by Annette Lavers. London: Paladin, 1972.

Blossfeldt, Karl. *Urformen der Kunst.* Munich: Schirmer/Mosel, 1994.

Eco, Umberto. "Die Welten der Science Fiction." In: *Über Spiegel.* Munich: dtv, 1990. 214–22.

Jameson, Fredric. *Postmodernism, or, The Cultural Logic of Late Capitalism.* Durham: Duke University Press, 1991.

Krau, Ingrid. "Utopie und Ideal — In Stadtutopie und Idealstadt." In: Winfried Nerdinger (ed.), *Architektur wie sie im Buche steht. Fiktive Bauten und Städte in der Literatur.* Salzburg: Anton Pustet, 2006. 75–82.

Luther, Diane. "Phantastische Architektur im Comic." In: Winfried Nerdinger (ed.), *Architektur wie sie im Buche steht. Fiktive Bauten und Städte in der Literatur.* Salzburg: Anton Pustet, 2006. 128–36.

More, Thomas. *Utopia.* London: Penguin Books, 2003.

Peeters, Benoît. "Reisen in die Geheimnisvollen Städte." In: Winfried Nerdinger (ed.), *Architektur wie sie im Buche steht. Fiktive Bauten und Städte in der Literatur.* Salzburg: Anton Pustet, 2006. 137–45.

Schuiten, François and Peeters, Benoît. *Le Guide des Cités.* Brussels: Casterman, 1996. Published in German as *Führer durch die geheimnisvollen Städte.* Stuttgart: Feest Comics, 1997.

Schuiten, François and Peeters, Benoît. *Urbicande* [website]. http://www.urbicande.be (accessed November 15, 2008).

Notes

1 On the series' official website (http://www.urbicande.be) the number of cities listed is only nine, due to the omission of Armilia. As Armilia is already described as a sunken, subterranean city in *Le Guide des Cités,* published in 1996 (and, before that, in *La route d'Armilia*), we have to assume that it has now become completely inaccessible, and that this fact is reflected in the updated list. (Another "official" website of the Fantastic Cities is OBSKÜR (http://www.ebbs.net.)

2 Of the 11 volumes of the core series, only six have been translated into English: *The Great Walls of Samaris* (1987), *Fever in Urbicand* (1990), *The Tower* (1993), *Brüsel* (2001), *The Invisible Frontier I* (2002) and *The Invisible Frontier II* (2004), all published by NBM (Nantier Beall Minoustchine), New York. There are no English editions of any of the books published *hors série.* In this chapter,

those books which have not been translated are given a "provisional" English title when they are first mentioned; otherwise, the full or abbreviated French title is used.

3   The most recent is *La théorie du grain de sable II / The Theory of the Grain of Sand II* (see Schuiten and Peeters 2008).

4   I take this information from the German edition of *Le Guide des Cités* (see Schuiten and Peeters 1997: 49).

5   There is a certain affinity between utopian literature and travel writing. Utopia is never "around the corner," and the idea of distance, both literal and metaphorical, is constitutive to the genre.

6   My translation. Original text: "Das genaue Verhältnis der beiden Welten ist nach wie vor rätselhaft: Es existieren sicherlich Querverbindungen, aber wie diese genau beschaffen sind, konnte noch immer nicht geklärt werden" (Schuiten and Peeters 1997: 7).

7   In this sense, all science fiction is mostly "about" plausibility and probability which, according to Eco, makes it a proto-academic enterprise (see Eco 1990: 216).

8   As a matter of fact, this tour, or at least part of it, has already been turned into a story of its own, which is told by Schuiten and Peeters in *La route d'Armilia / The Road to Armilia* (Schuiten and Peeters 1988).

9   This observation is made by Mary von Rathen, one of the few inhabitants of the Fantastic Continent who has made the passage to our world and back, and has long acted as the main correspondent and informant of Schuiten and Peeters on all facts pertaining to the history of the Fantastic Continent (see Schuiten and Peeters 1997: 20–1).

10   Verne himself is reported to be a frequent traveler on the Fantastic Continent, and a chance encounter between him and the Schuiten and Peeters character Axel Wappendorf is depicted in one episode of *L'enfant penchée* (see Schuiten and Peeters 1996: 125–9).

11   The effect of "glossy mirage" that Jameson discovered in certain Hollywood films of the 1980s is also to be found in Schuiten and Peeters's rendering of the Fantastic Continent and its settlements (see Jameson 1991: 21).

12   It also provides a frame for self-reflection, because, as Jens Balzer has pointed out, the era of early modernism is also the era which saw the beginnings of comics, and any reference to this era seems to suggest a look at the origin of comics, either in a "lost world" of more innocent and optimistic modernity, or in a world that is already marked by failed projects and a more skeptical outlook (Balzer 2005: 152–4).

13   The term "urbitect" first appears in *La fièvre d'Urbicande / Fever in Urbicande* where it is used to define the profession of the protagonist, Eugen Robick (see Schuiten and Peeters 1985).

14   Among the female characters of Schuiten and Peeters, Sophie may be the most interesting. A woman with a past, she sees her future in the administration of Urbicande's sex business, thus making the transition from illegal to regulated business and from the margins of society to the center.

6

Paris au pluriel: Depictions of the French Capital in Jacques Tardi's Comic Book Writing

MICHAEL CUNTZ

I T MIGHT NOT BE TOO obvious a choice to start this article by mentioning Edmond Choupard. Even the knowledgeable Tardi expert, or the dedicated fan for that matter, might need a moment to remember this character that is explicitly introduced as secondary. Nonetheless, it is he whom we follow on his daily — or should we say nightly — walk home at the beginning of *Momies en folie*, the fourth episode of Jacques Tardi's *belle époque* series *Adèle Blanc Sec* from 1978. In the voice-over narrative boxes he is described to the reader as a stupid, fat, and saturated bourgeois, threatened by gout and cholesterol, spending his nights drinking and playing cards with men similar to him. It is a routine that inevitably ends in his taking the same way home, a short stroll leading past some of Paris's most famous monuments. This routine is suddenly interrupted by an unexpected and horrifying event. A blood-dripping corpse with a goat's head is hanging from the Arc de Triomphe du Carrousel. Two days later, at almost the same time of night, Choupard is confronted again with a similar cadaver hanging from the fences of the Tuileries garden.

In addition to the ridiculousness of the character, it is the paradigmatic repetition of the scene of discovery that works as a generator of a comic relief counterbalancing the atrocity of the crime, and thus maintaining the equilibrium of the *Adèle* series' approach to death and manslaughter. This repetition comes to a climax in the middle of the book when it is again Choupard who runs into what we have learned, in the meantime, to be the third victim of a sect engaging in human sacrifice to worship ancient idols. That corpse is dangling from a monument standing next to the small Arc de Triomphe. The enormous "A" in the speech bubble, a conventional sign in Tardi's universe, is confirmed in next day's newspapers — Choupard does not survive his third encounter with these gruesome instances of archaic horror. He succumbs to a heart attack (Tardi 1978: 3–6).

The whole episode is far from trivial. When focusing on the story in the foreground, which revolves around the activities of a secret sect, this death is certainly no more than collateral damage. Nevertheless, I would argue that Choupard does not die incidentally but is punished for clinging stubbornly to his routine, ignoring all signs of warning. Even repetitious confrontation with horror cannot make him consider the possibility of taking the long way home. His topographical inflexibility can thus be interpreted as an expression of a deathly sin — sloth — a twist that could go unnoticed by the casual reader had Tardi not chosen in his last work to date, *Le secret de l'étrangleur* (2006), to elaborate on this motif, from which one could go as far as extrapolating a rule: Those who shut their eyes to the possibilities offered by the maze of the city, callously following their daily routines and repetitive itineraries, will be punished severely. At the same time, being reduced to running around in circles in the same confined area is a punishment in itself.

In *Le secret de l'étrangleur,* where the action takes place during a period of foggy days in November 1959 while the Parisian police forces are on strike, a strangler sets out every night to kill a man on his way home (Tardi and Siniac 2006). Again, what seals the victims' fate is the absolute predictability of their itinerary. Even in the dense fog, the murderer follows his prey easily, knowing beforehand the location most appropriate for the fatal assault. As we learn from the surprising denouement of the story, there is another uncanny feature: What we actually eye-witnessed throughout the book was a series of mock stranglings performed by someone who was in fact only the accomplice of the real murderer, acting in order to cover up the real crimes, which are perpetrated *hors cadre,* outside the panels. The different victims we believe that we were seeing were in fact one and the same person, the real murderer disguised as his victims. In this case, it is not only the daily — or nightly — repetition of the same itinerary through Paris that is predictable, but also the style of

clothing, which the assassin imitates perfectly. The lack of verisimilitude
(and in fact, at the end of this comic book verisimilitude gives way to
a *nouveau roman*-like variety of different, contradictory denouements
excluding each other) of this staged murder-scheme makes reading it
as a poetological allegory even more possible. The victims are strangled
by their doppelganger who not only follows their footsteps closely, but
whose outward appearance is a perfect copy of the original. I would
argue that these two aspects — itinerary and way of dressing — point to
the two major aspects of Tardi's approach to the city: topography and
style. The danger of being strangled by a doppelganger (and this doppelganger could turn out to be a genuine doppelganger in the Romantic
understanding, a split-off part of one's own personality) is particularly
high in the case of Tardi, since not only is his style characteristic and
easily recognizable and thus prone to imitation, but, unlike others, he
has confined himself almost exclusively, when he deals with cities, to
drawing the city of his residence of several decades. As we shall see, this
concentration itself is not the only reason why Paris can rightly claim
to be not just the setting of most of his work, but also to have become,
over time, its most prominent protagonist.

By incessantly coming back to Paris, looking for ever new ways and
means of exploring the city, Tardi creates a body of work that is characterized by a dialectics of repetition (or confinement) vs. variation (or
extension) of space and style. From the perspective of production, this
dialectics seems to be convenient for Tardi. The necessity (and often the
outright dilemma) of choice can be addressed by a confinement of artistic means, while on the other hand, such confinement generates new
possibilities. In many regards, Tardi's approach seems to be comparable
to that of the French writer Georges Perec, one of the most prominent
members of the OuLiPo movement, who explored the writing of texts
according to fixed formal rules — and, like him, he is a postmodern
artist who cannot be reduced to that label. Both artists' works follow, to
some degree, the logic of the *contrainte*. This is most obvious in Tardi's
best-known adaptations, those of the crime novels of Léo Malet. Not only
the genre itself but also the fact that the investigations of Nestor Burma
(Malet's private eye protagonist) are restricted to a single *arrondissement*
in three of the four adaptations — a bureaucratically and thus somewhat
arbitrarily constituted secluded social environment that diminishes
freedom of choice and yet, at the same time, generates new options.
Tardi himself compares this topological constraint to the situation of

a writer who repeatedly has to describe a given situation or mood and will strive to avoid clichés by looking for alternative ways to depict or express them (Tardi and Sadoul 2000: 126). Although one could argue that Tardi has not failed to create his own clichés of Paris (an argument supported by ample evidence in his depiction of weather, for example, in a specific Tardian atmosphere created by rain, fog and snow, reflections of the city lights on wet pavement and blurred lines serving as a counterpoint to the tradition of *ligne claire*), we should consider Tardi as an artist becoming more and more skeptical about classical clichés and postcard views,[1] the so-called typical or representative views of the city he was mainly drawing at the beginning of his *Adèle* series and other early works. The problem Tardi is dealing with could thus be condensed into the question: How does one make a specific city recognizable? By drawing famous buildings? The more certain well-known buildings are identifiable, however, the more they turn into mere shallow signs, providing a readily available visual currency.

Besides their interest in artistic constraint, Tardi and Perec share rather conflicting predilections for, on the one hand, stories full of suspense — one tends to devour them like those of Jules Verne (one of Tardi's first albums, *Le démon des glaces*, was a Verne pastiche both on the story and the image level) — and, on the other hand, a deep obsession with what Perec called the *infra-ordinary*: objects and linguistic and visual material from everyday life. Tardi is famous for the referentiality of his work, the research and documentation he does for the sake of reconstructing historical aspects of Paris. Still, to simply speak of realism, or even hyperrealism, does not quite do justice to his work. Neither does he claim or strive for hyper-veracity. Rather, like Perec, he uses banal objects of everyday life and banal sites of the city as generators of memories that go beyond personal reminiscences but are nonetheless unlikely to become a part of official cultural memory.[2]

However, the positivistic reconstruction of Tardi's sources of documentation is not my major concern here. I am not going to say much about photography either, since its role as a major source for his work is rather blatant — and yet it is far from being the only visual medium that becomes a reference for Tardi's style. Depending on the temporal setting of the respective album, Tardi borrows features from or counterfeits visual media such as the nineteenth-century book illustrations (*Adèle/Le cri du peuple*); etchings; nineteenth-century stereoscopy and panorama (*Le cri du peuple*); the aesthetics of post-war French black-and-white movies and film noir (the Malet adaptations/*Griffu*); and even the lurid colors of Technicolor (for *Jeux pour mourir*).

I would like to refer to just one example of how Tardi uses a photograph to reconstitute a specific site at a specific historical moment: the Place de l'Opéra during the celebration of the armistice in 1918. In doing so, my purpose is not so much to point to what is identical in his rendering of the original photograph but to what has changed for the sake of composition. First of all, as one can see, the black-and-white photograph has been transformed into a colored panel for the *Adèle Blanc-Sec* album *Le Noyé à deux têtes* (Tardi 1985: 20). Moreover, Tardi slightly shifted the perspective, added a lantern on the left, probably for reasons of symmetry, replaced the missing lamp on the lantern on the right, replaced and added different flags, erased the vehicles, and so forth.

Fortunately, there is always a market for cheap books, which in the case of *Le noyé à deux têtes* gives access to an uncolored version of Tardi's drawing of the Place de l'Opéra. Its differences from another drawing of the same location are thus made more noticeable, namely a panel in Tardi's 1995 black-and-white adaptation of *Le petit bleu de la côte ouest* by Jean-Patrick Manchette (Tardi and Manchette 2005: 66), one of France's finest and most innovative crime novel writers. The difference is not only a matter of the presence or absence of coloration, but a matter of the choice of two different styles of drawing: meticulous accuracy in the case of *Adèle*, a more summary scribbling for *Le petit bleu de la côte ouest*, thereby translating the carefully neglected, deliberately non-literary style of Manchette into the comic medium.

Figure 6.1.   **Jacques Tardi, *Le noyé à deux têtes*, Paris: Casterman 1985, 20 (*Les aventures extraordinaires d'Adèle Blanc-Sec*, Vol. 6). © Casterman.**

Figure 6.2. **Jean-Patrick Manchette/Jacques Tardi: Le petit bleu de la côte Ouest,
Paris: Les Humanoïdes Associés, Paris 2005, 66. © Futoropolis.**

Taking the dialectics of repetition and innovation or variation as a
starting point, one could distinguish between features that are constant
in Tardi's depictions of Paris and those that are not. One could use this,
then, as a guideline for the exploration of Tardi's versions of Paris and
ask what they all have in common and where they differ. In so doing
one could establish the central features at the heart of Tardi's very own
view of Paris. Things are more complicated, however. As a matter of
fact, Tardi's comic book work can be divided into at least three main
categories:

1   His work as both writer of the story and comic book artist. The *Adèle
    Blanc-Sec* series as well as *Adieu Brindavoine* or *Le démon des glaces*
    belong in this category.
2   His collaboration as a comic book artist with other scenario writers.
    This is the case with, for example, *Griffu* (scenario by Manchette)
    and *Rumeurs sur le Rouergue* (scenario by Pierre Christin).
3   His adaptations of novels, such as *Brouillard au pont de Tolbiac, 120 rue
    de la gare, M'as-tu vu en cadavre, Casse-pipe à la nation* (all by Léo
    Malet); *Jeux pour mourir* (Geo-Charles Véran); *Le secret de l'étrangleur*
    (Pierre Siniac); *Le cri du peuple* (Jean Vautrin); *Le petit bleu de la côte
    ouest* (Manchette).

According to this classification, Category 1, in which Tardi figures
both as the writer and as the artist, would be the one representing
his most personal work. Shouldn't we be looking in this category for

a representation of Paris that epitomizes his very own perspective on the city?

I would like to argue that, at least at the outset, the Paris of *Adèle* indeed differs considerably from the city's representations in his other work. Strangely enough, though, from a topographical and topological point of view, Tardi's representations of Paris stemming from his collaborative works and his adaptations have more in common with each other than *Adèle* has with any of them.

But is *Adèle* really more original than the rest of Tardi's work? What was original at the time Tardi started the series, in 1976, was his choice of the historical period, the Paris of the *belle époque*, and his choice of a heroine rather than a hero. To those familiar with these albums, however, it is rather obvious that they can be legitimately labeled as postmodern, being clearly indebted and referring ironically to nineteenth- and early twentieth-century French (popular) literature, as well as to Tardi's Belgian heroes Edgar Jacobs and Hergé. This means that, paradoxically, Tardi's "genuine" creation, Adèle Blanc-Sec's Paris, is a multiple adaptation and thus no more personal than the rest of his comic books and, what is more, its topographical and topological features stand alone in his plural universe. This observation has nothing to do with the historical distance of the story itself, which does not allow for Tardi to rely on personal first-hand memories of the time. In this context, the Vautrin adaptation *Le cri du peuple* is quite revealing: Although it takes place during the short-lived Commune (March to May 1871) and is thus four decades earlier than *Adèle*, it has more in common with Tardi's depiction of the Paris of the 1950s than with the *belle époque* version depicted in *Adèle*. Still, to come to the conclusion that in Tardi's work we witness the peaceful coexistence of two conceptions on a par with each other would be premature. As we shall see, with the progression of the *Adèle* series the heroine's initial conception of her universe comes under attack from all sides.

In the *Adèle Blanc-Sec* comics, Paris is depicted as one of the uncontested centers of the world, picturesque and powerful — and I think this owes a lot to the London of Edgar Jacobs in *La marque jaune*, and to the recurrent "mad scientist" theme. It is a cosmopolitan city as well as a colonialist metropolis. In other words: Paris is the whole world in a nutshell. This means that it constitutes a central junction in a worldwide network of communication: Space and time seem to be under total control. Thus, we see pictures of Marseille, Nantes, Lyons, and so forth, in all of the first volumes of the series. A peak of global communication is reached in the fifth episode, *Le secret de la salamandre*. From New York to Egypt to China, the whole globe is encompassed in the narration of a worldwide conspiracy of capitalist warmongers while Adèle's revived mummy speaks to stand-in protagonist Brindavoine via telepathy from Egypt. Likewise, Adèle moves effortlessly within Paris, belonging to the affluent few who can afford motorcars, moving easily from the center to the outskirts of the city. Interesting enough, Adèle ranges freely over the rich western suburbs like Neuilly where she meets people. Before moving to an apartment in the center herself, in the first episode, *Adèle et la bête*, the heroine stays in a house in Meudon, a village southwest of Paris, near Versailles. So what underlies the initial design of the series is the statement *belle époque* = *beaux quartiers*, "the nice quarters," or the nice *arrondissements*.

This topographical pattern reaches a peak in the second volume, *Le démon de la Tour Eiffel*. Tardi chooses not only the city's most recognizable landmark but *the* most emblematic picture postcard view as the location for the final showdown. Throughout the whole album he shows the reader around the most beautiful parts of town, confronting him with the strange beauty of exoticism in all its aspects, from the contemporary Orientalism of interiors to the historicizing Orientalism of stage settings and costumes, while Adèle herself lives in a fashionable art nouveau house on the *rive gauche*.

Complementary to this centripetal horizontal extension, there is a vertical dimension: the city's horrible, bizarre and fantastic secrets hiding in the underground, in secret caves, tunnels and subterranean laboratories. All these criminal and/or insane subterranean activities are linked to creatures or idols from the past: dinosaurs, cavemen, and mummies coming alive, or ancient idols worshiped in gory cult rituals by members of the Parisian high society. Paris is characterized by the accumulation and appropriation of the entire planet's space *and* time. It is the objects, tokens, trophies, and specimens belonging to prehistoric, ancient or so-called exotic cultures, which were consumed in a frenzy in this period of French art in which syncretism prevails while academic painting is indulging in prehistoric scenes. In short, Adèle's fantastic is the fantastic of the museum.[3] Choosing these objects and specimens as triggers for action, Tardi remains quite close to Hergé. Like the Tintin adventure *L'Oreille cassée*, *Adèle et la bête* begins in a museum. Whereas Hergé sends his young reporter out into the world, there is no need for such sending in the *belle époque* Paris of Tardi. The whole world has already been gathered in one place.[4] Adèle is not a reporter traveling the world, but rather a relative of Eugène Sue, author of the *roman feuilleton* called *Les Mystères de Paris,* a serialized novel published in newspapers (Adèle is exploring the new mysteries of Paris in the different adventures centered around her character). The first scene of *Adèle et la bête,* where a pterosaur first hatches out of its egg and then breaks through the glass of its display case and the glass of the roof of the *belle époque* museum is a *mise-en-abyme* of the whole project: The classified and contained objects of ancient time and other places escape their controls. Likewise, effort-less worldwide communication creates its uncanny counterpart when the flying dinosaur is revived by the telepathic powers of a scientist living in Lyons. Possession and telepathic thought control are recurrent themes throughout the series. Unlike Sue, however, Adèle seems to hesitate before moving among the poor in the *quartiers populaires,* the dwellings of the working-class and the poor.

Turning to Tardi's adaptations and collaborations, two major differences can be noticed. First and foremost, Paris becomes decentered. Certainly, in this process the Banlieue becomes more and more important — yesterday's Banlieue, to be more precise. What is at stake is not only the opposition of city vs. Banlieue though. In many of his adaptations, be it the Nestor Burma albums based on Malet, or *Le cri du peuple* or *Le secret de l'étrangleur,* Tardi remains within the boundaries of Paris, which is now an east-biased Paris. The eastern crescent, with the 10th, 12th, 13th, 19th and 20th *arrondissements,* as well as the corresponding Banlieue, become the most prominent or even the exclusive settings in his adaptations and collaborations. The western axis of power stretching out from the Louvre to the Champs Élysées and to the western Banlieue has shifted out of focus.[5] But the urban space has not only become decentered, it has lost its open, boundless character. Tardi shows us various versions of Paris as a mousetrap. Within these versions, we can distinguish between two models: Either there are parts of Paris and its surroundings, an *arrondissement* or a suburban town the characters cannot escape from, or it is the entire city that is cut off, disconnected from the rest of the world.

As a consequence, communication media and transport only work in a very restricted manner. Nestor Burma constantly uses telephones in his investigations, but only to make calls within Paris. Means of transportation become dysfunctional. In *Jeux pour mourir* and *Brouillard au pont de Tolbiac,* characters are run over and killed by trains while trying to escape, instead of escaping on a train. The Manchette adaptation *Le petit bleu de la côte ouest* begins and ends with the protagonist's nocturnal driving in endless loops on the Boulevard Périphérique circumventing the city. *Jeux pour mourir* obsessively returns to the same places, indicating that the characters are desperately running around in circles. It is not a coincidence that in this book, a police station, site of arrest and torture, features in a large number of panels identical in format and point of view. On the map of the 13th *arrondissement* indicating the locations of *Brouillard au pont de Tolbiac,* there is only one place marked outside of this *arrondissement* — it is the morgue on the other side of the river Seine.[6]

And yet it is by confinement that Tardi seems to become confident in making the city the real protagonist of his work. It is through the adaptation of Malet's *Brouillard au pont de Tolbiac* that he unfurls his characteristic techniques. Wandering, strolling, and any form of locomotion become an end in themselves. We see Paris from the viewpoint of a person — generally a pedestrian moving through the city. We do not find a lot of panoramic views of Paris in Tardi; they do not even occur as establishing-shot panels.[7]

In analogy to homodiegetic narration in a novel or short story, clinging to the perspective of a pedestrian is a visual narrative technique creating a reality effect. In fact, Tardi's representation of the city can be linked to the way naturalist writers like Zola integrated description into their narrative (see Hamon 1972: 465–85). Yet Tardi's protagonists, like Burma, differ from those of the naturalist novel in so far as they are only focalizers in a very restricted way. There are practically no subjective views; in each panel we see the character walking in the streets. This allows for the maintenance of a narrative economy according to the convention of the comic medium. We follow the progression of the protagonist from panel to panel and can still read this as a panel translation of the action-to-action type (McCloud 1994: 70–88). Tardi refrains from openly breaking up the chain of narration and thereby obscures the fact that generating multiple vistas of the city might be the narrative's ultimate purpose. According to the terminology of Benoît Peeters, his conception of the panel could be referred to as "productive," which means that the panel generates the course of the action, action consisting in motion (Peeters 2002: 49–82). Outside motion can easily go on for four or more pages. To increase the number of outside views, Tardi systematically resorts to the artistic means of "talking houses" and "talking cars." Instead of showing the characters inside, speech bubbles emanate from buildings and vehicles. Characters walking the streets recapitulate actions taking place in closed rooms retrospectively.

Speaking of the specific possibilities of the comic as medium, I would like to briefly point out that Tardi's urban spaces are spaces of signs, and thus of written words and word-text combinations. Besides shop signs and brand logos, we constantly see the characters walk by wallpapers and proclamations, posters on advertising columns, movie posters, and so forth. Tardi thus reflects upon his medium as the sequential art of still images. As such, it allows for building narrations with the combination of text/words and still images and thus can do what no other medium, not even photography, is able to achieve: to show, *en passant*, written information in the (public) urban space, thus at once exposing and hiding the most obvious.[8]

To sum up, strolling while distancing oneself from the nice and rich quarters of town is what characterizes Tardi's adaptations. As the *Adèle* series evolves, the heroine, too, becomes affected by this approach. Returning to the beginning of *Momies en folie*, one can see one of the first seeds of this evolution there. Not only does Tardi mock the "sites of cultural memory," first in the voice-over, for example calling the statue of Joan of Arc pointless, and then through the profanation of monuments by grotesque corpses. Here we see a three-page sequence that follows the itinerary of a single person.[9]

By far the most interesting episode of the series, however, is *Le noyé à deux têtes* from 1985, which takes place immediately after the armistice that ends World War I and where the movement of decentering (to the east) has reached Adèle's Paris. Once again, Tardi begins his story by following two secondary characters on an extremely extensive itinerary, making it clear from the very start that the true protagonist is the city itself. The reader sees the Canal St. Martin situated in the 10th *arrondissement*, which, together with the 19th and the 11th *arrondissements*, will provide the locations for this book. It is an urban landscape indeed very typical of Tardi: a multilevel maze of brick, steel, rubble and water.[10] Whereas before Adèle visited famous painters and the theater, in this volume she is going to see the circus.[11] We leave the beautiful quarters and the richly decorated façades lining regular streets for shabby and irregular streets disrupted by large gaps between houses. Eventually we reach the *terrains vagues* where caravans supplant the houses. The parts of Paris we find in this sixth volume of the *Adèle* series are quite the opposite of the cliché postcard views of the sights and places of interest that seem to be so representative of and emblematic for the city, and which, for this very reason, are a currency available all over the world without even the obligation to visit these sites.[12]

In agreement with this topographical and topological reorientation, *Le noyé à deux têtes* is full of allusions to the two adaptations of Malet that Tardi had already made at the time. When Brindavoine visits Adèle's place on the *rive gauche*, he takes the long way, crossing the Pont de Tolbiac,[13] while a mysterious character watches the scenery from the Hôtel chez Leo. A parallel Tardi universe irrupts into Adèle's universe, whose immune system breaks down.

What has happened? In the preceding episode, *Le secret de la salamandre* (1981), the infantry soldier Brindavoine, who experienced the folly of the war in the trenches, was introduced into the series and became the hero of the story, while Adèle herself was waiting in a survival tank to be brought back to life. In *Le noyé à deux têtes* Adèle has survived World War I in the shelter of her tank; the original design of the *Adèle* series, however, did not survive the shock of the war.

As a consequence, what is even more striking than the modification of space in this sixth volume of the series is its conception of time: It becomes obvious that Paris is not a mere static backdrop to the story. Tardi does not content himself with showing fixed, frozen views of Paris. For a more conventional comic series like *Adèle*, there was no obligation to follow the course of historical time. Adèle could have continued to resolve *belle époque* mysteries for another 10 or 20 albums. Instead, she is aging, changing her haircut, and finds herself waking up to a Paris she is not entirely familiar with because the city, too, has changed over time. Taking up terms used currently to distinguish between different types of TV series, one can consider this as a shift from the "series" (paradigmatic, no evolution in time, episodic structure) to the "serial" (syntagmatic, evolution in time, overarching narration connecting the episodes).[14]

With this shift in space *and* time, it is the whole plot structure, which is based on subterranean "mysteries" needing to be "uncovered," that collapses. Compared to the blatant crimes and insanities of World War I and the frenetic celebration of "victory," the official plot of the *Adèle* series revolving around mad scientists and the sustained effort to unravel a secret conspiracy in order to save the life of a general who sacrificed the lives of thousands of soldiers has become futile.[15]

There are no hidden mysteries anymore, at least not the kind Adèle Blanc-Sec used to resolve. The true crimes are plain and obvious. Like Nestor Burma in *120 rue de la gare*, the reader is confronted with the well-known lesson from Poe's *Purloined Letter* — the best place to hide something is where everybody sees it without noticing it.

The deconstruction of the crime novel investigation scheme is pushed to the limit in *Le cri du peuple*. Like Eco's *Nome della rosa* (*The Name of the Rose*), this album mixes elements of the crime novel with those of the historical novel, but only to demolish the conventions of both genres. Instead of using the Commune and the massacre perpetrated on the Communards as a thrilling background for the suspense of a detective story, Tardi turns the multitude and the city from a mere backdrop (as in a conventional historical novel) into its actual protagonists, thus redistributing agency from the story's heroes to the constituents of their milieu that reach the status of actors. The grim repetition of execution scenes, abounding throughout the last two volumes of the adaptation, destroys the very possibility of entertainment by time travel, reviving instead a counter-memory buried beneath the postcard cliché monuments.

It is no coincidence that I close with some thoughts on these two works of Tardi outside the *Adèle* series. From a chronological point of view, the *belle époque* Paris of the *Adèle* series is framed by *Le cri du peuple*, set in 1871, and the Malet adaptation *120 rue de la gare*. By far Tardi's longest adaptation of Malet — about 180 pages — it does not belong to the cycle of the *Nouveaux mystères de Paris* and thus is not confined to a single *arrondissement* and not even to Paris. Situated in 1940–1, it starts in a prisoners' camp between Bremen and Hamburg only to continue for half of the book in Lyons. But what is central here is that this shift of location allows for the representation of Paris as a cut-off, disconnected city. France is divided in two, and while Lyons is the real capital of the Vichy regime, Paris is under German occupation. The difficulties of inter-zone communication and the troubles of getting back to Paris are a constant theme of the album. In Tardi's versions of Paris, the city never seems to recover from this isolation. Paris under occupation corresponds to the Communard Paris under siege. In *Le cri du peuple*, the hope for a better Paris lasts only a few weeks — and in retrospect is known to be doomed to failure from the very start. The whole city has become a mousetrap and will be the grave of tens of thousands of the Parisian multitude. This survey of Tardi's versions of Paris leads to a last remarkable paradox: From a chronological point of view, the freely communicating *belle époque* world capital of the *Adèle* series is under siege itself from all sides, circumvented by past and future sceneries of confinement.

Works Cited
Comics

Tardi, Jacques. *Le noyé à deux têtes*. Paris: Casterman, 1985.

Tardi, Jacques. *Momies en folie*. Paris: Casterman, 1978.

Tardi, Jacques and Malet, Léo. *120 rue de la gare*. Paris: Casterman, 1996.

Tardi, Jacques and Manchette, Jean-Patrick. *Le petit bleu de la côte ouest*. Paris: Les Humanoïdes Associés, 2005.

Tardi, Jacques and Siniac, Pierre. *Le secret de l'étrangleur*. Paris: Casterman, 2006.

Tardi, Jacques and Vautrin, Jean. *Le cri du peuple 4. Le testament des ruines*. Paris: Casterman, 2004.

Secondary Literature

Certeau, Michel de. *L'invention du quotidien, tome 1: Arts de faire*. Paris: Gallimard, 1990.

Foucault, Michel. "Des espaces autres." In: Daniel Defert and François Ewald (eds.), *Dits et écrits II, 1976–1988*. Paris: Gallimard, 2001.

Hamon, Philippe. "Qu'est-ce qu'une description?" In: *Poétique. Revue de théorie et d'analyse littéraire* 12 (1972).

McCloud, Scott. *Understanding Comics: The Invisible Art*. New York: HarperCollins, 1994.

Peeters, Benoît. *Lire la bande dessinée*. Paris: Flammarion, 2002.

Tardi, Jacques and Sadoul, Numa. *Tardi. Entretiens avec Numa Sadoul*. Brussels: Niffle-Cohen, 2000.

Notes

1   Those who open up an *Adèle* album know that at the bastard title they will find a drawing of the stereotypical view of a Parisian boulevard as a historical postcard, as is indicated by an obliterated stamp in the upper right-hand corner.

2   One of the most valuable aspects of cultural semiotics is the open-minded stance it affords one in picking up on the less solid objects and cultural productions of everyday life — at least if it succeeds in getting beyond considering them as mere containers for ideological messages. Both Georges Perec's novel *La vie mode d'emploi* and his project about a non-personal/non-official memory, *Je me souviens*, are indebted to this approach, as is the latest novel by the Italian master semiotician Umberto Eco, *La misteriosa fiamma della regina Loana*.

3   The museum thus works as a heterochronic heterotopia (see Foucault: 2001: 1571–81, 1578).

4   Hergé himself inverted the model of his *Tintin* series in one of the last albums, *Les bijoux de la Castafiore*, in a still more radical way. The protagonists never leave the premises of Castle Moulinsart, home to Tintin and Captain Haddock. Yet, it is not the whole world that gathers there — only the famous

diva Bianca Castafiore attracting the media who promptly broadcast pictures of the opera singer and the heroes around the globe.

5 Even though the suburban town Le Troncy, where *Jeux pour mourir* as well as *Une gueule de bois en plomb* take place, is fictitious, it can easily be identified as an imaginary and representative part of the wider circle of this eastern crescent.

6 In *M'as-tu vu en cadavre,* Burma even has to abandon his office and flat in the 2nd *arrondissement* and move to a hotel room in the 10th *arrondissement* where he investigates.

7 Nonetheless, one cannot easily use de Certeau's distinction between *carte* and *parcours* (see Certeau 1990) and file Tardi under the heading of *parcours*: Taking up Malet's practice of including cuttings from maps of Paris in his novels, Tardi draws maps of the *arrondissements* serving as settings and places them at the end of the albums, as a reference charting all sites of action. Within the diegesis, the panoramic view is not totally absent, but is mainly reserved for views of disaster in *Le cri du peuple,* for example, the view of the city in flames after the assault of the "regular" government troops (see Tardi and Vautrin 2004: 6–7).

8 See, for example, Tardi and Malet (1996: 67, 90, 167, 184). In a novel a sort of insert would be needed to achieve a similar effect — writers such as Louis Aragon (*Le paysan de Paris*) and Georges Perec (*La vie mode d'emploi*) used this device — while a movie would have to resort to an extremely long shot lending excessive weight to any writing displayed in this way.

9 It is hard to say if, in McCloud's terms, this is still an action-to-action or rather a moment-to-moment transition (McCloud 1994: 70–81).

10 Strolling, too, becomes more important in order to intensify the exploration of the urban landscape. The weather has changed: We find Paris in the rain, the wet pavement reflecting the streetlights.

11 This is another heterotopia, the sedentary circus paradoxically becoming a perpetuated version of what is "*absolument chronique*" (see Foucault 2001: 1579).

12 However, one has to admit that a growing predilection not only for the Banlieue, but also for what the French call "the zone," for the aesthetics of the ugly or banal parts of town, is not an exclusive feature of Tardi — at least if we widen our focus from the *bande dessinée* to contemporary French literature. The work of authors like Jean-Philippe Toussaint, François Bon, Jean and Olivier Rolin and the late Georges Perec goes in the same direction — and one could also mention Céline or Aragon for that matter.

13 Alluding to the *Nestor Burma* adaptation *Brouillard au pont de Tolbiac* (1982) (see Tardi 1985: 21–2). Inter-textual — or inter-pictorial — references to this album are numerous and obvious.

14 However, to complicate things, in his *Tintin* series, which rather belongs to the "series" type (Tintin and Milou never age), Hergé constantly points back to earlier episodes, using the device of footnotes.

15 Tardi even mimics his own topography of the subterranean when Adèle, once again, is kidnapped and led into the canal system of Paris. This displacement, however, has become totally dysfunctional. Although one could argue that only the subterranean provides enough space for all the personnel presented in this scene, I would suggest that what takes place in the underground is an empty convention that only serves to point out that the vertical topography of

mysteries has become totally obsolete (see Tardi 1985: 36–8). Yet, in *Le mystère des profondeurs*, a rather disappointing sequel whose title is thus paradigmatic, Tardi returns, in a somewhat uninspired fashion, to the original "series" design of *Adèle*.

III

Superhero Cities

7

The Batman's Gotham City™: Story, Ideology, Performance

WILLIAM URICCHIO

THE TRADEMARK AFFIXED TO BATMAN'S Gotham City in this chapter's title suggests something of its special status. Plastered across games, amusement park rides, toys, and other collectables, Gotham City as a brand is a highly valued asset not only of the Batman franchise, but of the larger corporate entities of DC Comics and Warner Bros. As a place marker and invocation of urban space, Gotham City's protected legal status in fact extends to little more than a ten-letter sequence. It lacks borders, elected officials, citizens — none of which is surprising given its fictional status. But it does have a history and a *raison d'être*, and with them an accretion of representational strategies, icons and, of course, characters. This chapter will side-step the value of Gotham City as intellectual property and generator of profits, looking at it instead as a generative element in the production of Batman narratives and related ideological value systems, both of which offer an opportunity to rethink urban cartographies as enacted rather than objective spaces.

As the Riddler once put it, "When is a man a city?" "When it's Batman or when it's Gotham . . . It's *huge* and contradictory and *dark* and funny and threatening" (Gaiman 1989). It is difficult to argue with this broad spectrum of descriptors. And yet the Riddler's remarks regarding the mutual definition of the character and the city bring with them a crucial implication. The interdependence of the Batman and Gotham City is as essential to sustaining the logic behind the endless iterations of the narrative as the Batman's oft-invoked origin story. In fact, the origin story sets the terms not only for a narrative economy that has driven over 70 years of comics, films, acted and animated television episodes, games and other tangibles, but it also establishes the link between character and setting, defining forever the nature of Gotham. The darkly lit crime-ridden streets of Gotham set the stage for the birth of the Batman, a primal scene in which young Bruce Wayne witnesses the murder of his parents. And those same streets and conditions provide the locus, condition and cause for Batman's obsessive battle with crime. Gotham's value in this case is far greater than a mere setting for the adventures of a superhero: it turns on its generative relationship to the narrative, the source of the franchise's endless iteration.

We will also be concerned with value of a different sort: The ideological notions bound up in Gotham's history and particularly its *pas de deux* with the Batman character. Gotham City seems ideologically skewed, locked forever by the origin story into a place of property crime, where the extraordinarily wealthy Bruce Wayne disguises himself to combat obsessively the most trivial of transgressions. Sometimes crime serves as the vocabulary of his equally obsessed counterparts (the Joker, Riddler, Penguin, etc.). In many of these narratives, Gotham provides little more than a generic urban backdrop against which grandiose rhetorical flourishes compel spectacular scenes of confrontation. But at other times, Gotham's dark passages and anonymous urban canyons are home to far more familiar notions of transgression: crimes against property and threats to life and limb. In those narratives — populated not by supervillains but by nameless crime bosses, thugs, and petty criminals like those responsible for the death of little Bruce Wayne's parents in the origin story — we can find evidence of a preoccupation with property crimes. But this recursive fixation comes with a refusal to address or even suggest that the city itself is a generator of social inequities such as poverty, poor living conditions, inadequate education, corruption, and the absence of opportunity. By day, the wealthy Bruce Wayne seems unable to change these conditions despite the Wayne Foundation's charities and his own civic engagement (indeed, his disproportionate wealth might be seen as symptomatic of the problem of inequitable wealth distribution, a point underscored by his day job as a playboy); by night, the Batman obsessively enforces the laws of the propertied classes against those who would illegally share the profits. The reluctance across the vast majority of Batman narratives to address underlying social inequities and urban conditions is as striking as the unity of the Wayne/Batman figure as both paragon of wealth and vigilante enforcer of the law.

By the conclusion of the chapter, we will have traced the intertwined uses of the city for purposes of story and ideological implication, mapping Gotham's particular geographies through their sites of enactment. Because we can only know this imaginary city through its moments of character-driven action and articulation, we might re-read the corpus of Bat-texts as something of a performative cartography, a space continually (re)produced and modified through the actions of its inhabitants. Fleeting encounters, everyday routines, and affective intensities are the stuff of "non-representational" theory, and we will conclude by exploring the affordances of this turn in cartographic theory for our understanding of Gotham.

Locating Gotham City

Despite its trademarked status, Gotham City is pinned between the twin challenges of trademark dilution (it remains a widely used sobriquet for New York City, frequently appearing in book titles and everyday parlance) and its ample historical precedent. In use as early as the fifteenth century to refer to places with foolish inhabitants, it was picked up by Washington Irving in the early nineteenth century as a term for New York in his satire *Salmagundi* (1807). By the century's end, Jacob Riis would document the squalid living conditions of Gotham Court in his exposé of tenement life in New York City's Lower East Side in *How the Other Half Lives* (1890). In fact, the confusion between New York and Gotham may owe something to the fact that Batman's home *was* New York City until he moved to Gotham in *Detective Comics* 48 (February 1941), and Gotham is explicitly modeled on the "dark and brooding" aspects of New York City's architecture and atmosphere. Dennis O'Neil, long-time Batman editor, made the reference explicit in the "Batbible" issued for continuity purposes to Batman's creators, describing Gotham as "a distillation of everything that's dark, moody and frightening about New York. It's Hell's Kitchen. The Lower East Side. Bed Stuy. The South Bronx. Soho and Tribeca off the main thoroughfares at three in the morning" (O'Neil 1989). Writing a few years later, O'Neil softened his characterization slightly, but maintained the same conflation when he described Gotham as "Manhattan below 14th Street at eleven minutes

past midnight on the coldest night in November" (O'Neil 1994: 344).
Frank Miller wrote that "Metropolis is New York in the daytime; Gotham
City is New York at night" (see MacDonald and Sanderson 2006). DC
Comics president and publisher Paul Levitz described Gotham as "New
York from 14th Street down, the older buildings, more brick-and-mortar
as opposed to steel-and-glass" (see Rousseau 2008). And *New York Times*
journalist William Safire seemed to get O'Neil's message, describing
Gotham City as "New York below 14th Street, from SoHo to Greenwich
Village, the Bowery, Little Italy, Chinatown, and the sinister areas around
the base of the Manhattan and Brooklyn Bridges" (Safire 1995). For the
(trademark) record, DC is careful to state that Gotham and New York
City exist separately from one another.

The diegetic history of Gotham City is amply documented in the pages
of Wikipedia and a number of fan websites, offering comparisons of the
city's various maps, architectural references, locations, episodes, variations in reference (for example Batman artist Neil Adams and director
Christopher Nolan both see Gotham as Chicago) and, of course, artists'
interpretations. As such, it enjoys a visibility and reception history that
would be the envy of many moderately sized "real world" cities. Like
the character of the Batman himself, the representation of the city
undulated throughout its long history, reflecting the concerns of the
day: depression and urban decay; war and the need to look beyond
urban conditions in the interests of fighting a larger enemy; the post-
war era with its reorientation to civilian and above all family life; the
uncertainties of the 1960s and 1970s manifest in the counterculture, the
camp and beyond; the gritty 1980s marked by media representations
of urban crime, governmental corruption; and the steady slide into
darker, more obsessive concerns that have continued to the present.
With the exception of a few periods in which Gotham might have been
mistaken for Superman's far more sunny and optimistic Metropolis
(and during which time, the Batman was also a creature of the day),
and despite a few curious sojourns to other times, Gotham has, through
it all, remained an emphatically American inner city, indebted to the
urban photographic tradition of Charles Sheeler and Dorothea Lange,
informed by the compositional angularity and lighting contrasts of art
deco and German Expressionism, and responsive to the vocabulary of
film noir. Stylistic variations have been many, as artists and set designers
moved among gothic, machine age, and retrofuturist references. But
through it all, dark shadows and extreme angles enabled a half-hidden

Batman, perched on ledges and brooding with the gargoyles, to revel in his outsider status, swooping down as needed by the citizenry.

If Gotham is both rooted in New York and torn among stylistic references, a specific tonality nevertheless persists and dominates. Fritz Lang's *Metropolis* meets Peter Kuper's *The System*; Michael Hardt and Antonio Negri's *Empire* meets Guy Debord's *Society of the Spectacle* (Thissen 2001). It is difficult not to read retrospectively the stinging ambivalence that has characterized the recent critical fascination with the modern urban condition back into earlier renderings of Gotham. The far simpler rendering style of the comics' early years avails itself of a bleak reading. And at the same time, this contemporary attitude has crystallized into the iconography that now serves as shorthand for an urban space and condition. This is perhaps nowhere more clear than on sites where Gotham's iconography is reduced to silhouettes of darkened skyscrapers, urban canyons and lonely streets — comic book covers, games, toys, even Gotham-decorated birthday cakes. Cities, of course, are more than spatial amalgams, and O'Neil's invocation of time and temperature evokes the stark conditions that accompany the desolate-to-threatening Gotham scene. Add to this space the human factor — endemic corruption, urban blight and rampant criminality — and the dark and decaying spaces of the city take on the feel of a dystopian nightmare.

Generating Narratives and Ideology

As mentioned at the outset, a number of these associations are driven by the Batman character's origin story, and the elegance of this particular narrative universe can be found in the efficient coherence of the character's defining elements and his diegetic universe. The invocation of the bat, a nocturnal flying mammal, brings with it not only the fear that Bruce Wayne hoped to induce in criminals, but a preferred time of day (night), locations (the eaves of isolated buildings), and associations of darkness, silence, and surprise. The contrast to Superman's rather garish ensemble, best appreciated in radiant sunlight and in the public spaces of Metropolis, couldn't be sharper.

One of the Batman's striking narrative features is the endless reiteration of his original trauma: first in *Detective Comics* 33 (Fox and Kane 1939) and next in *Batman* 1 (Finger and Kane 1940). It has reappeared many hundreds of times over the intervening years. Batman continuously avenges his parents' murder by apprehending those perpetrators

Figure 7.1. ***Batman & Superman: World's Finest*** (Book One, Year One). New York: DC Comics, 1999. Written by Karl Kesel, Artwork by Dave Taylor, Peter Doherty, Graham Nolan, Tom Morgan, Robert Campanella, and Sal Buscema. © DC Comics.

Figure 7.2. ***Batman & Superman: World's Finest*** (Book One, Year One). New York: DC Comics, 1999. Written by Karl Kesel, Artwork by Dave Taylor, Peter Doherty, Graham Nolan, Tom Morgan, Robert Campanella, and Sal Buscema. © DC Comics.

who blight Gotham's landscape, in the process metaphorically reenacting the primal scene. Terms like obsession, revenge and trauma are central to the character's brand of justice, and they are particularly salient when directed towards faceless thugs, nameless hirelings and episode-specific crime bosses. By contrast, those episodes that pit the Batman against costumed supervillains such as the Joker and Penguin, even though driven by the same narrative engine, are nevertheless distinguished by the fact that all of the characters mirror the Batman in having generative origin stories, obsessions, and an overall demeanor that we (with luck) will never encounter in real life. Their world is self-referential, in contrast to the episodes with everyday criminals that reflect and extend to the realities of the urban condition.

Batman's origin story is centrally bound up with Gotham — a prosperous family out for an evening in the city . . . the theater district with its shadowy alleys and unsavory urban mix . . . an attempted robbery . . . a struggle . . . a shot . . . then another . . . Echoing the logic of Germany's "street films" such as *Die Strasse* (Grune, 1923) and *Dirnentragödie* (Rahn, 1927), Gotham's respectable classes are endangered when they venture into the wrong neighborhoods. The death of Bruce Wayne's parents takes place in the Gotham that will forever serve as Batman's domain — a Gotham generally characterized by darkness, debris, and physical dereliction, and a portion of the city inhabited by the unruly and criminal underclass. The parallels noted earlier by Dennis O'Neil to the Bronx or Bed Stuy or downtown Manhattan at three in the morning point to places still resonant as sites of danger for the well-heeled, and it is this nexus of time, space, and the potential for violent crime that serves as the defining springboard for the character of the Batman and his subsequent obsessive reenactments of his defining trauma. Gotham, in this sense, is inseparable from the narrative logic of the character, and serves not only as a background but also as a *condition* for the iterative generation of endless stories.

Frank Miller has said, "Batman only really works as a character if the world is essentially a malevolent, frightening place" (Miller 1986: 37). This depiction of Gotham helps Batman to work as a character by persuading the reader to empathize uncritically with the hero's actions. Gotham — or at least the parts inhabited by the Batman — is indeed "dark, moody, and frightening." But we might more closely examine what comes along with our instinctual flight response, and, if we are witness to crime, the uncritical empathy that accompanies those who,

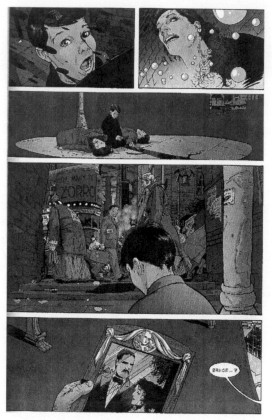

Figure 7.3.   ***Batman & Superman: World's Finest*** (Book One, Year One). New York:
DC Comics, 1999. Written by Karl Kesel, Artwork by Dave Taylor, Peter
Doherty, Graham Nolan, Tom Morgan, Robert Campanella, and Sal
Buscema. © DC Comics.

like the Batman, restore order. The origin story, so important to the
Batman's narrative logic and the generative place of Gotham City within
it, carries more than just the basis for iterative enactments of revenge,
obsession and justice set in a malevolent urban space. It also establishes
a particular relationship to authority and property rights. Batman's
childhood trauma stemmed from an incident in which resistance to a
petty violation of property rights (the theft of a necklace) gave rise to
a capital crime (murder). Bruce Wayne's wealthy father was willing to
give up his and his wife's lives to defend property — a necklace — and
to uphold the law. The motive for the robbery was unspoken, undif-
ferentiated from the sorts of petty street crime that plague most large

American cities (although in some later retellings, it was occasionally positioned within larger frameworks of meaning). The motive for defending property was equally unspoken, in the way that "doing the right thing" needs no reflection or articulation. And the son followed in his father's footprints, with an obsessive twist.

"Uncritical empathy" seems a reasonable response to a child's oath to extract justice for the death of his parents. And it may even extend to a man, particularly one battling to extract justice in an urban setting that looks "as if hell had erupted through the sidewalks." But this view elides a significant absence. As Roberta Pearson and I have argued,

> this representation of Gotham certainly gives a compelling image of late-twentieth century urban decay, as any New Yorker can attest, and the astute reader will certainly see these conditions as a causal factor in the high Gotham crime rate. Yet, like the criminals, Gotham is largely removed from a socio-economic context. The narratives deal with the crime rate; they deal with criminal brutality, but not the brutalizing slum landlords; they deal with the greed of petty theft but not poverty and hopelessness — in short, they deal with the transgressions of the underclasses but not the conditions that give rise to these transgressions.
>
> (Uricchio and Pearson 1991: 206)

And as suggested at the outset, the general failure to address these conditions so central to the identity of Batman's Gotham takes on a particular character when we consider the character's larger conceit.

Millionaire ("billionaire" in some tellings of the tale) Bruce Wayne — playboy industrialist, landowner and, it must be added, philanthropist — spends his days both accumulating capital and sharing his wealth through the Wayne Foundation. Wayne epitomizes an economic system of extreme wealth distribution. But where there are highs, there are sure to be lows. And while we are privy to life at the top in Wayne Manor, we see little of life at the other end of the spectrum, an end that drives its members to acts of desperation, risk, and hopelessness. Indeed, the narrative effectively trades on the failure of trickle-down economics to make a significant difference in the city's underclass. Despite the best efforts of one of Gotham's wealthiest residents, its streets remain crime-ridden and dangerous, and the nature of the crimes that Wayne-as-the-Batman obsessively fights by night remains petty even at its most grandiloquent. Again, this argument excludes the costumed supervillains for whom economic drivers are not a primary motive but rather a site of expression, since they are bound up in logics and story economies that closely parallel the Batman's (little wonder that they predominate in an era increasingly sensitive to socio-economic contradiction). Significantly, the criminality in Gotham-as-the-Bronx or Bed Stuy or south of 14th Street at three in the morning has an additional characteristic: it excludes crime of the "white collar" variety. The evils of market manipulation, insider trading, large-scale fraud — to mention acts that explicitly contravene the law — as well as the grey zone of influence-peddling, speculation, and the many small and socially sanctioned acts that enable crimes against humanity, are all striking in their absence from Batman's world of crime fighting. And again, were this the real world, one would likely find criminals of this variety on the various corporate boards that Bruce Wayne also inhabits, or at social gatherings at which he is a prized guest or even patron. The world of Bruce Wayne is complicit in the conditions that sustain Gotham's troubled criminal character, which he polices by night as the Batman.

The ideological slippage seems easy to miss, particularly in a nation that unabashedly claims first place in the percentage of its citizens behind bars and clamors for ever greater levels of crime fighting and ever longer jail sentences. The "uncritical empathy" generated and actively reinforced by the ever refreshed origin story does much to keep our eye focused on petty hoodlums with grand plans, the ne'er-do-wells with broken noses, low foreheads and, in earlier generations of the comics, a decidedly ethnic appearance. But the contradictions of extreme capital accumulation, like the vague status of white-collar crime — contradictions that directly contribute to the need for Bruce Wayne's night job — pass by largely unnoticed. The symbiosis of Bruce Wayne/Batman, each needing the other to support their own condition, plays out over the bodies of the underclass in the streets of Gotham.

Performing Gotham

Gotham City is a trademarked term; it is the site of an origin myth and generator of a related iterative narrative; and it is both setting and condition for the Batman's Sisyphean struggle to extract justice from an irrepressible criminal underclass. But Gotham as a fictional, if heavily referenced, city offers something more. To Batman's writers and artists, it provides a site where the urban imagination takes form, resulting in maps, street plans, architectural details, and spaces of interaction. To fans of the Batman, it is a site of the pleasures of accreted memory, of shifting connections and references, of obsessively chronicled details and hotly contested orthodoxies, and above all, it provides a space of shared interest, collective knowledge and social endeavor. And, were one to imagine Gotham through the narrative actions of its characters, we might find it to be an accumulation of enacted spaces, of landmarks and buildings and streets brought to life through action, event and reference: Crime Alley (aka Park Row), Arkham Asylum, Wayne Tower, Old Gotham, Amusement Mile, Blackgate Isle, and the many locations named for Batman's creators (from the Robert Kane Memorial Bridge to Grant Park). These shifting references and enacted spaces offer a particularly interesting take on the city, one of growing relevance for academic cartographers. And although embedded in a fictional universe, *longue durée* serial narratives of the type Batman emblematizes help to illuminate the workings of non-objectivist cartography in a compelling way — and with it, our understanding of the city.

The field of cartography has shifted over the past few decades from a largely technical enterprise concerned with the production of objective representations, whether static or dynamic, to approaches more behavioralist and culturalist in character. The availability of high-resolution satellite imaging, most recently in the form of Google Maps, supported this shift in interest. Add to this the impact of thinkers such as Michel de Certeau, Gilles Deleuze, and Karen Barad who take up notions of creativity, improvisation, and transmutation, and the conditions for new understandings of the spaces we inhabit and describe seem inescapable. Among the implications of the new cartography movement has been the deconstruction of older representation systems in terms of their power and knowledge claims, and a turn instead towards alternate mapping systems more sensitive to the needs of marginal social formations and more responsive to the transient and dynamic character of social spaces. Among the theories with a specific impact on these strategies has been "non-representational" theory, associated primarily with Nigel Thrift (see Thrift 2007; Thrift and Dewsbury 2000: 411–32; Lorimer 2005: 83–94; Kwan 2007: 22–34; Kitchin and Dodge 2007: 331–4; and Laurier and Brown 2008: 201–16) and informed by the phenomenological tradition (Merleau-Ponty to Heidegger), as well as the work of Foucault, Deleuze and Guattari, Latour and Serres.

Non-representational theory examines the geographies of what happens; that is, how life, cities, the economy, landscapes, and so on are continually (re)produced and modified in ordinary actions. Everyday routines and interactions become the stuff of the geographer's attention, as do fleeting encounters and even affective intensities (calling to mind Baudelaire's notion of modernity as "the transient, the fleeting, the contingent") (see Baudelaire 1972: 395–422). In a move that brings this aspect of geography extraordinarily close to certain strands of sociology, what is significant exists in and through *practices*, ephemeral and non-reproducible though they may be. Cartography, in this view, becomes something processual rather than representational (thus the oxymoronic moniker), and navigation becomes an act of *bricolage* as we piece together landmarks, memories, conversations, road conditions, and buildings into a coherent and meaningful process.

And so to the question: What is Gotham City? Beyond trademarked property, narrative generator, and ideological conceit, it is an accumulation of narrative and graphic acts. We know Gotham through the actions of its inhabitants, and thus we know it not as an objective space, but as a highly selective and ever shifting accretion of parts, of encounters between characters, favorite episodes, rendering styles, even perspectives. Those few maps of Gotham that exist, attempting to define, fix, and represent a fictional entity from an objectivist perspective, are from this view absurd, unless positioned within the tight semiotic frame of a particular story. But if we take Gotham as a site of performance and a set of enacted practices, we have something much closer to the experiential cartography just described. Gotham is not so much a site of contradiction as a palimpsest of half-remembered episodes, out-of-sequence encounters with the text, selectively accruing landmarks, and ever reinvented spaces. Gotham is a space where the variant renderings of decades of multi-authored Wayne Towers or Arkham Asylums do not so much compete with one another as inconsistencies but rather cohere together as an experiential *bricolage*. It is a space whose dynamic flux is the source of its vitality.

This view emerges from our everyday encounters with "real" cities as articulated by the non-representational turn in cartography, encounters that — extended to the world of Gotham City — provide a means of accounting for our familiarity in an always reinvented (transient, fleeting, contingent) place. And it offers a potentially powerful way to account for the experiences of those artists and writers who occupy themselves by creating the details that constitute this ever shifting whole, as well as those readers whose engagements with the text allow them to navigate and make sense of the Gotham of their encounters, memories and dreams. Gotham City stands as an aggregation of the ever-changing events depicted on its rooftops, alleys and streets rather than as a stable and coherent street grid. It stands as an enacted space, a space whose identity and meanings are bound up in the dynamic logics of performance rather than the fixed terrain of material artifact.

The trademarked term "Gotham City" indicates far less than the grand legal claims made on its behalf, and yet is positioned as a reality of last resort. By contrast, the accumulated actions of Gotham's inhabitants, the ever shifting character of its buildings, streets and vistas — together with the experiences of their authors and readers — constitute a rich and compelling set of practices, sharing much with our encounters with reality and potentially helping us to see reality more clearly.

Works Cited
Comics
Finger, Bill and Kane, Bob. *Batman.* New York: DC Comics, 1940–current.
Gardner, F. Fox and Kane, Bob. *Detective Comics.* New York: DC Comics, 1939–current.
Kesel, Karl, Taylor, Dave, Doherty, Peter, Nolan, Graham, Morgan, Tom, Campanella, Robert and Buscema, Sal. *Batman & Superman: World's Finest* (Book One, Year One), New York: DC Comics, 1999.

Secondary Literature
Baudelaire, Charles. *Selected Writings on Art and Literature,* trans. P. E. Charvet. New York: Viking, 1972. 395–422.
Gaiman, Neil. "When is a Door: The Secret Origin of the Riddler." In: *Secret Origins Special* 1. New York: DC Comics, 1989.
Kitchin, R. and Dodge, M. "Rethinking Maps." In: *Progress in Human Geography* 31 (2007). 331–4.
Kwan, M.P. "Affecting Geospatial Technologies: Toward a Feminist Politics of Emotion." In: *The Professional Geographer* 59 (2007). 22–34.
Laurier, E. and Brown, B. "Rotating Maps and Readers: Praxiological Aspects of Alignment and Orientation." In: *Transactions of the Institute of British Geographers* NS 33 (2008). 201–16.
Lorimer, H. "Cultural Geography: The Busyness of Being 'more-than-representational'." In: *Progress in Human Geography* 39 (2005). 83–94.
MacDonald, Heidi and Sanderson, Peter. "New York Is Comics Country." In: *Publishers Weekly* (January 30, 2006). Available online at: http://www.publishersweekly.com/article/CA6302532.html (accessed March 1, 2009).
Miller, Frank. "Spotlight: Dark Knight." In: *Comics Interview* 31 (1986).
O'Neil, Dennis. "A Brief Batbible: Notes on the Dark Knight Detective." Unpublished manuscript (April 1989).
O'Neil, Dennis. "Afterword." In: *Batman: Knightfall: A Novel.* New York: Bantam Books, 1994.

Rousseau, Caryn. "Dark Knight's Kind of Town: Gotham City Gets Windy." *Salon.com* (July 21, 2008). Available online at: http://www.salon.com/wires/ap/entertainment/2008/07/21/D922CNGG0_monday_movie_buzz_chicago_as_gotham_/index.html (accessed March 1, 2009).

Safire, William. "On Language: Jersey's Vanishing 'New'." In: *New York Times* (July 30, 1995).

Thissen, Siebe. "BATMAN vs. GOTHAM CITY: Het wereldbeeldmerk van de kraker." Available online at: http://www.siebethissen.net/Kunst_en_Theorie/2001_Batman_vs_Gotham_City.htm (accessed March 1, 2009).

Thrift, William Nigel (ed.). *Non-Representational Theory.* London: Routledge, 2007.

Thrift, William Nigel and Dewsbury, J.D. "Dead Geographies — and How to Make Them Live." In: *Environment & Planning D: Society and Space* 18 (2000). 411–32.

Uricchio, William and Pearson, Roberta E. "'I'm not Fooled by that Cheap Disguise'." In: Roberta E. Pearson and William Uricchio (eds.), *The Many Lives of the Batman: Critical Approaches to a Superhero and his Media.* New York: Routledge, 1991.

8

A Tale of Two Cities: Politics and Superheroics in *Starman* and *Ex Machina*

ARNO METELING

The Superhero Narrative

In his study *Strukturwandel der Öffentlichkeit* (*The Structural Transformation of the Public Sphere*) the German philosopher and sociologist Jürgen Habermas makes an interesting remark about the historical situation of the protagonist in Johann Wolfgang von Goethe's paradigmatic *Bildungsroman* ("novel of formation") *Wilhelm Meisters Lehrjahre* (*Wilhelm Meister's Apprenticeship*) (1795). According to Habermas, Meister's primary aim in life is not education or the formation of his character. He does not want to achieve balance between his creative self and his social involvement in order to lead a life in harmony, as required by the genre. Therefore, the so-called "theater episodes" in the novel are not the beginning of his education. Instead, as Meister admits in a letter to his brother-in-law, Werner, the reason for his acting on stage is his wish to be a "public person" and to be acknowledged like a nobleman at court. But, as Habermas points out, Meister's ideal is something of an anachronism because the lifestyle of a nobleman was already considered as something to be criticized by the middle class at the end of the eighteenth century. Even more, Meister's audience is composed of enlightened and bourgeois citizens representing a new public sphere that is opposed to the idea of an absolutist monarchy. These people no longer admire or even identify with the roles of noble people, and aristocrats actually grew to be the villains in the new enlightened and *Sturm und Drang* plays, for example those by Gotthold Ephraim Lessing or Friedrich Schiller. So the "theater episodes" in *Wilhelm Meister,* Habermas concludes, show Goethe's criticism of a contemporary theater that still acts anachronistically, as if it had a noble audience at court. Goethe's Meister is too late in wanting to become a part of an absolutist "representational regime" (see Rancière 2006) that is on the verge of becoming obsolete at the end of the eighteenth century, and the institution of the theater has to realize that it has become part of a new enlightened and bourgeois public sphere instead, a society which is actually based on the critical perception of life at court or the remains of it.

But what does Habermas's remark about the asynchronicities of Wilhelm Meister have to do with superhero comic books? It is a fact that the superhero comic book is not only hybrid in its mediality, composed of text and pictures, but its narrative is a something of a "mixed zone," too. So, while the diegetic world of the superhero is recognizably a more or less realistic version of ours, that is, of the late modern urban world of the twentieth and twenty-first centuries, it is still inhabited by strange protagonists who do not have anything in common with realistic characters, who can be found in modern novels. Superheroes are not only graphically inconsistent with a realistic backdrop when wearing spandex costumes in primary colors, displaying hypertrophied muscles and performing miraculous feats with their super powers, they also seem to belong to another time and to another narrative genre. Like aristocrats at the end of the eighteenth century in *Wilhelm Meister* superheroes are anachronisms in their own diegetic worlds, representing gods, demigods, and classical heroes from a prehistoric and mythical time, while fighting crime in a realistic and urban context. The reason for the superhero comic book being graphically and narratively hybrid is, as Umberto Eco has already remarked in his essay on Superman, the mixed literary origin of the superhero (see Eco 1986). Superheroes are products of classical mythology as well as of serial mass literature, particularly the dime novels and pulp magazines of the early twentieth century. In a diegetic world with realistic people, modern urban life and especially modern crime, in terms of power and politics, the superhero anachronistically takes the position of an absolutist sovereign. His super powers allow him to have absolute power over every citizen. He even has the power to supersede any law, acting as a vigilante. If a superhero is involved, every situation becomes a "state of exception," and the superhero is the one who dictates it. This makes him, according to Carl Schmitt's definition, the sovereign ruler of his world (see Schmitt 1996). As the superhero comic book reader has known since *Amazing Fantasy* 15 (1962), "With great power there must also come-great responsibility!" the superhero is aware of his unique existence, usually taking the role of the "protector of the constitution" (Carl Schmitt) in his city, and reigns over it like a sovereign in the *ancien régime*. As a side effect, the superhero city is transformed into some kind of autonomous city state.

History of the DC Universe

Superheroes live and act in the modern society of the twentieth and twenty-first centuries, in a society that shows, according to Habermas or Richard Sennett (2002), the rapid decline of the public sphere due to the overwhelming success of mass media, which pervades all aspects of life, making everything private public and vice versa. But superheroes still act as absolute sovereigns over the cities or city states they have sworn to protect. They belong to some mythical feudal or even divine elite, being able to roam freely in the city or flying over it, watching the people from high above, neglecting property laws, and ultimately acting as vigilantes, taking the law into their own hands. Superheroes even have a kind of "political theological" legitimation like absolutist sovereigns, for example, in the form of a special mission from a higher being, as is the case with Captain Marvel, Green Lantern, or the Spectre. Or they belong to an aristocratic dynasty of superheroes who have been protecting their designated cities since the Golden Age. Seminal superhero comic books like Stan Lee and Moebius's *Silver Surfer: Parable* (1988), Kurt Busiek and Alex Ross's *Marvels* (1994), or Mark Waid and Alex Ross's *Kingdom Come* (1996) have touched on the problems that arise when modern man meets these incarnations of gods or demigods in their cities. These comics show superheroes from the worm's-eye view of ordinary citizens watching them fly and fight between the skyscrapers, not only doing impossible things but also wrecking buildings around them, which leads to one categorical question: How do superhero comic books cope with the asymmetric clash of different historical epochs and what asynchronicities ensue when the anachronistic, mythical, and literally "timeless" concept of a superhero confronts a recognizably modern and especially urban situation?

One can observe different strategies employed by superhero comics

Figure 8.1.   **The worm's eye view of men.** *Marvels,* **Vol. 1, No. 2, February 1994. New York: Marvel Comics. Written by Kurt Busiek, Artwork by Alex Ross. © Marvel Comics.**

to handle this situation. As Scott McCloud comments in *Reinventing Comics:*

> In the 80s, those who best understood superheroes began decon-structing the genre, hoping to kick some life into the old clunker by breaking nearly every one of the tried and true "rules." [. . .] The deconstruction of the 80s laid bare the inner workings of the genre and became the foundation of a sturdy and streamlined reconstruc-tion by writers in the 1990s.
>
> (McCloud 2000: 117)

While having a generous understanding of the term "deconstruction," McCloud nevertheless marks two relevant breaks in the post-Silver Age history of superhero comic books. Showing pictures from Frank Miller's *The Dark Knight Returns* (1986) and Alan Moore and Dave Gibbons's *Watchmen* (1986), he cites not only the two most important "deconstruc-tionist" works within the superhero genre, but the very comic books

responsible for the implementation of Sigmund Freud's "reality principle" in the genre — both comics stress the private lives and mundane
problems of their heroes and sometimes even sketch them as neurotic
or psychotic. These two comics, Geoff Klock remarks,

> are the first instances of . . . a superhero text that, in Harold Bloom's
> words, is a 'strong misreading' of its poetic tradition, a comic book
> whose 'meaning' is found in its relationship with another comic book
> . . . *The Dark Knight Returns* and *Watchmen* are a judgment, and the
> superhero narrative's first sense of memory . . .
>
> (Klock 2002: 25–26)

After the new grim and gritty superheroes that were spawned by Miller's
interpretation of Batman and Moore's *Watchmen* character Rorschach,
in the 1990s the genre then got into the so-called "reconstruction"
mode and indulged in reimagining and revisiting its Golden and Silver
Age heroes. McCloud cites Alan Moore's *Tom Strong* (1999–2006) and
Kurt Busiek's *Astro City* (1995–current) as examples. But one could
also mention Brian Michael Bendis's *Alias* (2001–2004) and *Powers*
(2004–current), or Warren Ellis's take on *Stormwatch* (1996–7/1997–8),
its "sequel" *The Authority* (2000–current), and especially *Planetary*
(1999–current), a comic book series that literally explores the history
of the superhero genre.

One of the first and most influential superhero comic books that
initiated this "reconstruction" in the 1990s is James Robinson and Paul
Smith's four-issue mini-series *The Golden Age* (1993–4). It tells the story
of the DC Universe's superheroes after World War II, facing different
aspects of McCarthy-like politics in the 1950s. This series is about the
U.S.A. losing its innocence by dropping the atom bomb on Japan and
about the decline of the Golden Age heroes afterwards, fighting among
themselves and fighting their government. Although *The Golden Age* is
part of DC Comics' "Elseworlds" branch, which means that it does not
belong to the official continuity of the DC Universe, its tagline ("An
Elseworlds too close for comfort") shows that it is not only a nostalgic
rehash of some old stories, but an important "revisionary narrative" of
the DC Universe's history. At first glance, *The Golden Age* seems to run
in the vein of comics like *The Dark Knight Returns* or *Watchmen*, as it lays
out the inner mechanisms of superhero comics and "deconstructs" the
transcendental signifier of the Golden Age, that is, the innocence of the

American Nazi-, Communist-, and crime-fighting superhero. But this — and in particular the reinterpretation of the Golden Age superhero Starman — is the starting point for a major "reconstructionist" overhaul of the DC Universe.

Nostalgia Mode in Opal City

This development is realized fully in James Robinson and Tony Harris's series *Starman* (1994–2001). Discussing the notions of appreciating history and tradition, *Starman* deals with collectibles, nostalgia, myth-building, father–son issues, family duties, and especially the dynastic lineages of DC superheroes. It tells the story of every incarnation of Starman that has ever appeared in the history of DC Comics, however short and unimportant. One of *Starman*'s most striking features is the creation of a realistic and complex, if highly esoteric and pop-mythological, universe by filling in all the gaps and flattening all paradoxes in the history of the DC Universe. By subtly retconning incidents and characters it achieves a new level of historical depth and sense of continuity for the DC Universe that is fully responsible for what can be called a "new wave" of superhero comic books, all based on Golden Age heroes and their descendants. Popular examples of this new wave are *Doctor Mid-Nite* (1999), *Stars and S.T.R.I.P.E.* (1999–2000), *Hourman* (1999–2001), *Hawkman / Hawkgirl* (2002–7) and, most importantly, the revival of *Justice Society of America / JSA* (1999–current). This reconstructionist wave of Golden Age-related heroes, presenting superheroes to be as mythical as possible, also reintroduced one of the DC Universe's most interesting narrative devices, namely the unique relationship between a superhero and the city he has sworn to protect. While in the Marvel Universe almost every hero seems to live in New York City (e.g. the Fantastic Four, the Avengers, Spider-Man, or Daredevil) and therefore meets his super colleagues on a daily basis, in the DC Universe the superhero is the designated and sole protector of a fictional city, for example Superman and Metropolis, Batman and Gotham City, Nightwing and Blüdhaven, Hawkman and St. Roch, Captain Marvel and Fawcett City, the Question and Hub City, Green Arrow and Star City, the Golden Age Flash and Keystone City, the Silver Age Flash and Central City, or Stargirl (the former second Star-Spangled Kid) and Kid Flash sharing Blue Valley, Nebraska. The advantage of this concept is the possibility of touching all the political fantasies that usually accompany fictional city states found in utopian literature. Although some of the cities are recognizable as counterparts of real cities, for example, Metropolis and Gotham City seem to be complementary parts of New York City, most of them are based on imaginary models exemplifying certain ideas and visions, whether they be utopian or dystopian.

Starman's designated city is Opal City. It is not only treated as a beautiful but dark gem that has to be watched over by its superhero, the police, and even the former immortal supervillain the Shade, who resides in Opal City, according to the allegory traditionally used as propaganda in medieval warfare, the city is also regarded as a maiden to be protected, a damsel who is constantly in distress and is always in need of her "knight," of course in the shape of Jack Knight, the latest incarnation of Starman. Opal City also has a rich history, with a lot of stories from its past that are often referenced, for example, it was a port for pirates in the sixteenth century and a frontier town in the Wild West. Sometimes this past even literally haunts the present, for example, in the shape of Brian Savage, a westerner, best friend of the Shade, and former sheriff of Opal City, who is reincarnated in the body of police detective Matt O'Dare. There is also Jon Valor, the Black Pirate, who keeps haunting the city. *Starman*'s final story arc "Grand Guignol" consequently deals with a citywide threat that originates in the nineteenth century: Simon Culp, a villain from nineteenth-century London, has taken over the personality of the Shade and uses his super powers of shadow to cover the whole city with a dome of material blackness. Opal City is then completely isolated from its surroundings, actually looking like a black ball, or an opal. Starman and other heroes are forced to save the city by literally using their powers of light. Finally, the Golden Age Starman Ted Knight has to sacrifice his life in order to save the city one last time.

Jack Knight, the Golden Age Starman's son, is a reluctant successor at first, forced to become a superhero by emergency and then by acknowledging the Starman heritage. His private interests are focused on the history of art and pop culture, and he is the owner of an antique and collectibles store. Even as a superhero, he does not wear the iconic colorful red-and-green costume of Starman, instead wearing 1950s-style street clothes. Significantly, he puts a sheriff's star on his leather coat, drawing from the paradigmatic American figure of city law. Knight has no super powers *per se*, but wields the "cosmic rod," an energy device invented by his father. It gives him the power to fly, to levitate objects, and to

Figure 8.2 **Jack Knight and his cosmic rod.** *Starman*, **No. 63, March 2000. New York: DC Comics. Written by James Robinson, Artwork by Andrew Robinson, cover art. © DC Comics.**

manipulate energy in different forms, for example, as energy blasts or force fields. Although Knight appears to be quite ordinary in private and does not seem to change his demeanor when acting as a superhero, the instant he dons his Starman outfit he clearly belongs to some elite group of super-people. So, even if he does not wear a costume, his instruments and garb are parts of a superheroic representational regime that can be regarded as a form of absolutist regalia. The tank driver's goggles he usually wears on his head when he is not flying resemble some form of crown or diadem; the sheriff's star, of course, marks him as a lawman; and his cosmic rod is unmistakably a scepter and a sword. Like other superheroes he operates on different levels in his city, often working with its architecture. He fights on street level as well as in the sewers or high above the city, not only flying in the city's sky, but also standing on high buildings, or even (but less than other, more gothic heroes) clinging or crouching on some ledge. He has to take this kind of sovereign position because the panoramic view is most important for a superhero in the role of guardian. Akin to a divine or Olympic gaze, it allows him to keep watch over the whole city. One can add that there are two ways for a superhero to do this: First, he lets himself be seen in order to show citizens his might and his alertness. Second, he tries to stay invisible, thereby taking a panoptic stance as understood by Jeremy Bentham and Michel Foucault. Either way, the sublime gaze from above conveys the superhero's power over his city and gives the comic book's penciller the chance to make establishing shots by drawing panoramic views of the city and even implying ambivalence — these views may be the comic reader's gaze or they may be focalized by the superhero.

The notion of history is the most important subject in *Starman*. Opal City operates as a harbor (or archive) for the forgotten superheroes and villains of DC Comics' history, like the Black Pirate, Ralph Dibny the Elongated Man, the Black Condor, or even the second-rate superhero Starman himself. As a paratext there is also "The Shade's Journal" in the letters column, telling anecdotes from the immortal villain's life. Furthermore there are special issues of *Starman* dedicated to Opal City's past, which are called "Times Past" and tell stories about important historical characters and incidents that not only have repercussions on the present but also establish the image of a coherent and mythological DC Universe. In that way, James Robinson's *Starman* comic book project on the history of Opal City as a synecdoche for the history of the DC Universe is very much alike to Walter Benjamin's project on the urbanity of the nineteenth century, for example, on Charles Baudelaire, the Arcades, Paris as the capital of the nineteenth century, or Berlin during his childhood around 1900. This project was accurately described as an "archaeology of the latest past" by Burkhardt Lindner (see Lindner 1984: 27–48), for Benjamin not only tries to write down historical facts, but very much describes the urban aspects of the nineteenth century as surreal and mythological. Even the latest inventions and objects in the nineteenth century are regarded as something very old, something to be discovered again, or to be read as traces from some imaginary past. Benjamin's protagonists, the surrealist artist, the *flâneur*, or the child, observe the city's past as something to be discovered archeologically or to be understood as something mythological. They invest the remnants, traces, or ruins of the past with ideas from the present, irrevocably mixing the present of the twentieth century with the latest past of the nineteenth century in order to miraculously save both periods from the catastrophes in history. The *Starman* project is very similar in its approach to order and the revitalization of everything in the DC Universe's history. It is not only the superhero and collectibles dealer Jack Knight who appreciates all things from the past, but the comic book *Starman* even tries, one could say with Benjamin, using a "weak messianic energy," to save the diegetic universe of DC Comics from chaos, paradox and especially from being forgotten. *Starman* is literally an archeological and a mythological comic book, imagining the DC Universe's past as real and as cohesive as possible. The consequence of this approach of creating a hermetic universe, like in most fantasy novels, is its avoidance of all references to reality. *Starman* therefore exemplifies the final consequence of DC Comics' decision to have a mythological world filled with fictional cities, existing only as the territories and playgrounds of their designated superheroes.

Super Politics in New York City

In stark contrast to *Starman*'s obvious "nostalgia mode" (see Jameson 1991), with its portrayal of the DC Universe's history, its celebration of the halcyon days of Golden Age superheroes and its hermetic and self-referential concept of fictional cities, is Brian K. Vaughan and Tony Harris's comic book series *Ex Machina* (2004–9). Ten years after *Starman* and only a few years after 9/11 this comic book ostentatiously deals with political problems outside the superhero-only world of the DC Universe. The narrative of *Ex Machina*, which is published under the Wildstorm imprint, is self-contained and does not belong to the continuity of the DC Universe. It takes place in an alternate version of a very realistic, semi-fictional New York City in the present and can be regarded as a comment on DC Comics' superhero line. The protagonist of this comic book is Mitchell Hundred, Mayor of New York City and former civil engineer. As mayor he has to handle realistic and sometimes very mundane problems such as the security of protest marches, school education, cannabis use, racist art, or gay marriages. As a politician Hundred does not belong to any party. He calls himself a "realist" and shows a very liberal attitude towards most political subjects. The point of this series is that the protagonist is not only an important politician having to handle all the problems of New York City, he is also the first and only superhero in this diegetic world and once tried to protect the city as a vigilante. After a series of more or less successful rescue actions and crime-fighting under his superhero guise, Hundred was able to save the second tower of the World Trade Center on September 11, 2001.

Figure 8.3. **The Great Machine flying over New York City. *Ex Machina*, No. 1, August 2004. New York: DC Comics (Wildstorm). Written by Brian K. Vaughan, Artwortk by Tony Harris. © DC Comics.**

This got him a lot of popularity, which he used afterwards to get himself elected mayor of the city. *Ex Machina* tells of his political work after his election, with his life as a superhero and his origin story told in flashbacks. These stories not only shed light on Hundred's character, they are almost always connected to his problems in the present, whether directly or on a metaphorical level.

Hundred's transformation into a being with extraordinary powers is the result of a strange explosion under the Brooklyn Bridge, caused by a machine that is supposed to be of alien origin. The explosion left him scarred with fragments of this machine on half of his face, reminiscent of a circuit board. Since the accident he is able to communicate with and control all mechanical and electronic devices. An avid comic reader, after this incident he styled himself the superhero "Great Machine." The name refers to the description of society by Thomas Jefferson, but can also be read as a reference to Thomas Hobbes's theory on society reigned by the mortal and mechanical god, the Leviathan (1651), of course. The Great Machine's appearance is an obvious homage to the

Golden Age-style or pulp superhero. He is armed with a ray gun, wears a helmet with goggles, and flies by means of a jet pack, very much like the Rocketeer. Unfortunately, Hundred was not very successful as a masked crime fighter and got into a lot of trouble. Superficially, *Ex Machina* deals with the realistic problems the mayor of a big city like New York has to face, but Hundred's superhero past leads to an interesting mixture of political and superhero narratives. The fact is that he is not only haunted by his past, for example, by enemies he has made as a superhero or by copycats he has inspired — Hundred is still in need of his powers, for example to protect himself from assassination attempts.

Starman and *Ex Machina* are similar in many ways. They are both atypical mainstream superhero fare, and they both show superheroes protecting their respective cities (Opal City and New York City) while stressing the private aspects of their protagonists. Jack Knight does not wear a traditional superhero costume, and Mitchell Hundred has retired from his superhero work. But while both heroes strongly identify with their cities the ways they do it and the ways their cities are depicted are quite different. *Starman* works with the history and mythology of the DC Universe in a self-referential way. Furthermore, it uses the camouflage of a conventional superhero narrative, for example, by having the Justice League of America as guest stars, or showing Starman traditionally fighting supervillains to set up a discourse on the notions of history and tradition. *Ex Machina* does it the other way round. Ostentatiously showing a mayor at realistic work in his office, the superheroics in *Ex Machina* are slowly revealed as a "necessary supplement" (Jacques Derrida) of the main subject "politics." This can be regarded as the punch line of *Ex Machina*. The series' title, referring to the theatrical device deus ex machina, is also its program because the godlike super powers are actually needed to protect New York City: not only to save one tower of the World Trade Center, but in a lot of other situations in the series, too. This means that Hundred, his politics and New York City face a lot of problems that cannot be solved in a conventional way. Sometimes, Hundred just has to fall back on his super powers or he has to reactivate his former superhero identity to save the city in the present. The interpretation of this is quite obvious: Politics are not enough. They are always prone to depend on some third power or the belief in it, for example, divine intervention, which translates in *Ex Machina* as the use of super powers and superheroic management in post-heroic times.

The Aesthetic Regime of the Superhero

The superhero, as stated in the beginning, can be read as an incarnation of the absolutist sovereign, ruling over his designated "city state." This perspective is even more convincing if one remembers how strongly the absolutist system in the *ancien régime* was bound to the body of its sovereign. It unified the authority and dignity of the state, representing it emblematically not only by the doctrine of divine right (*dei gratia*), but also by representing the social body of the nation, like in the famous frontispiece of Hobbes's *Leviathan*. The most precise comment on the relationship between a sovereign and his state is supposed to be from the paradigmatic absolutist King of France, Louis XIV: "L'état c'est moi." The king's public body or royal state persona is composed of different symbols displaying its transcendent legitimation, e.g. the royal garb, given to the sovereign at the investiture, and it is purely superficial. Ernst Kantorowicz was the first to systematically define the two bodies of the king, the private and mortal one, and the sovereign and immortal body of the public image, only composed of signs and symbols (see Kantorowicz 1994). This constellation of two related bodies has been the center of all political theology since the middle ages and it is also the premise for the unique situation of the superhero. Not only is the superhero's legitimation often of transcendent or supernatural origin, but he also possesses two bodies and identities. His private body is that of an ordinary citizen, but when he goes public, dons his costume, and displays his powers, he takes the guise of the undisputed champion, guardian, and ruler of his city, unfettered by mundane problems such as obeying laws that are valid only for ordinary people. Even if a superhero, like Jack Knight in *Starman* or Mitchell Hundred in *Ex Machina*, tries to lead a life in a more or less ordinary way or wears civilian clothing in superhero mode, or even if a superhero works together with politicians and the police, for instance Batman and Commissioner James Gordon or Starman and the O'Dare family, the superhero is nevertheless recognizable as someone who has to be judged by different categories.

The superhero comic book shows two distinct strategies in dealing with political subjects and the strange confrontation between the archetypical and mythical character of the superhero and the modern urban setting. The first strategy is the self-referential and esoteric world-building of the DC Universe with its fictional cities, paradigmatically executed by *Starman* and thereby creating a mythologically coherent fantasy world. The second strategy is to implement extradiegetic political problems and to deal with them through the work of a superhero, as is done in *Ex Machina*. But these strategies are not mutually exclusive. Although *Starman* seems to concentrate on the hermetic universe of its superheroes, there are always historical, judicial, or political questions that have to be dealt with and that can be transferred to problems of the real world. As Jack Knight is a realistic character with a private life, he also has to deal with general problems in his diegetic world that occur in real life, too. The alternative is shown in *Ex Machina*: It seems to be very realistic and referential to the extradiegetic world, but also shows that not only the superhero Mitchell Hundred and New York City are in need of his super powers, but the comic also.

As a consequence, the superhero comic book can be read as a stage, as an "aesthetic regime" in the terms of Jacques Rancière (see Rancière 2006) that curiously incorporates and displays the workings of the older "representational regime" performed and represented by the superhero. Therefore, the superhero comic book cannot be non-political. It may be escapist in showing alternate histories and realities and building a world that is clearly divided into good and evil, but it cannot escape political referentiality. This may not be intended (in *Starman* and *Ex Machina* it obviously is), but the narrative, the structure and the aesthetics of a superhero comic book always show politics at work. Rancière's definition of the modern "aesthetic regime of art" acknowledges the singularity and autonomy of art, but at the same time, by being singular and autonomous, art has a political capacity. It does not simply mirror political intentions such as the older representational regime that is focused on the referentiality of the displayed. It is the "mixed zone" of referentiality and autonomy that offers a specific political stage for conflicts and for "disagreement," to add another central concept of Rancière's (see Rancière 2002). This does not mean a simple argument between opposing parties — "disagreement" is the center and definition of all things political and is in need of a stage and therefore of aesthetics. The "disagreement" does not refer to the conventional meanings of politics, policy, or polity, but is a form of the basic struggle in a society where everybody is able to speak and therefore to change things. Therefore, superhero comics — if they are considered a form of art — can be as escapist as they want to be, but they will still transport some political meaning because they not only literally show politics as a form of struggle by different parties (e.g. showing superheroes fighting supervillains, each other and also ordinary criminals), but, they show different political systems and different aesthetical grasps of reality at work: absolutist or mythological systems, represented by the superhero, and a modern realistic society, represented by the urban setting and particularly by its crime rate.

Finally, one can read this aesthetic regime of the relationship between the superhero and his city, graphically as well as narratively, as the comic book realization of Marshall McLuhan's figure/ground concept (see McLuhan 1997). This is a variation of McLuhan's famous concept, "the medium is the message," as only figure and ground together constitute the whole picture. The idea behind it is the fact that the "figure" is defined by the attention of the observer. It has a specific shape in contrast to the generic and unstructured "ground." But each figure only exists because of the ground and when the attention wanders, the ground becomes the figure. This interplay is called the "resonating interval" and, according to McLuhan, is getting faster in the "electric age," so in the end one will not be able to distinguish between figure and ground any more because all information will be gained simultaneously. Transferred to the interplay between a superhero and his city one can say that the longer a superhero represents a certain city, the higher the level of identification gets, even to the extent that the city becomes a reflection of the hero's psyche and appearance. Therefore, Superman's Metropolis is big, bright, and important; Batman's Gotham City is dark, dangerous, and psychotic; Starman's Opal City has a rich and colorful history and is full of interesting old architecture and objects; and the Great Machine's city is a very realistic depiction of New York City, only that it is imaginary and does have its own superhero.

Works Cited
Comics

Bendis, Brian Michael and Gaydos, Michael. *Alias*, Nos. 1–28. New York: Marvel Comics (Imprint: Max), 2001–4.

Bendis, Brian Michael and Oeming, Michael Avon. *Powers*. Berkeley, CA: Image Comics, 2000–2004/New York: Marvel Comics (Imprint: Icon), 2004–current.

Busiek, Kurt and Anderson, Brent. *Kurt Busiek's Astro City*. Berkeley, CA: Image Comics (Imprint: Homage)/New York: DC Comics (Imprint: Wildstorm/ Homage), 1995–current.

Busiek, Kurt and Ross, Alex. *Marvels*, Nos. 1–4. New York: Marvel Comics, 1994.

Ellis, Warren and Cassaday, John. *Planetary*, Nos. 1–27. DC Comics (Imprint: Wildstorm), 1999–current.

Ellis, Warren and Hitch, Brian. *The Authority*. New York: DC Comics (Imprint: Wildstorm), 2000 current.

Ellis, Warren and Raney, Tom. *Stormwatch*, Vol. 1, Nos. 37–50/Vol. 2, Nos. 0–11. Berkeley, CA: Image Comics (Imprint: Wildstorm), 1996–7/1997–8.

Johns, Geoff and Eaglesham, Dale. *Justice Society of America*. New York: DC Comics, 2006–current.

Johns, Geoff and Moder, Lee. *Stars and S.T.R.I.P.E.*, Nos. 0–14. New York: DC Comics, 1999–2000.

Lee, Stan and Moebius. *Silver Surfer: Parable*. New York: Marvel Comics, 1998 [1988].

Miller, Frank. *The Dark Knight Returns*, Nos. 1–4. New York: DC Comics, 1986.

Moore, Alan and Gibbons, Dave. *Watchmen*, Nos. 1–12. New York: DC Comics, 1986–7.

Moore, Alan and Sprouse, Chris. *Tom Strong*, Nos. 1–36. New York: DC Comics (Imprint: Wildstorm/America's Best Comics), 1999–2006.

Peyer, Tom and Morales, Rags. *Hourman*, Nos. 1–25. New York, DC Comics, 1999–2001.

Robinson, James and Smith, Paul. *The Golden Age*, Nos. 1–4. New York: DC Comics, 1993–4.

Robinson, James, Harris, Tony and Snejbjerg, Peter. *Starman*, Nos. 0–80. New York: DC Comics, 1994–2001.

Robinson, James, Johns, Geoff and Morales, Rags. *Hawkman*, Nos. 1–50. New York: DC Comics, 2002–6.

Robinson, James *et al. JSA*, Nos. 1–87. New York: DC Comics, 1999–2006.

Simonson, Walter and Bennett, Joe. *Hawkgirl*, Nos. 50–66. New York: DC Comics, 2006–7.

Stevens, Dave. *The Rocketeer: Cliff's New York Adventure*. Milwaukee: Dark Horse Comics, 1995.

Vaughan, Brian K. and Harris, Tony. *Ex Machina*, Nos. 1–50. New York: DC Comics, 2004–current.

Wagner, Matt and Snyder, John K. *Doctor Mid-Nite*, Nos. 1–3. New York: DC Comics, 1999.

Waid, Mark and Ross, Alex. *Kingdom Come*, Nos. 1–4. New York: DC Comics, 1996.

Wolfman, Marv and Pérez, George. *Crisis on Infinite Earths*, Nos. 1–10. New York: DC Comics, 1986.

Wolfman, Marv and Pérez, George. *History of the DC Universe*. New York: DC Comics, 2002 [1986].

Secondary Literature

Benjamin, Walter. *Charles Baudelaire. Ein Lyriker im Zeitalter des Hochkapitalismus*. Frankfurt am Main: Suhrkamp, 1992.

Benjamin, Walter. *Das Passagen-Werk. Gesammelte Schriften*, Vol. V, 1 and 2, ed. Rolf Tiedemann. Frankfurt am Main: Suhrkamp, 1998.

Eco, Umberto. "Der Mythos von Superman." In: *Apokalyptiker und Integrierte. Zur kritischen Kritik der Massenkultur*. Frankfurt am Main: Fischer 1986. 187–222.

Foucault, Michel. *Überwachen und Strafen. Die Geburt des Gefängnisses*. Frankfurt am Main: Suhrkamp, 1994.

Goethe, Johann Wolfgang von. *Wilhelm Meisters Lehrjahre* [Wilhelm Meister's apprenticeship], ed. Ehrhard Bahr, Stuttgart: Reclam, 1982.

Habermas, Jürgen. *Strukturwandel der Öffentlichkeit. Untersuchungen zu einer Kategorie der bürgerlichen Gesellschaft* [The structural transformation of the public sphere: An inquiry into a category of bourgeois society]. Neuwied and Berlin: Luchterhand, 1975.

Jameson, Fredric. *Postmodernism, or, The Cultural Logic of Late Capitalism.* Durham: Duke University Press, 1991.

Jones, Gerard and Jacobs, Will. *The Comic Book Heroes: The First History of Modern Comic Books from the Silver Age to the Present.* Rocklin, CA: Prima Publishing, 1997.

Kantorowicz, Ernst H. *Die zwei Körper des Königs. Eine Studie zur politischen Theologie des Mittelalters* [The king's two bodies. A study in medieval political theology]. München: dtv, 1994.

Klock, Geoff. *How to Read Superhero Comics and Why.* New York and London: Continuum, 2002.

Lindner, Burckhardt. "Das *Passagen-Werk,* die *Berliner Kindheit* und die Archäologie des Jüngstvergangenen." In: Norbert Bolz and Bernd Witte (eds.), *Passagen. Walter Benjamins Urgeschichte des neunzehnten Jahrhunderts.* München: Wilhelm Fink, 1984. 27–48.

McCloud, Scott. *Reinventing Comics.* New York: DC Comics (Imprint: Paradox Press), 2000.

McLuhan, Marshall. "The Global Village." In: Marten Baltes *et al.* (eds.), *Medien verstehen. Der McLuhan-Reader.* Mannheim: Bollmann, 1997. 223–35.

Rancière, Jacques. *Das Unvernehmen. Politik und Philosophie.* Frankfurt am Main: Suhrkamp, 2002. Originally published as *La Mésentente : politique et philosophie* [Disagreement: Politics and philosophy]. Paris : Galilée, 1995.

Rancière, Jacques. *Die Aufteilung des Sinnlichen. Die Politik der Kunst und ihre Paradoxien.* Berlin: b_books, 2006. Originally published as *Le Partage du sensible: Esthétique et politique* [The politics of aesthetics: The distribution of the sensible]. Paris: Fabrique, 2000.

Schmitt, Carl. *Politische Theologie. Vier Kapitel zur Lehre von der Souveränität.* Berlin: Duncker and Humblot, 1996 [1922].

Sennett, Richard. *Verfall und Ende des öffentlichen Lebens. Die Tyrannei der Intimität.* Frankfurt am Main: Fischer, 2002. Published in English as *The Fall of Public Man.* London: Penguin, 2003.

9

The Radiant City: New York as Ecotopia in *Promethea*, Book V

ANTHONY LIOI

A PLAYGROUND FOR SERIAL KILLERS, a hive of petty criminals, and a locus of crooked cabals, led by a mayor who is possessed by demons: This is New York City in *Promethea*. *Promethea* is a graphic novel published in 32 individual issues from 1999–2005 by America's Best Comics. It is a collective work by writer Alan Moore, penciller/painter J.H. Williams III, inker Mick Gray, colorists Jose Villarubia and Jeremy Cox, and letterer Todd Klein, though for the sake of simplicity, this team will be represented by the synecdoche "Moore." But I digress. Throughout much of *Promethea*'s run, New York is Babylon, the city of sin, a place badly in need of heroes — in other words, the New York of the noir tradition, a properly gothic Gotham. In Book V, the end of the series (Issues 26–32 in the original run) however, New York is transformed, through the work of a superhero, into the "heavenly, radiant city" of the New Jerusalem. And not just any Jerusalem, but a city for the twenty-first century, the center of an ecological culture that is planetary in scope and cosmic in vision. This transformation is possible because Moore calls *Promethea* an "apocalyptic series," in the strict biblical sense: A book that reveals a divine vision, a successor to Ezekiel, Daniel, and the Book of Revelation itself. *Promethea* hews closely to the plot of Revelation: Where there is Babylon the Great, the center of imperial evil, there must be its successor, the New Jerusalem. I intend to explain how Moore uses the medium of the superhero graphic novel to depict this transformation; why it is so important, in an American and planetary context, to depict an *urban* ecotopia; and what the consequences of this depiction might be for readers and the environmental movement at large.

First, an explanation of the problem of urban ecotopias in an American context. "Ecotopia" is a contraction of *ecological utopia,* a community in harmony with its environment as depicted in Thomas More's *Utopia.* The contemporary term ecotopia usually signifies the small town as an experiment in ecological living, such as Arcosanti in Arizona or Toyosato in Japan, small intentional communities in revolt against the modern city. This is ironic because *ecotopia* originated in a novel — Ernest Callenbach's *Ecotopia* (1975) — which depicts a nation that secedes from the U.S. in order to form a Green polity. Because Ecotopia includes the old states of Oregon and Washington, it also includes at least two major cities, Seattle and Portland. Callenbach's vision included cities unequivocally, and at least one later novel — Starhawk's *The Fifth Sacred Thing* (1993) — founds an ecotopia centered on San Francisco. Nonetheless, the idea of an ecological city runs contrary to the mainstream of American thinking; an urban ecotopia is a contradiction in terms to the canons of American literature and environmentalism. The aversion to the urban originates in the nineteenth-century protest against the evils of the Industrial Revolution centered in Eastern cities, and New York most of all, as the antithesis to the virtuous farmer and the brave settler (Marx 2005: 39–62). This literary tradition arose at the same time as the conservation movement associated with Gifford Pinchot and Theodore Roosevelt. (By comparison, the Environmental Protection Agency, which remediates urban land polluted by industry, dates only from 1974.) Though there was a burst of technological utopianism between the Civil War and the Great Depression, this tradition centered on the control of nature and never influenced Green philosophy in the U.S. (Segal 2005: 19–44).

Consequently, American environmentalism has been, until quite recently, a pastoral affair, rooted in the urge to flee the city altogether. Pastoral republicanism is the ideal: Escape to the country or the wilderness liberates the citizen.[1] Aside from the Puritan notion of the "city on a hill," which never had much purchase outside of New England, there are few examples in American culture of the city as the site of enlightenment. The New York of *Promethea* Book I is no exception to this rule.

Moore's first depictions of New York rely on the Marvel Comics tradition of calling the city by its real name, emphasizing the grittiness of street life and the panorama of Midtown seen from the air. These are gestures toward Spider-Man and the Fantastic Four; Moore gives us a super-group called "The Five Swell Guys" as a wink in this direction. This depiction of dystopian technopolis, the city-as-crisis, will be dispelled by *Promethea*'s inclusion of civilization as part of the unfolding cosmic drama. Where standard environmental utopias imagine the death of technopolis, *Promethea* sings about whales, butterflies *and* the Chrysler Building. "Poisoned cities" are included as part of the glory of divine emanation in the material world (*Promethea*, No. 31: 11). New York is not burned, drowned or buried as it is in Hollywood films; it is reconnected to the cosmos by a sacred narrative that is ecological and cosmocentric. Technopolis is redeemed as part of a larger whole. This end is something that Marvel could not allow because it makes superheroes redundant: The radiant city needs no *übermenschen* because many more than four are fantastic. The superhero moves inside the ordinary citizen and, by implication, inside readers themselves. This movement gives the city its light: In ecotopia, everyone is their own hero, and the city is its own end. In order to understand this metamorphosis, we need to contend with three models of New York that operate throughout *Promethea*: the Manhattan of Marvel Comics; the "Radiant City" of the architect Le Corbusier; and the city as apocalypse.

The exoteric Manhattan of classic Marvel titles like *The Fantastic Four, X-Men, The Avengers,* and *Spider-Man* must first be examined in its original context. During the Golden Age of DC Comics, superheroes lived in places that suggested real cities but never named them directly. The disguise of the city mirrored the superhero's own disguise, signaling the importance of keeping dual identities secret. The thrill of Marvel's New York was the thrill of identity unmasked, but also of shared community: Marvel's Silver Age heroes give the sense that they are just around the corner in Midtown. The collapse of the fictive and the real worlds parallels the thrill of pulling off the mask to discover someone you already know, of recognizing the hero as one New Yorker among others. This pleasure is where the story of Promethea begins in Book I, with a college student, Sophie Bangs, doing research for a term paper on a comic book heroine named "Promethea." Through her intense involvement in writing about Promethea, Sophie *becomes* Promethea, the latest in a series of hosts for the immortal Spirit of Story. This trope of becoming-the-story-you-tell is the central metaphysical structure of the

Promethea narrative, as many reviewers have discovered. What has not been discovered is the way Sophie's transformation is the microcosmic version of New York's macrocosmic transformation. Douglas Wolk believes that Promethea's career as a New York superhero is actually "a rather wonderful excuse for the 51-year-old Moore to explain his version of hermetic Kabbalistic philosophy" (Wolk 2005). This dualism between the fake superhero story and the real Kabbalah is unnecessary: As Promethea's weapon, the caduceus of Hermes, explains to her, it is two snakes twined around a central rod because one represents the microcosm and the other the macrocosm.[2] Sophie's adventure in New York is the outside of her experience in the realm of the soul. It is her inner journey that makes the outer transformation of New York possible in Book V. This union between inner and outer self is brilliantly expressed in Michael Chabon's analysis of the superhero costume as "secret skin." Chabon, whose novel *The Amazing Adventures of Kavalier & Clay* is based on the Golden and Silver Ages of comic books in New York, argues that "the self you knew you contained, the story you knew you had inside you, might find its way like an emblem onto the spot right over your heart" (Chabon 2008). This, he says, is the reason fans always fall short when they don a hero's costume; it is impossible to wear someone else's inner self.

There is another aspect to this confusion that relates to Sophie's identity as microcosmic New York: the idea that Promethea is a revision of Wonder Woman. In *How to Read Superhero Comics and Why*, Geoff Klock explains: "Promethea is Wonder Woman as Wonder Woman could have become, a powerful heroine in her own right rather than something for young male readers to ogle" (Klock 2006: 116). Notwithstanding the appropriation of Wonder Woman by American feminism — the first cover of *Ms.* magazine in 1972 featured Wonder Woman as feminist icon — Klock's point is that Promethea repudiates the tits-and-ass model of the female superhero that took over American comics in the 1990s. Though Promethea exerts a powerful erotic influence, she is the subject of her own sexuality, and the division between sexual and spiritual love is another dualism she overcomes. Promethea's Hellenistic costume, especially her golden breastplate and winged tiara, evoke Wonder Woman visually, but her origin myth points to a difference. Whereas Wonder Woman is an Amazon princess from Paradise Island, the original Promethea was the daughter of a pagan priest who sent her into the Immateria, the divine story world, to protect her from fourth-century Christian zealots in Alexandria, Egypt. This back-story evokes the philosopher Hypatia, the last head of the Library of Alexandria, who was torn apart by a Christian mob before the Library was burned to the ground. Moore's recuperation of Hypatia is an attempt to resurrect a lost figure of wisdom whose work was cut short by murderers. Unlike Princess Diana, who voluntarily enters "man's world" as Wonder Woman to stop World War II, Promethea is driven out of the physical realm and seeks to incarnate again and again to bring about a spiritual revolution. Though her powers manifest physically, she is not primarily a warrior, but a bringer of light to dark times, a role suggested by her name, the female form of Prometheus, the Titan who gave fire to humanity.

If Wonder Woman is not the only archetype at work here, what other options are there? If we return to the idea of New York in the Marvel Universe, we remember that, among the creations of Stan Lee and his collaborators is the sorcerer Dr. Strange, an overlooked companion to the exoteric heroes. If Midtown is the symbol of the powers released by science in the modern age, the domain of mutants and monsters, then Greenwich Village is the symbol of the mystical New York, the home of psychedelic "soul-manifesting" adventure. This is where Dr. Strange lives, and where he protects his city from magical threats. I suggest that Dr. Strange — and, by implication, the whole panoply of mystical heroes such as Dr. Fate, Zatanna, the Scarlet Witch, Phoenix, Iron Fist, and so forth — is one of the hidden archetypes for Promethea. Like Sophie herself, Stephen Strange stumbles into a career as hero by other means: He was a brilliant surgeon taken into the care of a mysterious Eastern mystic after a car accident cripples his hands. The Ancient One teaches Strange the esoteric arts of the East, through which he wins the Eye of Agamotto, a golden amulet that emits a beam of overpowering radiance — a weapon of wisdom, like Promethea's caduceus. Though one might be tempted to see Stan Lee's Orientalism as less sophisticated than Moore's ceremonial magic, Lee created an original mythography of the occult at a time when modernity was identified with secularity. In doing so, he signaled the existence of another New York, the layer inhabited by the Beats, by experimental music, by the drug culture, and cross-cultural disciplines like Zen meditation, yoga, and the martial arts. As shown by her meetings with Jack Faust, a magician who introduces Sophie to Tarot and Theosophy, Promethea inhabits both the magical and the scientific New York, the modern and the eternal Manhattan, in ways that set the stage for the final revelation of Book V. Nonetheless, this expanded New York is far from ecotopian; in the mystical as in the mundane worlds of Marvel, the city is still a fire whose ashes need to be swept away.

This sense that the old city must perish to make way for the new is one of the central architectural ideas of the French modernist Le Corbusier, whose manifesto *La ville radieuse / The Radiant City* (1935) — imagines the destruction of Victorian cityscapes in favor of modern towers raised above the ground, surrounded by grass. According to Alice Sparberg Alexiou, Corbusier loved the skyscrapers of Midtown but he "hated New York's streets" (Sparberg Alexiou 2006: 37). Corbusier wrote:

> I am not able to bear the thought of millions of people undergoing the diminution of life imposed by devouring distances, the subways filled with uproar, the wastelands on the edges of the city, in the blackened brick streets, hard, implacably soulless streets — tenement streets, streets of hovels that make up the cities of the century of money — the slums of New York or Chicago.
>
> (Sparberg Alexiou 2006: 37)

Though Corbusier accurately describes the dystopian environment inherited from the nineteenth century, with its split between pastoral suburb and pestilential city, many critics, including Jane Jacobs and Lewis Mumford, believe that his attempt to combine the skyscraper with the lawn produced what Mumford called "yesterday's city of tomorrow," a failed urban ecotopia (Mumford 1962: 139–44). In the New York of *Promethea* Book I, Sophie would readily identify Corbusier's vision as "the Projects," where the urban poor are cut off from the promise of the city. Moore's gesture to Corbusier's idea — "the radiant, heavenly city" of Book V, is unambiguous, though not un-ironic. If his gestures to the Marvel universe define the dystopia out of which ecotopia must emerge, his gesture toward modernism might acknowledge that others have offered a vision of New York as paradise and failed. In "Le Corbusier and the Radiant City contra True Urbanity and the Earth," Rachel Kennedy critiques his vision in just these terms:

> Corbusier's designs for the city are grounded in the desire to escape the earth. The vertical street, the skyscraper, the death of the street, the destruction of the sensuality of city life, are all proof positive that

he was terrified of the earth and others. In the *Contemporary City*,
Corbusier describes the view from the skyscraper as not of this earth;
it is placid, serene, and harmonious.

(Kennedy 2009)

This is Corbusier as ecophobic, as patriarchal Neoplatonist. Kennedy
continues:

Of course, Corbusier saw himself as the fatherly redeemer of human-
kind. He was *le grand initié* who could step outside of history and
uncover the good society. He was the good Calvinist who would make
the world over for the glory of rationalism. Obviously, the flux of history, the uncertainty of being was too much for him.

(Kennedy 2009)

What is fascinating in this characterization is the light it sheds on
Moore's own feminist Neoplatonism. Though the story of Sophie's
ascent to the Godhead dominates the middle books of *Promethea*, Moore
does not use a vertical metaphysics to demean matter with the purity
of spirit, as Kennedy claims Corbusier does. Instead, he envisions an
erotic economy in which spirit desires incarnation and matter desires
revelation. The journey away from the earth results in a descent back to
the earth to renew, not negate, it with spiritual power. In such a scheme,
the residents of New York, and the whole planet, are not confused children waiting for a great initiate to lead them, but the protagonists of
their own story who must confront enlightenment. This economy leads
inevitably to the apocalypse of Book V.

Book V opens with a meeting between two federal agents and Tom
Strong, a "science-hero" who led a super-team, "America's Best,"[3] that
included the 1950s version of Promethea, an incarnation prior to
Sophie's. The agents tell Strong that Sophie's Promethea is now a "terrorist" who plans to "end the world" (*Promethea*, No. 26: 7). Though
this is news to him, it is not news to readers: At the climax of her ascent
through the "sefirot," or divine emanations, Sophie is told by Binah,
the third "sefirah" and highest origin of Promethea's power, that she
is the Promethea of the apocalypse. Binah reveals that Promethea's
power is grounded in the Merciful Mother who is also the Whore of
Babylon: Binah as the Vessel of God's Mercy poured out to everyone, a

deconstruction of the virgin/whore dichotomy at the most fundamental level. (This identity is coded into the character's name itself: "Sophie Bangs" translates readily into "Wisdom Explodes," with connotations of cosmic creation, spiritual enlightenment, and sexual excess.) Sophie begins Issue 26 with the same appraisal of the situation as the federal agents: If she becomes Promethea again, the world will end. She takes a new identity in order to disappear and prevent herself from ending the world. This situation is a parody of the secret identity of the superhero: It obstructs the hero's mission, and is therefore unsustainable. We see this at the end of Issue 26 and the beginning of Issue 27 when the government compels Tom Strong to track down Sophie and put an end to her threat. Though he tries to reason with her, Sophie's shock at being discovered leads her to summon Promethea as an act of self-defense. In a splash page that extends across pages 8 and 9, the new version of Promethea appears, dressed in the scarlet and gold costume she gained during the encounter with Binah. The gold indicates continuity with her old identity as a wisdom-figure, and the scarlet identifies her with the mercy of the Whore of the Apocalypse, symbolized as a golden chalice spilling blood into the world. She turns to Strong and announces "I am the Final Fire," exhorts him to make peace with God, and flies off to end the world (*Promethea*, No. 27: 10).

In order to understand what happens next, it is necessary to clarify what apocalypse means in biblical and environmental contexts. In the Bible, an apocalypse is an "un-veiling" of a divine mystery in visionary form, and encompasses the Books of Ezekiel, Daniel, parts of the Gospels, and the Book of Revelation. Apocalypse as a worldview is generally considered to be a fusion of prophetic and wisdom writing, in which an oppressed people — first, the Jews under Babylon and later both Jews and the early Christians under Rome — imagine the end of imperial domination (Gabel *et al.* 2000: 146–61). Thus, in Revelation, the power of the Beast, the Anti-Christ, and the Whore all symbolize the idolatrous power of Rome in opposition to the Reign of God. The conflict between Rome and Christ includes a battle, Armageddon, which has become identified in later tradition as the essence of apocalypse itself. This is a misunderstanding of the plot of Revelation, which does not end with a battle, but with the descent of the New Jerusalem as the union of heaven and earth. This is the "heavenly city" Moore refers to when he calls New York "the radiant, heavenly city," combining the modernism of Le Corbusier with the original City of God:

Then I saw a new heaven and a new earth, for the first heaven and the first earth had vanished, and there was no longer any sea. I saw the holy city, new Jerusalem, coming down out of heaven from God, made ready like a bride adorned for her husband. I heard a loud voice proclaiming from the throne: 'Now at last God has his dwelling among men! He will dwell among them and they shall be his people, and God himself will be with them. He will wipe away every tear from their eyes; there shall be an end to death, and to mourning and crying and pain, for the old order has passed away!'

(Revelation 21: 1–4, NEB)

It is impossible to underestimate the importance of the visionary mode — "Then I saw" — to the climax of *Promethea*. One of the advantages of sequential art is that images and words can mutually interpret one another. If Promethea is an incarnation of the spirit of narrative, she does not manifest only as words, but as the "picture-stories" that Hermes identifies in Book III as the divine language (*Promethea*, No. 15: 17). This self-referential quality of a comic book talking about comic books is not merely ludic postmodernism — it is a claim about the revelatory power of sequential art. *Promethea* is meant to unveil itself to the reader as much as the characters. This is reinforced by the idea that the heavenly city is the "dwelling" of God among the people. In later Talmudic thought, the Hebrew word for God's dwelling will be personified as a female figure, the Shekhinah, who is identified with Malkuth, the tenth sefirot, co-extensive with the material creation (Green 2004: LII). The Shekhinah is the Presence of God in the world; Promethea is that Presence manifest as the radiant city, the instrument through which the old order passes away.

It is this narrative of world-transformation that has made apocalypse a central trope in contemporary environmental writing. In Greg Garrard's primer, *Ecocriticism*, he begins with Lawrence Buell's assertion that "Apocalypse is the single most powerful master metaphor that the contemporary environmental imagination has at its disposal" and cites Rachel Carson's *Silent Spring*, Al Gore's *Earth in the Balance* and Bill McKibben's *The End of Nature* as texts that depend on apocalypse for their rhetorical coherence (Garrard 2004: 93). While he criticizes this literature for its reliance on a rhetoric of crisis, which easily dissolves into factional strife and demonization of the opponent, he goes on to distinguish between tragic and comic apocalypse, drawing on the work of Kenneth Burke and Stephen O'Leary. He quotes O'Leary's version:

Tragedy conceives of evil in terms of guilt; its mechanism of redemption is victimage, its plot moves inexorably toward sacrifice and the 'cult of the kill'. Comedy conceives of evil not as guilt, but as error; its mechanism of redemption is recognition rather than victimage, and its plot moves not toward sacrifice but to the exposure of fallibility.

(Garrard 2004: 87)

Using these terms, we can see that the central contribution of *Promethea* to urban ecotopias is its rope-a-dope plot structure, which makes readers believe they have entered a tragic apocalypse in Book I, only to encounter a comic apocalypse in Book V. This is a misunderstanding that Sophie believes right up to the moment she becomes Promethea for the last time. The climax of the narrative is a prime example of O'Leary's comic structure: Promethea brings an apocalypse that unveils human error about the nature of reality, and the mechanism of redemption is not violent destruction but realization of the truth. As Promethea flies past the Statue of Liberty toward the center of Manhattan, what seems to be mass psychosis strikes the people. In the beginning of Issue 28, this change in perception is represented as the imposition of super-vivid color on the Chrysler Building and other skyscrapers, next to which the Great Pyramid at Giza suddenly appears, joined by the Parthenon and a profusion of giant flowers several pages later. The language of Revelation is applied and parodied by an anonymous narrator who says "everybody suddenly remembered that each brick, each busted tail-light in this mad stampede of world and time was Holy, to be loved, and there was no more and so on and so on, no more yadda yadda" (*Promethea*, No. 28: 2). Meanwhile, the human characters, including the federal agents and the Five Swell Guys, are still drawn in a realistic style, in which they confront the growing psychedelia as if it were a supervillain's attack. In a striking visual effect, one of the agents, Karen Breughel, is overcome, and experiences enlightenment as she is swept off the page of the comic book into a splash page in which she can read the comic book itself, and recognizes herself as a character. Giant figures in blue with multiple statue-faces address her, saying, in multiple fonts, "remember Karen hello us are WE here you AGAIN," while the panels of her comic book curve off to a vanishing point. The jumble of syntax — which does not quite resolve into "Hello Karen, here we are again, remember us" — suggests the disruption of perception through the disruption of language. The agent is then abruptly dumped back into the scene she left, where she struggles to articulate what has happened to the other characters (*Promethea*, No. 28: 10–11). Scenes like this repeat all over the city, until everyone is swept away into a world where they speak to the dead and to angels, are attacked by demons and surrounded by fairies, become Mary recognizing the Christ child, and so on, until the whole city is engulfed in the enlightenment effect. The other government agents try to explain it as an electromagnetic effect on the brain, as temporal lobe seizures causing false religious experiences, until agent Lucille Ball — one of Moore's jokes about comedy — says, "Well, I mean, what if, you know . . . what if it's the other way around?" (*Promethea*, No. 30: 1–2). In other words, what if spiritual events cause the restructuring of the brain?

As the effect visibly spreads over the globe, the government in Washington panics, and orders a nuclear strike on New York. If launched, this strike would inaugurate a tragic apocalypse in which the center of revelation is consumed in atomic fire. The commanding officer barks "We have to remove Manhattan to save America!" Then, in a classic moment of anti-authoritarianism that resonates with Moore's *V for Vendetta*, the junior officers refuse to activate the bomb, saying "Sir, no Sir, I won't do that, Sir" and "Fuck you, Sir. I ain't doing that. No way" (*Promethea*, No. 30: 14–15). By the time the commander responds, it is too late, and Promethea's vision overwhelms the planet. What happens next is true to the pattern of micro- and macrocosmic harmony. Along with all humanity, the reader enters a small, firelit room, where each person meets Promethea alone. The same message is delivered. In the margins around three double splash pages — quite the gesture by traditional comics standards — Promethea narrates the creation and evolution of the universe according to modern astrophysics and biology, but in the mode of a sacred creation myth (*Promethea*, No. 31: 8–13). Around the edges of the first splash page, the four animals of the Gospel writers — a lion, an eagle, a cow and a man — surround a planisphere of constellations, with Promethea superimposed on the stars to underline the simultaneity of sacred and scientific discourse. The second splash page is a picture of the whole earth, full of fish, snakes, tyrannosaurs, birds, and humans: "All things are precipitated by the nature of existence. Therefore, nothing is unnatural, be it bee-hive or termite-mound or all our shining, poisoned cities." The final splash page is a double circle of deities looking at humans looking at deities: "Know that our universe is all one place, a single firelit room, all time a single moment. Know that there has only ever been one person here." The vision ends back in that firelit room, where Promethea leaves the reader with the exhortation, "Stay awake" (*Promethea*, No. 31: 15).

Turning the page after the darkness of fadeout, the vision of "The Radiant, Heavenly City" — the title of Issue 31 — is now shown to have permanent effects on the shape of New York. All of the characters, even the ones who had been enemies, are shown walking together in the sun, trying to make sense of the vision they shared (*Promethea*, No. 31: 17). To represent their transformation of consciousness, they and the city are now drawn in a new way, neither the realistic style from before the vision nor the overwhelming psychedelia of the vision itself, but a middle ground of Technicolor intensity. In a spiritual revolution of aesthetics, realism — and the postlapsarian consciousness it represents — has been overcome. In place of the dark technopolis is a city of brilliance, mirrored by individuals drawn in graceful, unique styles, their secret skin made visible to each other. People seem, at last, to be their own superheroes; yet this utopia is not perfect, or finished — the dialogue reveals that not everyone could assimilate the shared vision to the same extent. Yet as Sophie walks through a Central Park whose boundaries blur into the streets, the message is clear. The individual is the city, the city is the planet, the planet is the universe where the sacred and profane are one, and still evolving. Even a chastened ecotopia, where tears must still be wiped away, cannot be summoned simply by reading a comic book. The representation of enlightenment is not the fullness of enlightenment; like other kinds of sacred art, *Promethea* is proleptic. It suggests, however, that readers, as citizens of the radiant city, can take their place for the final fire, moving to a post-pastoral environmentalism that inhabits the city, no less than the wild, as hearth of the world.

Works Cited
Comics
Moore, Alan *et al. Promethea*, Nos. 1–32. New York: DC Comics (Imprint: America's Best Comics), 1999–2005.

Secondary Literature
Chabon, Michael. "Secret Skin." In: *The New Yorker Online* (March 10, 2008). Available online at: http://www.newyorker.com/reporting/2008/03/10/080310fa_fact_chabon?currentPage=4 (accessed January 3, 2009).
Gabel, John B. *et al. The Bible as Literature: An Introduction*. New York: Oxford University Press, 2000.
Garrard, Greg. *Ecocriticism*. New York: Routledge, 2004.

Green, Arthur. "Introduction." In: *The Zohar*, Vol. 1. Pritzger ed. Trans. Daniel C. Matt. Palo Alto: Stanford University Press, 2004.

Kennedy, Rachel. "Le Corbusier and the Radiant City contra True Urbanity and the Earth (January 2, 2009)." Available online at: http://www.uky.edu/Classes/PS/776/Projects/Lecorbusier/lecorbusier.html (accessed January 3, 2009).

Klock, Geoff. *How to Read Superhero Comics and Why*. New York: Continuum, 2006.

Marx, Leo. "The Idea of Nature in America." In: Nadia Tazi (ed.), *Keywords: Nature*. New York: Other Press, 2005.

Mumford, Lewis. "Yesterday's City of Tomorrow." In: *Architectural Record* CXXXII (1962). 139–44.

The New English Bible: With the Apocrypha. Oxford Study Edition, ed. Samuel Sandmel *et al*. New York: Oxford UP, 1976.

Segal, Howard P. *Technological Utopianism in American Culture*. Syracuse, NY: Syracuse University Press, 2005. 19–44.

Sparberg Alexiou, Alice. *Jane Jacobs: Urban Visionary*. New Brunswick, NJ: Rutgers University Press, 2006.

Wolk, Douglas. "Magic Comic Ride." *Salon.com* (January 5, 2009). Available online at http://dir.salon.com/story/books/review/2005/07/01/promethea/ (accessed January 3, 2009).

Notes

1 The "American Renaissance" in literature was constructed around this idea, though Walt Whitman was considerably more positive about cities than Emerson, Thoreau, or Melville (see Marx 2005).
2 *Promethea* 12. The snakes call themselves "Mic" and "Mac" accordingly.
3 Tom Strong is the flagship character of Moore's line of comics, also called "America's Best Comics." His appearance as a character in *Promethea* is meant to emphasize the continuity between *Promethea* and the other titles in America's Best Comics.

10

"I Am New York" — Spider-Man, New York City and the Marvel Universe

JASON BAINBRIDGE

Introduction

New York has always haunted the pages of comics. It was, after all, the birthplace of the American comics industry — commencing with the comic strip in the newspapers of William Randolph Hearst and Joseph Pulitzer, the comic book in the 1930s and the superhero in June 1938 with the debut of DC Comics' Superman (Benton 1989; Jones 2004). It was the birthplace of comics writers like Stan Lee and of comic artists like Jack Kirby and it remains the location for the offices of both DC and Marvel Comics, the two major American comic book publishers. Aspects of New York appear in Will Eisner's stylized Central City in *The Spirit*, in Batman's Gotham City wrapped around letters and right angles, in Scrooge McDuck's Duckberg, dotted with oversized typewriters and billboards, in Flash's Central City, Green Lantern's Coast City, and Superman's Metropolis; indeed, as has been attributed to everyone from Frank Miller to John Byrne, Metropolis is often referred to as New York by day and Gotham as New York by night. But, as comics historian Peter Sanderson describes it, in each of these comics New York City was given "a fictional veneer [which] removed the fantastic series even further from reality" (Sanderson 2007: 9). This meant that the comic book city remained largely archetypal, a backdrop that was endlessly adaptable to the demands of the narrative. It wasn't until 1961 that the fledgling

Marvel Comics brought New York City into the foreground, rolling out a collection of characters and titles that were set *in* New York rather than inhabiting fictional cities that were simply extensions of themselves.

Giant-Size Astonishing X-Men, No. 1, the special concluding TV writer/director/producer Joss Whedon's two-year run on Marvel's *Astonishing X-Men*, opens with a double-page spread of Spider-Man web-slinging across the New York skyline. It is a common scene in Marvel Comics, the gaudily dressed hero juxtaposed against the familiar landmarks and locales of New York. This particular spread is a composite image of artist John Cassaday's drawn buildings (in the foreground) with a photograph of the real New York skyline behind, literally suturing the comic book New York to the real New York City. Spider-Man's monologue captions make these links explicit:

> You can't say 'I love New York.' Tourists can love New York. Me? Who grew up here? Who's lived here my whole life, who's crawled over every stone and swung off every cornice . . . I *am* New York. It's in me, in my blood, like a disease . . . you know, like a blood disease but a good one, like a happy . . . cancer . . . So clearly I was not bitten by a radioactive *poet*. But you get what I'm saying. When you're part of a greater whole . . . when you're . . . enmeshed . . . you know when something's coming.
>
> (Whedon and Cassaday 2008: 1–2)

Spider-Man's comments about a "whole life" spent in New York, about being "part of a greater whole" and "enmeshed," speak largely to the enduring importance of New York City in the Marvel Universe. In this chapter I want to explore the role New York plays both textually and extratextually in Marvel's relationship with its readers and in its movement into other fields of media. To do this I will primarily be focusing on Spider-Man, as he is Marvel's flagship character, predominantly based in New York City and arguably the template for Marvel's other superheroes (Everett *et. al.* 1939). Through Spider-Man I want to interrogate the relationship between New York City and the Marvel Universe and how, over the 70 years of their coexistence on the printed page, each has come to depend on the other.

New York and the Marvel Universe

The Marvel Universe is named after the first comic produced by pulp publisher Martin Goodman, *Marvel Comics*, No. 1, released in response to DC's superhero comics, which Goodman saw as threatening his pulp empire. The idea of a cohesive Marvel Universe emerged as early as 1941 with a 60-page epic depicting a lengthy battle between the original Human Torch and Namor, the Sub-Mariner, that culminated with the Sub-Mariner flooding and devastating New York (Everett *et. al.* 1941). The caption announcing the success of Namor's "anti-American blitz," the product of "five whales with turbines" reads:

> They say New Yorkers have seen everything . . . But here's something they never saw . . . a mamouth [*sic*] tidal wave, so high it surmounts the city's tallest building, so wide it stretches from Battery to the Bronx, so terrific it slams down the worlds [*sic*] most famous skyline as if it were built with cards and then, its fury still unspent, spans the Hudson River and roars westward! Goodbye Broadway! So long Times Square! Down goes the Empire State Building! Down goes the George Washington Bridge! But the spirit of the populace stays up! Forewarned by the President to prepare for such an emergency they respond to "water raid" sirens, don diving helmets and enter water-tight shelters below the flooded subways!
>
> (Daniels 1991: 47)

New York was therefore present at the very beginning of the Marvel Universe and it would take on even greater significance when the Marvel Universe, as we understand it today, relaunched itself with the publication of *The Fantastic Four*, No. 1 twenty years later. Once again, this was Goodman's response to DC Comics' popularity and more particularly the resurgent success of their superheroes, principally their "superhero team," the Justice League of America. This time Goodman's company (after calling itself both Atlas and Timely) renamed itself Marvel Comics (after its 1939 debut issue) and with the return of Namor in *Fantastic Four*, No. 4 and Captain America in *The Avengers*, No. 4 confirmed that this was indeed the same Marvel Universe that had commenced with the original Human Torch back in 1939 (Lee and Kirby 1961, 1962, 1964).

The differences between the Marvel superheroes and their predecessors, particularly the DC superheroes, have been canvassed at length elsewhere (Bainbridge 2009) but it is perhaps instructive to recall director Christopher Nolan's comments regarding the DC superhero Batman when approaching the direction of *Batman Begins*,[1] the film tasked with relaunching the Batman movie franchise:

> Previous movie versions created a world so exotic that Batman naturally fit in. I felt there was this odd cinematic gap — no one had taken Batman on as a *realistic* character. Batman is, after all, a mortal guy. Even the Gotham of the comics, of all the comic locations, while certainly heightened and exaggerated, still reflects people's very real worries about their own society. What hadn't been done, for better or worse, was the notion of an extraordinary man in an ordinary world.
>
> (McCue and Bloom 1993)

Nolan's comments point to the fundamental difference between the Marvel and DC superheroes: Marvel superheroes are very much these "extraordinary" figures "in an ordinary world" as opposed to DC superheroes — including Batman — who function more as archetypes in "heightened and exaggerated" cities, kept removed from our own. Marvel superheroes are the very definition of the Silver Age superhero, ordinary people — like Peter Parker, Matt Murdock, or Bruce Banner — affected by "modernity." They are, as Sanderson notes, "a popular culture icon for a more modern, urban America, where the new frontiers lie in rapid, revolutionary scientific advances . . . an ordinary city dweller whom science endows with the abilities to make a difference in a city of millions" (Sanderson 2007: 13). Whereas Carmine Infantino's cities in *The Flash* were "stylized compositions of futuristic slanted spires . . . [that] reflected the crystal-clean images of America promulgated then by Hollywood and Madison Avenue in its entertainment and advertising" (Schumer 2003: 8–9), Steve Ditko's *Spider-Man* pages were "bleak and grey, peopled by equally drab characters of plain, everyman appearance" (Schumer 2003: 9).

This emphasis on urbanity is important for, as Ben Highmore notes, the debut of Marvel's Silver Age superheroes "coincides with a range of significant 'moments' in the changing history of work patterns and transformations of the urban environment" (Highmore 2005: 124), chief among them being vertical expansion "in the shape of [the] high-rise office building . . . [and] New York City can serve as the most vivid example" (Highmore 2005: 127). Citing the work of Leonard Wallock (Wallock 1988: 43), Highmore goes on to point out that "eleven million square feet of office space was built in Manhattan . . . between 1960 and 1961" (Highmore 2005: 127). Little wonder then that the "ordinary world" of the Marvel Universe is, for the most part, New York City, mirroring what Highmore describes as the "enormous centrifugal (horizontal) expansion" (Highmore 2005: 127) of this urban centre throughout the 1960s, collapsing what Guy Debord saw as any meaningful opposition between city and country (Debord 1995) and replacing it with an indiscrete kind of "viral urbanism" (Highmore 2005: 127).

With the relocation of the Fantastic Four from the generic Central City to New York City in *Fantastic Four*, No. 2, (Lee and Kirby 1961) New York was confirmed as the very center of the Marvel Comics Universe. It is what grounds the "civil wars," "secret invasions," and "dark reigns" of its heroes and villains; it gives an immediacy to the actions of cosmic villains like Terrax (when he levitates Mahattan Island) or Onslaught (when he attacks Central Park) and provides a spine that links the most disparate parts of the Marvel Universe, from the technologically advanced African nation of Wakanda to the inner spaces of the Microverse; Marvel confirmed what New Yorkers had long suspected, New York was not just the center of the world, it was the very center of the universe!

Virtually all of Marvel's major superheroes are "city dwellers" (Sanderson 2007: 12) with the Fantastic Four basing themselves in the Baxter Building (a Manhattan office building) and the Avengers in their mansion on the Upper East Side, later the Hydrobase off the New York coast and more recently in Avengers (formerly Stark) Tower, also located in Manhattan. Dr. Strange could be found in Greenwich Village (on 177A Bleecker Street); Tony Stark (Iron Man) in the offices of Stark International on Long Island; Peter Parker (Spider-Man) commuting between Forest Hills, Queens, and the *Daily Bugle* building in the Murray Hill neighborhood; while Daredevil patrolled Hell's Kitchen and Ben Grimm (the Thing) and Steve Rogers (the as-at-the-time-of-writing-still-late Captain America) both had roots in the Lower East Side (Sanderson 2007: 12).

Marvel's superheroes are therefore modern in two senses. They are the *dark* side of modernity, the result of scientific accident (as in the case of Spider-Man, Daredevil, the Thing, or the Hulk) or genetic mutation (as in the case of the X-Men) and they are also the product of modernity's industrialization and urbanization. For Highmore this makes them "a new species, a species that has adjusted to the modern city and overcome its obstacles" (Highmore 2005: 124), as depicted in the almost fetishistic repetition of Marvel superheroes ducking, weaving, swinging, and climbing through, over and under cityscapes in Marvel comic books. For Highmore, part of the pleasure of the Marvel hero is that they offer "a compensatory fantasy of remasculinization: from feminized office-bound weakling [reporter, scientist, lawyer] to muscle-bound hero" (Highmore 2005: 128); Marvel's superheroes are therefore products of the city but they are "super" in that they can transcend those limitations (of gridlock, crime, and other urban constraint) that the city places on the rest of us.

Of all cities, New York also seems the most suited for the comic page as New York City itself is structured around an abstract grid of buildings and streets just as the comic page is (most often) structured into grids composed of panels and gutters. In this way New York becomes the grid for the Marvel Universe; it makes the Marvel universe *legible* for the reader by offering both connectivity (a city-based community) and an element of realism (in that New York is a real place). This is aptly demonstrated in a sample panel from Denny O'Neil and Frank Miller's *Amazing Spider-Man Annual*, No. 14 where Spider-Man is swinging through a stormy New York night looking for Dr. Strange: "Who'd'a thought that on the rottenest Friday night of the year, ESU's campus would be like Grand Central at rush hour? Lessee . . . Last time I was there, Doc Strange's pad was in the village — on Bleeker near the Hudson" (O'Neil and Miller 1980).

In this moment Spider-Man is simultaneously a superhero, web-slinging his way to a master of the mystic arts, and a real New Yorker, navigating his way through a real New York City to find another member of his community. The city both connects and grounds the Marvel superhero.

Community-building

As one of Marvel's creators, Stan Lee, describes it:

> if the superheroes and their colorful cohorts all lived in the same city, it seemed reasonable to suppose that their paths would cross from time to time . . . That was the start of the Marvel Universe, a universe in which the Human Torch is apt to run into Spider-Man while chasing the Hulk down a busy street.
>
> (Lee and Mair 2003: 137)

The Marvel Universe is therefore predicated on connectivity and social networks (Alberich *et al.* 2002: 1–14). of both its titles and its individuals and, in its early years, the Marvel Universe benefited from the unified vision of its architects — Lee together with Jack Kirby, Steve Ditko, and John Romita[2] — whose creative cross-pollinations resulted in crossovers, guest appearances, and ongoing narratives, especially during 1963 when the Marvel logo started appearing on the covers and the issues began carrying checklists of all the titles Marvel published at the time. Innovations like these quickly contributed towards the idea of a cohesive whole, a community of characters and titles that could collectively be thought of as "the Marvel Universe" the "greater whole" Spider-Man is referring to in the opening splash panel of *Giant-Size Astonishing X-Men*, No. 1. This idea of a "greater whole" was confirmed in the 1980s with the release of the first edition of *The Official Handbook of the Marvel Universe*[3] and the *Marvel Super Heroes Secret Wars* mini-series, *The Official Handbooks of the Marvel Universe*[4] both of which highlighted the importance of New York City; Marvel's first map of Manhattan was published in *The Official Handbook* and the Beyonder's citadel in Central Park served as the crossover point for the Marvel superheroes (and villains) to enter the *Secret Wars* (in April cover-dated issues of their individual titles). As if to make clear the importance of connectivity in the Marvel Universe, just as cities are often metaphorically represented as bodies, since they both share cultures of connectivity (Highmore 2005: 137–8), so too does the Marvel Universe appear as a universal body, the cosmic being known as Eternity (a humanoid figure whose entire body is composed of stardust, planets, and suns).

Beyond storytelling, establishing a community of titles and characters is also important for commercial reasons as it allows the community to be holistically branded as a corporate product (the Marvel Universe) rather than the product of any one individual (e.g. Stan Lee and Steve Ditko's *Spider-Man*). Writers and artists therefore contributed to a *universe*, developing a franchise or expanding the world (rather than actually producing something totally original or new). A community of titles also encouraged the acquisition of a range of titles to "complete the story" or "collect the entire set," leading to the development of the infamous "Marvel zombies," readers who only buy Marvel products (and attempt to buy all of the Marvel products on offer). The Marvel Universe thereby began to offer a completely immersive experience, a community that is accessible through a variety of different titles and (increasingly) across different platforms that can be as complex or as simple as a fan's investment allows.

But this sense of New York building communities extended beyond the creation of an integrated fictional universe for consumers to the development of a larger community between the producers and consumers of Marvel Comics. This commenced with the publishing of letters from readers (creating a communal space for fans that would later be channeled into fan clubs like the Merry Marvel Marching Society, debuting in 1965) and, in December 1965, the idea of the Marvel Bullpen Bulletin,[5] a "house page" that provided alleged insights into the creators and creative processes of the Marvel company. Originally (purportedly) written by Lee himself, Bullpen Bulletins continued in various forms throughout the 1980s and 1990s (by Jim Shooter and Tom DeFalco, among others), connecting readers from all over the world to the production offices of Marvel and creating a community of consumers and producers around an often idealized form of Marvel's creative Bullpen in New York City.

Realism

The main novelty of the Marvel Universe, in contrast to other superhero comics of the time, was *realism*. Indeed, in one of the first mass media pieces to be written about Marvel, Sally Klepton stated that Marvel was unique in evoking "even metaphorically, the Real World" (Klepton 1965, cited in Schumer 2003: 10) and once again Stan Lee points to the importance of New York City in connoting this realism:

> It should be abundantly clear that I've always tried to make our characters as realistic as possible, given the fact that they were living in a world of fantasy. In fact, I tried to inject reality into that world itself ... these colourful superheroes ... had to live somewhere, why not let them all live in the same city? That city would be New York, because that's where I lived and it was the one place I felt I could write about with a fair degree of accuracy.
>
> (Lee and Mair 2003: 137)

Whenever Marvel drifted too far away from this "realistic" approach (through its endless proliferation of characters or overly convoluted back-stories) endless reboots and retcons have sought to bring the

Marvel Universe back to this core premise of being about superheroes in the real world, by relaunching a hero with a new number-one issue, introducing some element of tragedy into the heroes' adventures or launching a completely new "realistic" setting, as unsuccessfully trialled with the "New Universe" concept of the 1980s and more successfully with the "Ultimate Universe" concept of the 1990s. Perhaps the best single example of this approach was Kurt Busiek and Alex Ross's *Marvels*, which rendered the Marvel Universe as realistically as possible, with a narrative taken from the street-level perspective of journalist Phil Sheldon and fully painted artwork (mostly watercolors and gouache) (Busiek and Ross 1994). Of course, the streets were New York streets and perhaps more than any other Marvel series before or since, *Marvels* confirmed New York's status as a character as important as any other in Marvel's pantheon.

This concern with realism certainly never translated into any serious consideration of the effects of super powers (as Paul Chadwick's *Concrete* would later do), the impracticalities of superheroes costumes or body proportions (despite the abilities of Alex Ross to make them appear as "realistic" as possible) or the impact superheroes might have on the world, economically, politically, or legally (as explored in Alan Moore and Dave Gibbons's *Watchmen*).[6] Rather, realism came from the melodrama of the storytelling (Bainbridge 2009) and, perhaps even more importantly, the real-world setting of New York City. As comics theorist Scott McCloud notes:

> In the mid-sixties, Jack Kirby, along with Stan Lee, staked out a middle ground of iconic forms with a sense of the real about them bolstered by a powerful design sense . . . Today, many American mainstream comics still follow Kirby's lead for storytelling, but the desire for more realistic art and more elaborate scripts has pushed art and story further apart in many cases.
>
> (McCloud 1993: 55)

Given the fact that Kirby and Lee produced so much of Marvel's early output and remained so influential on Marvel's subsequent development, McCloud is really referring here to the essence of "Marvel Style," that notion of "extraordinary individuals" — near-naked iconic forms with distorted proportions, what Kirby referred to as "figures that fought and twisted" (Jack Kirby cited in Danzig and Thibodeaux 1993: 17–21) "violent ballets" (Kirby cited in Harold May 1995: 7) — being grounded by real-world (if overtly melodramatic) concerns in a real world city, New York. As Kirby himself described his depictions of the city:

> If you grow up in a city and see the city . . . you'll get a city as it really is, with all the detail that you remember . . . I would draw that city exactly as it was, brick by brick: the garbage in the street and the things floating down to the sewer.
>
> (Kirby 1993)

New York City is therefore not only the spine of the Marvel Universe, it is a *suture* — suturing the Marvel Universe to the real world, providing a material context for these iconic forms.

When Spider-Man speaks of being "enmeshed" in New York (again, in the splash page of *Giant-Size Astonishing X-Men*, No. 1) he is really speaking to this idea of suturing and being so "enmeshed" allows both Marvel comics and their characters to interact with the real world in some interesting ways. One of these occurred in December 2001 where, following the terrorist attacks of September 11, 2001, the Marvel Universe heroes directly responded to the tragic events of that day in the pages of a black-covered *Amazing Spider-Man*, No. 36 (Straczynski and Romita Jr. 2001). This issue deals with the aftermath of the World Trade Center attacks through a series of scenes depicting Spider-Man and other heroes helping rescue workers from the rubble, concluding with a full-page splash depicting the real-life heroes of the NYPD, FBI, and NYFD together with the superheroes. The images are accompanied by Spider-Man's running monologue, which reinforces the fundamental strength of the human spirit, as he states: "We stand blinded by the light of your unbroken will," echoing the "Get back to work" ethos expressed in (then) Mayor of New York Rudy Giuliani's speeches following the attack.

Here we see Marvel *responding* to real events. Over Marvel's 70 years this has been relatively limited (perhaps born out of a fear of dating the storylines or offending the readership) with few direct references to politics (aside from Watergate and Vietnam) or celebrities (apart from New York figures like David Letterman, Jay Leno, and the *Saturday Night Live* team); like other comic companies, Marvel seems more comfortable operating at this metaphorical level. But because New York is a real-world location it always allows Marvel the possibility to respond to the real world in a way that their contemporaries, such as DC Comics, simply cannot.[7] As artist John Romita Jr. put it:

> Spider-Man is a part of New York City and New York City is a part of Spider-Man. It's only natural that he should confront the tragedy . . . The World Trade Center Towers are . . . were . . . a part of New York City, not Metropolis or Gotham City. The majority of Marvel's characters are based in New York, and the Twin Towers were depicted numerous times in the past. Visual acknowledgement of the destruction should be considered.
>
> (Romita 2004)

This idea of Marvel sutured to the real world through New York has also enabled the easy transition of Marvel product into other visual media, as demonstrated through Sony's highly successful *Spider-Man* movie franchise.[8] Unlike Warner Brothers, which have had to construct largely filmic cityscapes around their DC Comic characters (from the gothic surrealism of Gotham City in Tim Burton's *Batman* films through to the more minimalist use of CGI to shape Metropolis in Bryan Singer's *Superman Returns*),[9] *Spider-Man* embraced the reality of New York City with location shooting in Manhattan, Queens, and Forest Hills, the use of New York's famous Flatiron building for exteriors of the Daily Bugle and posters featuring images of Spider-Man swinging around a sun-drenched New York[10] — a recurrent poster motif for *Spider-Man 2* and *3*. Indeed, reviews of the first film reflected on "The great, joyous thrill in watching a costumed Peter Parker swinging through the New York cityscape . . . It's an image that fans of the comic book have been waiting for decades to see realized on the movie screen."[11] By the time *Spider-Man 3* was released in May 2007, the barriers between the Marvel Universe's New York and the real New York City, between the textual and the extratextual, between promotion and celebration, and between the comic book Spider-Man and the filmic Spider-Man had almost been completely broken down by "'Spider-Man Week in NYC' . . . the result of a partnership between Columbia Pictures and NYC & Company, the city's tourism, marketing and events organization" (Saffel 2007: 313). Marvel had previously used its real-world New York setting as a way of cross-promoting their stories, perhaps most notably in the recreation of Peter Parker and Mary-Jane Watson's wedding in 1987. This was officiated by Stan Lee at the start of a New York

Mets/Pittsburgh Pirates game at Shea Stadium in Flushing, Queens, on June 5, 1987, which publicized the couples' wedding in the comics.[12] Here the real and Marvel worlds blurred through the New York location; fans arranged bachelor parties for Peter Parker at comic conventions; they sent wedding gifts to Marvel's New York offices; Peter and Mary-Jane's clothes were even designed by a real-life fashion designer Willi Smith. But "Spider-Man Week in NYC" took this type of cross-media promotion to a new level. As Saffel goes on to describe it, from April 30 to May 6, 2007 all five boroughs of New York were involved in staging "interactive events, media appearances and unusual exhibits" (Saffel 2007: 313) including arachnid exhibits at the American Museum of Natural History, photographic awards and exhibitions "in honour of Peter Parker's freelance photography career with the Daily Bugle" (Saffel 2007: 313) together with events at specific locations in the film — a Spider-Man comic exhibit at the New York Public Library (where Uncle Ben was shot) and a premiere screening of *Spider-Man 3* at the Tribeca Film Festival in Aunt May's Queens.

Such a celebration/promotion seems to echo the relationship between the residents of the Marvel Universe and their New York City, as demonstrated in *Avengers*, No. 144 where Patsy Walker, former girls-comic star of the 1940s and current superheroine Hellcat, explains that she moved from her small-town home for "New York and the super heroes!" (Englehart and Perez 1976). Sanderson suggests that here the comic's writer, Steve Englehart, is establishing a metaphorical link between superheroes and New York:

> For generations young people, and no-so-young people, have migrated to New York to start their careers, to find fame and fortune, and even to remold their identities, not unlike Patsy did in donning her Hellcat costume. It's why immigrants, such as the parents of the first genera-tion of Super Hero comics creators, traditionally come and settle in New York City. This city has a reputation of being larger-than-life . . . Super Heroes fit this mythic image of New York. Marvel's New York is literally full of marvels. The Super Hero represents the potential within every individual to become extraordinary.
>
> (Sanderson 2007: 17)

This is, as Michael Chabon has noted, the essence of the superhero nar-rative, *transformation*: "the costumed hero — if not a mutant — is born powerless and unheralded like the rest of us . . . it takes the bite of a radioactive spider, or some other form of half-disaster . . . to give birth to the hero" (Chabon 2008: 14). But if, as Chabon goes on to suggest, "superheroism is a kind of transvestism . . . [an invitation] to wear what we knew to be hidden inside of us" (Chabon 2008: 22–3) then these Marvel comics themselves are offering New York a kind of transvestism, a way to make manifest the possibility of New York. "Transvestism" is a good word here because, like all transvestism, it reveals as much as it conceals because it "wears what [is] hidden inside" (Chabon 2008: 23). In this way we can think of Marvel, through their comics and their films, as actively connoting the "possibility" of New York, encouraging the city to reveal what it so often conceals; Marvel connotes the "fantasy" of New York just as New York connotes the "reality" of the Marvel Universe.

As a final aside, it should also be noted that Marvel's depiction of New York City also serves as a constant reminder of the artists who produced it. As Arlen Schumer notes: "students of Kirby see, in his many widescreen scenes of utter devastation . . . the influence growing up in the cacophonous, claustrophobic, crumbling tenement slums of New York's lower east side had on Kirby graphically" (Chabon 2008: 23). New York therefore connotes not only a general "realism" for the Marvel Universe but also some more specific understanding of how its creators feel about the city in which they often lived and worked. Kirby's New York and Ditko's New York are as much signatures of the artists as any panels which bear their names.

Conclusion

The banners promoting "Spider-Man Week in NYC" in 2007 carried the byline: "A Hero Comes Home." This seemingly confirms the role of New York City textually and extratextually in the Marvel Universe for, ultimately, New York City provides an elision of *space* and *place.* New York is simultaneously the diegetic place where the Marvel Universe is located and the extradiegetic place where the Marvel Universe is created. It connects the reader to both the fictional space of the Marvel Universe and the productive space of the Marvel Bullpen. It connects the various characters, titles, and products produced by Marvel and coheres them into a universal whole. And it sutures this fictional space of the Marvel Universe to the real place of New York City, assisting in the translation of its characters into different media forms.

But just as New York City makes Marvel comics legible, Marvel comics similarly make New York City legible to a comic-reading community who may be otherwise unfamiliar with the city. As such Marvel is part of a tradition Highmore identifies as providing "urban culture *via* textual renderings of city life: worldscapes of urban culture as they have been distilled and secreted within particular formal devices (novels, films, social architectures and so on)" (Highmore 2005: 140).

But, as Highmore notes, "to privilege the metaphorics of the city is not to leave the real city behind . . . but to insist that our 'real' experiences of cities are 'caught' in networks of dense metaphorical meaning . . . the mingling of imaginings and experience that constitute the urban" (Highmore 2005: 5). In this way New York City becomes a kind of "second-hand world", to use C. Wright Mills's phrase, "determined by meanings" (Mills 1963 [1959]: 405) we have received as readers of Marvel Comics, a real place informed by Marvel's fictional space. As if the lines between fictional and real New York were not blurred enough already after "Spider-Man Week in NYC," then the publication of Peter Sanderson's *The Marvel Comics Guide to New York* (Sanderson 2007) — offering readers the chance to "explore the most exciting city in the world through the eyes of comics' most exciting super-heroes" including "the bridge where Spider-Man tried — and failed — to save his girlfriend, Gwen Stacy" (back-cover blurb) — must be the final confirmation of this elision between space and place. Like the cities Highmore has described, Sanderson's book serves as a reminder that New York exists "not simply in the physical environment of the urban but also in its material imaginary" (Highmore 2005: 5). Just as New York has haunted the comics page, so too have the people and stories of Marvel comics come to haunt New York.

Works Cited
Comics
Busiek, Kurt and Ross, Alex. *Marvels*. New York: Marvel Comics, 1994.
Chadwick, Paul. *Concrete*. Milwaukee, OR: Dark Horse Comics, 1986.
Englehart, Steve and Perez, George. "Claws." In: *Avengers*, No. 144, New York: Marvel Comics, 1976.
Everett, Bill *et al. Marvel Comics*, No. 1. New York: Marvel Comics, 1939.
Everett, Bill *et al.* "The World Faces Destruction." In: *Human Torch*, No. 5, New York: Marvel Comics, Fall 1941.
Lee, Stan and Kirby, Jack. *Fantastic Four*, No. 1, New York: Marvel Comics, November 1961.
Lee, Stan and Kirby, Jack. *Fantastic Four*, No. 2, New York: Marvel Comics, 1961.

Lee, Stan and Kirby, Jack. *Fantastic Four*, No. 4, New York: Marvel Comics, May 1962.

Lee, Stan and Kirby, Jack. *The Avengers*, No. 4, New York: Marvel Comics, March 1964.

Michelinie, David and Romita, John Snr. "The Wedding!" In: *Amazing Spider-Man Annual*, No. 21. New York: Marvel Comics, 1987.

Moore, Alan and Gibbons, Dave. *Watchmen*. New York: DC Comics, September 1986 to October 1987.

O'Neil, Denny and Miller, Frank. *Amazing Spider-Man Annual*, No. 14. New York: Marvel Comics, 1980.

Shooter, Jim *et al. Marvel Super Heroes Secret Wars*, New York: Marvel Comics, May 1984.

Straczynski, J. Michael and Romita, John Jr. *Amazing Spider-Man*, No. 36. New York: Marvel Comics, 2001.

Whedon, Joss and Cassaday, John. *Giant-Size Astonishing X-Men*, No. 1. New York: Marvel Comics, 2008.

Secondary Literature

Alberich, R., Miro-Julia, J. and Rossello, F. "Marvel Universe looks almost like a real social network." In: *Preprint* 11 (2002). 1–14.

Bainbridge, Jason. "'Worlds within Worlds': The Role of Superheroes in the Marvel and DC Universes." In: A. Ndalianis (ed.), *The Contemporary Comic Book Superhero*. New York: Routledge, 2009.

Bainbridge, Jason. "'This is the Authority. This planet is under our protection' — An Exegesis of Superheroes' Interrogations of Law." In: *Law, Culture and the Humanities* 3 (September 2007). 455–76.

Benton, Mike. *The Comic Book in America: An Illustrated History*. Dallas, TX: Taylor Publishing Company, 1989.

Chabon, Michael. "Secret Skin: An Essay in Unitard Theory." In: A. Bolton (ed.), *Superheroes: Fashion and Fantasy*. New York: The Metropolitan Museum of Art and Yale University Press, 2008.

Daniels, Les. *Marvel: Five Fabulous Decades of the World's Greatest Comics*. New York: Harry N. Abrams, 1991.

Danzig, G. and Thibodeaux, M. "Jack Kirby Interview." In: *Jack Kirby Collector*, Vol. 5, No. 22 (1993). 17–21.

Debord, Guy. *The Society of the Spectacle*. Trans. D. Nicholson-Smith. New York: Zone Books, 1995 [1967].

Highmore, Ben. *Cityscapes: Cultural Readings in the Material and Symbolic City*. New York: Palgrave Macmillan, 2005.

Jones, Gerard. *Men of Tomorrow: Geeks, Gangsters, and the Birth of the Comic Book*. New York: Basic Books, 2004.

Lee, Stan and Mair, George. *Excelsior! The Amazing Life of Stan Lee*. London: Pan Macmillan, 2003.

McCloud, Scott. *Understanding Comics: The Invisible Art*. New York: HarperCollins, 1993.

McCue, Greg S. and Bloom, Clive. *Dark Knights: The New Comics in Context*. London: Pluto, 1993.

May, H. "Kirby." In: *Jack Kirby Collector*, Vol. 2, No. 5 (1995). 7.

Mills Wright, Charles. "The Cultural Apparatus." In: *Power, Politics and People: The Collected Essays of C. Wright Mills*. Oxford: Oxford University Press, 1963 [1959]. 405–22.

Romita Jr., John. "Sequential Thoughts." In: *Cinescape Comics*. November 11 (2004). Available online at: http://www.mania.com/sequential-thoughts-john-romita-jr_article_30953.html (accessed October 1, 2009)

Saffel, Steve. *Spider-Man the Icon: The Life and Times of a Pop Culture Phenomenon*. London: Titan Books, 2007.

Sanderson, Peter. *The Marvel Comics Guide to New York City*. New York: Pocket Books, 2007.

Saunders, Catherine *et al.* (eds.), *Marvel Chronicle: A Year By Year History*. London: Dorling Kindersley Limited, 2008.

Schumer, Arlen. *The Silver Age of Comic Book Art*. Singapore: Collectors Press, 2003.

Vaz, Mark Cotta. *The Art of Batman Begins: Shadows of the Dark Knight*. San Francisco, CA: Chronicle Books, 2005.

Wallock, Leonard. "New York City: Capital of the Twentieth Century." In: *New York: Cultural Capital of the World 1940–1965*. New York: Rizzoli, 1988. 17–50.

Notes

1 Christopher Nolan, director, *Batman Begins* (2005).

2 While this chapter acknowledges the ongoing debate over the authorship of Marvel characters, Lee, Kirby, Ditko, and Romita are presented as the four individuals most indicative of the unified vision of the architects of the Marvel Universe. Similarly, where excerpts from Stan Lee's biography (Lee and Mair 2003) are presented they should be viewed as being indicative of the structural choices made in each hero's creation, rather than as evidence of Lee being the sole creator, or even greatest contributor to the creation, of each hero.

3 An A–Z guide to Marvel's characters. See "The Marvel Bullpen." In: *The Official Handbook of the Marvel Universe*, New York: Marvel Comics, January 1983.

4 The first company-wide crossover (Shooter *et al.* 1984).

5 "Bullpen" was a term used to describe holding cells for prisoners in the nineteenth century and later the area where baseball pitchers warmed up. As Daniels describes it "at Marvel, the bullpen was a big room where close to twenty artists worked on salary, penciling and inking pages that were handed from one man to another until the job was done" (Daniels 1991: 65). The Bullpen commenced in 1950 and continued on and off in various forms over the ensuing decades.

6 See Chadwick (1986); Moore and Gibbons (1986–7). Additionally, Marvel has occasionally flirted with the idea of following up on the consequences of superheroes' actions, as in Dwayne McDuffie and Ernie Colon's *Damage Control* limited series (commenced May 1989) that explored the day-to-day activities of a construction company cleaning up property damaged after superhero brawls. For a more detailed examination of the relationship between superheroes and the law see Bainbridge (2007: 455–76).

7 DC's direct engagement with September 11 was quite differently inflected, through a tribute book (*9–11 — The World's Greatest Comic Book Writers and Artists Tell Stories To Remember, Volume 2*), featuring a mixture of true stories, reflections on the tragedy, and stories starring DC heroes, with all proceeds from the book's sale going to various relief organizations. For more detail again see Bainbridge (2009).

8 Sam Raimi, director, *Spider-Man* (2002), *Spider-Man 2* (2004), and *Spider-Man 3* (2007).

9 Tim Burton, director, *Batman* (1989) and *Batman Returns* (1992); Bryan Singer, director, *Superman Returns* (2006).

10 Famously, a pre-release teaser poster featured a close-up of Spider-Man peering between skyscrapers with the World Trade Center reflected in his eyepiece; the reflection was removed following the destruction of the Twin Towers on September 11, 2001.

11 The comic wedding was conducted on the front steps of New York's City Hall in Michelinie and Romita (1987) and the Stan Lee and John Romita Snr. syndicated newspaper strip, *Spider-Man* (New York: Kings Features Syndicate, June 14, 21, and 28). The event received coverage on *Good Morning America* and *Entertainment Tonight* and in the *New York Times* and *Sports Illustrated*.

IV

Locations of Crime

11

Will Eisner, Vaudevillian of the Cityscape

GREG M. SMITH

T O APPRECIATE WILL EISNER'S COMICS, the reader must juggle two seemingly
contradictory tendencies in his work. On the one hand, Eisner
demonstrates a masterful command of the formal expressiveness of
comics. His mature works frequently foreground comics as *comics*, making the reader aware of frame borders, panels, and gutters as devices,
not as simple conveyors of the depicted world. Eisner is, therefore, a
modernist extraordinaire, a twentieth-century artist deeply concerned
with the nature of the medium. On the other hand, Eisner appears to
be a retrograde figure bogged down in melodramatic content from
the nineteenth century. His stories can be maudlin, with sentimental
stock characters gesticulating wildly in emotional paroxysms. The
old-fashioned content of his stories seems to be at odds with the modernist impulses governing his formal play. This chapter argues that a
key backdrop for understanding the contradictions of Will Eisner's
comics is American vaudeville. This popular theatrical form not only
provides characters and dramatic structures for his stories, but it also
ties Eisner to the modern urban landscape. Melodrama is a response
to the changing face of the city, and Eisner's obsession with making the
city speak in his comics leads him to his formal experiments. Vaudeville
and melodrama are important underpinnings that structure Eisner's
work, creating the tensions between modernity and the past that exist
throughout his comics.

Will Eisner was born in 1917, the son of an immigrant painter who sometimes worked for the Yiddish theater in New York City.[1] Fairly early in his career, Eisner paired with Jerry Iger to form the Eisner and Iger studio, and the shop worked on various comic titles in the fledgling American comics industry (an era depicted in the thinly veiled fiction of *The Dreamer*). Attempting to capitalize on the comic book boom, Eisner and Iger tried a distinctive form of comic book distribution. In 1940 they began publishing a 16-page weekly comic book, which appeared as a Sunday supplement to newspapers in *The Des Moines Register* and *Tribune Syndicate*. The supplement contained stories involving a variety of Eisner-created characters (including Mr. Mystic and Lady Luck), but the focus was on the character for which Eisner became primarily known: the Spirit. The Spirit was Denny Colt, a detective whose presumed death provided a cover for him to work as a masked crime-fighter. The mask was a conciliatory gesture to the syndicate, who wanted a superhero, but in practice the Spirit was an all-too-human detective inhabiting the gritty nourish Central City, depicted in Eisner's stylish pages. The Spirit continued to appear in over 20 newspapers (with a combined circulation of five million copies) until the supplement stopped publication in 1952. At that point Eisner moved from mainstream comic publishing and worked primarily on instructional comics for the Army and other agencies, a practice he began during his World War II service. Thus Eisner dropped out of sight of most comic fans until he was "rediscovered" by comic fan conventions in the 1970s. Inspired by the highly personal work being done by contemporary comics artists and writers, Eisner wrote the landmark graphic novel *A Contract with God*. Although he was not the first person to create a "graphic novel," Eisner became the primary popularizer of that term, advocating for a broad canvas for expression by comics artists/writers. His later works (*To the Heart of the Storm, A Life Force, Dropsie Avenue*) extended the experimentation begun with the Spirit, adapting semi-autobiographical narratives with a growing visual panache. He became an emblem for creator-driven quality comics, eventually lending his name to the prestigious annual Eisner Awards for comics achievement.

Eisner asserted that throughout his career he argued for a more sophisticated vision of comics that took advantage of their full potential. He recalled one particular occasion when he was extolling the beauties of comics to his fellow practitioners: "[Newspaper cartoonist] Rube Goldberg told me that what I was saying was bullshit. He said, 'Shit, boy, you're a vaudevillian. Don't forget this is vaudeville'" (Brownstein

2005: 63). I contend that, although Eisner aspired to "serious" work, he never did forget the lesson he learned from Goldberg and from his early experiences with American popular theater. The expressive forms and narrative structures of vaudeville show their imprint throughout Eisner's career.

American popular theater of the late nineteenth and early twentieth century depends on an understanding of gesture that is quite different from the norms of "realism" and "naturalism" that eventually laid claim to American stage and film acting. Instead of comparing melodramatic theatrical acting to the styles that later displaced it, it is more helpful to situate these turn-of-the-century performance styles in the theories that governed their practice. The work of François Delsarte sought to provide a conventionalized language for actors and dancers to convey emotion to an audience. He advocated bold gestures to give acting power, as opposed to subtler movements that were less clear. Delsarte studied patterns of gesture in everyday life, and he honed a system of archetypal postures based on these investigations. Horror, for example, could be effectively displayed by putting one hand to the head and the other palm outstretched and upright to ward off the horrific being. When actors wished to depict moments of high emotion, it was necessary for them to put their bodies into a characteristic posture in order for emotion to transfer directly to the audience. Unlike later Stanislavsky-based theories that made conventional forms the antithesis of good acting, conventional gestures are crucial for Delsarte. Spoken language is conventional too, but it does not access the deeper structures of the emotions in the way that the expressive human body can. A codified system of characteristic gestures combines the clarity of language with the emotional power of the human figure.

Genevieve Stebbins's 1886 book *The Delsarte System of Expression* was a hit, influencing stage practice worldwide but particularly in America.[2] The drawn illustrations of this book resemble a comic, with figures demonstrating various conventional postures. These figures bear particular resemblance to the postures found in Eisner's comics. When Eisner wants to give a lesson on "expressive anatomy" in his *Comics and Sequential Art*, he produces an illustration that seems almost straight out of Delsarte. He sketches a "micro-dictionary of gestures": a series of silhouettes in exaggerated postures to demonstrate particular emotions: anger, fear, joy, surprise, and so on. His fictional comics repeatedly demonstrate this tendency to pose his characters in Delsartian expressive positions. In the Spirit story entitled "Wild Rice," the villainess tries to manipulate her captors with a display of theatrical acting. Her head back against the wall, tears flowing, she balls up her fists to rail against the world, saying, "Yes . . . Fun while it lasted . . . *While it lasted* . . . That's how it's been all my life . . . Is there no way to escape?" (Eisner 1948: 6; emphasis in original) He continues this emphasis on broad gesture in his later graphic novels. When Frimme Hersh's daughter dies in *A Contract with God*, the Hasidic man throws his head back and raises both arms, his knees buckled, crying out to God, "NO! Not to me! You can't do this . . . We have a contract!!" (Eisner 1985: 21). When Jacob Shtarka tells his wife Rifka that he wants a divorce in *A Life Force*, she runs through a series of dramatic postures, one after the other, depicting her excessive grief: She puts both hands to her head and opens her mouth wide; she lays one hand on her breast, the other clutching her head; then she collapses onto a chair maintaining her hand positions (Eisner 1995: 120).

Like many comic artists, Eisner recognized that he could depict his characters in any of a range of poses. In order for his visual storytelling to be clear, he needed to capture a particularly strong posture for his characters. When looking for a model of how to position figures in the most dramatically powerful way, he would reasonably turn to the American popular theater, influenced by the widely disseminated theories of Delsarte.

Theater provided structural principles for Eisner's page layouts as well. Eisner often treats the single page (or a pair of comics pages) as the comics equivalent of the stage scene, maintaining a unity of time and space across the page, then moving to another continuous time-space on the following page. Eisner frequently takes advantage of the "natural" break between pages to transition to another place and time, as if a curtain descends on the scene at page's end only to rise again at the top of the next page. Eisner explicitly acknowledged his theatrical roots in a published conversation with Frank Miller:

> . . . each page is . . . like theater, it's a scene. A [comic] book is a series of scenes, like what I first was exposed to when I saw vaudeville as a kid: there were scenes that were called blackouts. Blackouts were little vignette scenes where the joke was told visually, and at the end of the joke all the lights went out.
>
> (Brownstein 2005: 83)

Figure 11.1. **Eisner following Delsarte: This "microdictionary of gestures" depicts standard body postures for anger, fear, joy, surprise, deviousness, threat, and power**

From: *Comics and Sequential Art* (New York: Norton, 2008), 105.

In this anecdote, Eisner emphasizes the comic scene structure of vaudeville, but his own work leans toward the dramatic, and so it borrows also from the dramatic structures of vaudeville.

Eisner's page "scenes" tend to end at a moment of dramatic suspension of the action, a moment known in American popular theater as a "tableau." A tableau, according to Ben Brewster and Lea Jacobs, was a pictorial effect onstage in which characters "froze" into a static posture. This often occurred at the ends of scenes because once dramatic action has halted, it is difficult (though not unheard of) to put the characters back into motion in a somewhat believable fashion. The tableau, therefore, is a highly theatrical, non-naturalistic effect that suspends action in order for the audience to linger over, contemplating both the aesthetics of the frozen *mise-en-scène* and the dramatic tension between the characters.

The tableau often occurs at a narrative "situation." In the parlance of the time, a dramatic situation was a moment in which the "linear progress of the narrative is arrested or blocked" (Brewster and Jacobs 1997: 24). Situations are points at which opposing forces meet. The characters freeze because they reach a physical impasse: If one character moves, then the entire direction of the narrative changes. Brewster and Jacobs say: "Situations thus exist on the cusp of actions; they give rise to actions and are in turn altered by them . . . [They are] an unstable constellation of forces precariously held in check but nonetheless liable to break out into action" (Brewster and Jacobs 1997: 23). Tableaux, therefore, give pictorial embodiment to the narrative situation. A situation is more than just a stilled action; it is a highly energized pause where characters are on the verge of doing something narratively significant.

The scenes in Eisner's stories often end in a situation/tableau where the characters take an exaggerated posture at the height of the scene's action. When Willie's shop-owner father discovers that his son is making pro-union signs for a mass demonstration in *A Life Force*, he tells Willie and his friend to "get out of my house!" pointing one hand dramatically in the air, eyes closed, while the two youngsters look at each other in bewilderment. Sometimes such moments are quiet stoppages of action. When Father O'Leary tells Neil in *Dropsie Avenue* that both his parents have died, the priest asks "Is there anything I can do? After, all we are neighbors, Neil?" The final panel shows Neil slumped over his piano, his shoulders sagging as the father leaves, and Neil says, "Nothing!" At the ends of pages/scenes, Eisner loves to freeze the action with his characters at their most expressive position, depicting a moment where something must change before the story can move forward. In so doing, he duplicates the frozen tableaux and narrative situations developed in American popular theater.

In making the link to tableaux and situations, I want to say something more than the obvious observation that comics are composed of still images. Of course every image on a comics page is frozen, but the panels at the ends of Eisner's scenes tend to present a particular kind of stilled action. These scenes show us a moment of action halted at an instant where the opposing character forces have stalemated each other. This differs from previous panels in the scene that tend to show intermediate stages with actions in progress, one action leading to the next, and not the tense constriction of potential energy that characterizes the situation.

Theatrical situations become principles that operate in a variety of

Figure 11.2. **The tableau: A frozen moment of emotional tension**
From: *A Contract with God* (New York: Norton, 2005), 23.

narrative forms, but they most importantly serve as a structuring principle for melodrama.[3] Melodrama places less emphasis on a strong linear character-driven line of action than more realistic drama does. Instead, as Brewster and Jacobs argue, melodrama maximizes the number of sensational situations, stringing them together with minimal narrative connective tissue. Characters in a melodrama lurch from dramatic reversal to reversal in ways that can be psychologically implausible, and this causes melodrama to be maligned by those who do not understand its distinctive structures. The skill for a melodramatist is to lead an audience from one emotionally affecting situation to another.

Melodrama, then, models the experience of moving through the modern world, being battered from all sides by intense sensations that have little connection to each other. To the immigrants emerging into the strange new world of the modern city, the urban environment presented them with a series of shocks. Modernity severs the ties between the individual and their former cultural context, forcing them away from the insulation of rural life to deal with a dizzying array of unfamiliar people and situations. The modern city dweller develops the ability to evaluate strangers based on their public presentation of self, and melodrama is obsessed with this unveiling of the underlying moral order. Melodrama is concerned with revealing who is truly moral, in spite of their public face. The esteemed landlord can be exposed as a tyrant; the proper husband might be a brutal wife-beater behind closed doors; or publishers can renege on their dealings with struggling comics artists. By participating in a melodramatic narrative, audiences can hone their skills at the urban survival skill of evaluating strangers through close observation of their actions and emotions.

Modernity, then, places the individual in a disorienting world of speed and mobility. The promise of modernity is that it will bring the world under the rational control of planners, that people will be more protected from the vagaries of nature as they participate in the steady rhythms of scheduled industrial labor and modern leisure. However, the fear that modernity produces is that individuals are more susceptible to fortune's reversals. In this seemingly more rational world, disaster is outside the individual's control in the form of industrial accidents, factory layoffs during economic downturns, or violence at the hands of criminals. This provides the social justification for the lack of classical causality in the melodrama. If external events can intervene to cause chaos in an individual's life in the real world, then certainly melodrama can move from one sensational, relatively unmotivated emotional crisis to another. The spectacle of overwrought suffering is the central pleasure provided by melodrama, just as walking down the urban street can present a series of displays of strangers caught in moments of high emotion. Melodrama, to this way of thinking, is both a reaction to modernity and an attempt to gain a certain measure of control over its excesses. Melodrama, far from being a retrograde practice, can be seen as being deeply embroiled in the contemporary experience.

Vaudeville adapted the melodramatic form (which developed over centuries) into a modular form, as is befitting the compartmentalized world of the modern city. Vaudeville presented a conveyor belt of disparate emotional sensations, each one only minimally related to the preceding one. A juggling act might follow an operatic tenor singing an aria, followed by a comedian, a short dramatic scene, and a coterie of dancers. Vaudeville's structure took maximal advantage of a centralized distribution network of performers, thus allowing theater managers

to treat individual acts as interchangeable parts, following the lead of
the assembly line. Many different arrangements could result because
there was no necessary dramatic logic that forced the components into
a particular order.

The city encloses people into modules as well, providing standardized
domiciles (in the form of apartment buildings) and routinized work
schedules in factories. The city places people in a range of compart-
ments of different sizes and forms, and Eisner's comics explore the
multiple forms of urban compartmentalization and containment. His
stories present melodramatic narratives of people trapped by their
circumstances, railing against the cruel injustice of these narrative
impasses. Eisner's enclosed figures embody Delsartian postures, making
their emotional plight clearly legible to their audience.

Transposing these melodramatic narratives from their stage heritage
to the medium of comics creates a distinctive opportunity that could
not exist in the theater. In depicting these stories of enclosure, Eisner
begins to be interested in the formal possibilities posed by the urban
landscape. His work becomes increasingly concerned with tracing the
multiple forms of the cityscape and noting how each one can frame these
entrapped characters. Eisner's comics form a catalog of how architecture
can become a frame and how these frames can become prisons.

A whole host of architectural features become foregrounded formal
elements in Eisner's work. *New York: The Big City* presents a series of
short portraits of urban life, many of them explicitly centered around
features of the cityscape. The drama of "The Ring," "The Money," "The
Weapon," "The Key," and "The Treasure" all occurs on top of what
appears to be the same storm drain grate. "Stoops" stages its scenes
("Witnesses," "Supper Time," "Home," "Stoopball") on the stairs leading
to tenement buildings. Architecture in progress provides opportunities for Eisner to explore. When Jacob Shtarka is building a wall in the
rabbi's home, the rabbi interrupts the construction to ask Jacob to read
a narratively significant letter. Eisner stages this action within the skeletal
wood structure of the wall being built, with Jacob and the rabbi sticking
their heads out of the spaces between wood studs to deliver their lines
(Eisner 1995: 84). Even destroyed architecture can be useful to Eisner's
staging. In the Spirit story "Visitor," a bank robbery is foiled by a mysterious explosion that blows a hole in the wall, and Eisner frames the
Spirit and the investigating policeman through the irregularly shaped
opening left by the blast (Eisner 1949: 2).

Doors in particular function as frames in these comics. When Eisner introduces the notorious femme fatale P'Gell in Istanbul, he takes full advantage of the opportunity provided by the Turkish setting, framing her voluptuous figure in silhouette in an Orientalist domed doorway (Eisner 1946: 4). In a story featuring another of *The Spirit*'s dangerous women, Sand Saref tosses a suitor that she judges to be inferior out of her apartment, and Eisner depicts this in a black panel, showing only the door and the bright light from within the room splashing onto the floor (Eisner 1950: 3). Doors can serve as formal anchors for the action throughout a scene. For instance, when Jacob visits his estranged wife Rifka, the scene plays as a series of variations centered on the door: The rabbi exits through the door, Rifka's word balloon summons Jacob through the empty black doorway to her bedroom, and that same doorway frames Jacob as he exits, carrying her food to end the scene (Eisner 1995: 134).

Eisner's pages often begin and end with exits through doors, further accentuating the connection between his pages and the structure of theatrical scenes. Just as in film, there is no need for a comic's character to exit the scene. In theater, an actor who is onstage has to get off the stage. In film this can be accomplished with a cut; in comics with a simple transition to another time and place. Eisner's tendency to begin or end scenes in doorways both points to his fascination with the formal possibilities that doors present and the strong theatrical heritage that influences his comics' staging.

Figure 11.3. **The storm drain as stage: Urban architecture becomes theatrical set**
From: *New York: Life in the Big City* (New York: Norton, 2006), 12.

Windows similarly play a strong role in Eisner's formal architectural play. The cover to *Dropsie Avenue* is a brick-building front with each of the sets of characters in the neighborhood seen through various windows. The layout of the cover draws attention to the similarity between these windows and the layout of panels in a comic page. In one of Eisner's famous splash pages that often began his Spirit stories, the Spirit stares through the bars of the window of the police station as rain falls outside, and the bars duplicate the rectangular layout of the standard comics page (Eisner 1950: 1). The elegant flashbacks in *To the Heart of the Storm* often begin as World War II serviceman Willie looks out of the train as he returns home, and what he sees through the frame of the window triggers his memories. Similarly in one of the short pieces in *New York: The Big City* appropriately entitled "Theater," a man looks out a subway window at a passing scene of two lovers framed by their bedroom window, a frame within a frame (Eisner 2006: 32). The obvious connection between windows and doors is that they usually (but not always) echo the rectangular shape of the standard comic's frame. They offer a fairly naturalized opportunity to emphasize the relationship between the diegetic space and the usually unacknowledged border that frames the action. Eisner's formalist tendencies rarely extend so far that he calls attention to the expressive capacity of the panel border without some motivation. His modernist practice, therefore, is limited, seeking grounding in the story world instead of flaunting formal play with the frame for its own purposes.

An outgrowth of Eisner's interest in architecture is his emphasis on the shapes made by light. Once he began to play with doors and windows, there is a natural progression to the squares of light produced by these architectural features. After all, in comics both the doors and their attached shadows are simply rectangles, just as comics' frames often are. It is just as easy to draw an outline of cast light as it is to draw an outline of a window letting the light in.

In addition, comics can heighten dramatic "lighting" because drawing makes "lighting effects" possible that could not be achieved in real life. Real theatrical lighting requires very powerful lighting instruments in order to create a distinct edge, and no lighting instrument can define an outline as clear and sharp as an inked line. The lighting in Eisner's compositions is often described as following film noir practice, but this is not quite accurate. Eisner's lighting effects can be *more* noir than film noir, accomplishing effects that no actual film lighting could.

Figure 11.4. **The naturalized frame: Windows frame the flashback images within the panel**

From: *To the Heart of the Storm* (New York: Norton, 2008), 35.

These lighting effects eventually take on a kind of tangible form. As the connections between cast shadows and drawn frames become more foregrounded, it becomes possible for these lighting effects to serve as a kind of stage on which the action occurs. In the previously mentioned Sand Saref story, the light spilling through the open doorway illuminates a square in the black frame, providing a landing for the suitor's fall in the otherwise abstract space. In later works, the square of light begins to drift away from its moorings to become pure space. The short work "Sermonette" begins with a street preacher shouting in an alley between buildings. As the sermon continues, the buildings disappear, leaving the street preacher declaiming on an abstract rectangle of space. In these moments, the grounding in naturalism is tenuous at best. Here we see light and shadow as almost pure outline, using them to frame and enclose the action just as strongly as doors and windows do. Here we see light being used in ways that greatly exceed the theatrical practice that gave rise to these effects. Adapting melodramatic stories of entrapment to comics created opportunities for Eisner to experiment in distinctive ways with comics' depiction of spatial enclosures. Adapting lighting effects from theater to comics made them more theatrical in ways that exceed the source.

The naturalized play that Eisner is most known for is his handling of rain and water. This tendency is so pronounced in Eisner's work that Harvey Kurtzman gave it a name: "Eisenshpritz." Rain creates spectacular vistas in the Spirit's Central city, such as the splash page in "Life Below," in which rain drips across a stone structure that spells out the Spirit's name (Eisner 1948: 1). Rain functions like light in Eisner's comics, as a naturalized feature of the environment that greatly exceeds its grounding in reality. It hugs and flows around the urban landscape, accentuating its contours just as light does. Rain acts like shading, creating dramatic spatial effects. As Eisner works later in his life, he begins using less of the spectacular Eisenshpritz that distinguished his early career, instead using the same kinds of lines as shading. The lines that might have been rain in the Spirit become patches of shading in his later graphic novels. When Mr. and Mrs. Svensen are forced to leave Dropsie Avenue, they depart in a car depicted against a wall of shading lines (Eisner 1948: 117). These lines extend from the city skyline, but they could just as easily have been made into Eisenshpritz. Later Eisner uses thick shading lines to give texture and form to the increasingly abstract spaces of his city exteriors and interiors.

At the same time Eisner's artistic style begins to extend more and more outside the confines of the frame boundaries. This tendency has always been present in Eisner's work, although he does this only to a limited extent in his run on the Spirit.[4] When Eisner reemerges in mainstream comics with his graphic novel *A Contract with God*, he seems energized by the innovative work of comics artists in the 60s and 70s. Once practitioners such as Neal Adams and Jim Steranko began extending their art outside the classical container of the panel, this seems to embolden Eisner in his later graphic novels to make good on his nascent tendency to play with the panel border. Thus freed, Eisner's later works can fully explore the tropes of containment and liberation in his stories. His characters can be imprisoned within their narrative confines and within the borders traced by Eisner's lines, but they can also find freedom, expressed both in story terms and by having characters sail outside the classical panel. In his later works, Eisner's form and content are free to interact in lyrical counterpoint to present his vision of the city.

Will Eisner's city is both concrete and abstract. It ebbs and flows as needed to serve the pacing of his stories. He has bemoaned the use of hyperrealistic art in comics, particularly when depicting buildings:

> Part of your storytelling skill depends on how much detail you put in. And it has to do with the rate of story speed. [Frank Miller's type of]

story moves so fast that if you stop the reader and give him a wall
with five hundred windows carefully done, you're going to derail the
whole thing.

(Brownstein 2005: 267)

In spite of the possibility of derailing the reader, Eisner does at times
present his own buildings in lushly detailed fashion. Instances include
the opening page of "The Building" (a portrait of how major events in
four characters' lives occur in front of a single city structure) and the
oft-reprinted "Gerhard Shnobble," in which the title character flies
across a photo of a cityscape. More often, however, Eisner uses the city
as backdrop for dramatic action in the foreground. Once the drama of
"The Building" has begun, the lush details of the overall building are
hidden, leaving us with portions of the architecture as seen from street
level. The short piece entitled "Backdrop" literally positions the cityscape
as a theatrical backdrop for more intimate foreground action (dining).
Over and over in Eisner's later work he sketches in the merest outline
of the cityscape behind his characters, reminding us of the inescapable
influence of urban modernity on the petty melodramatic narratives.

Eisner's city is rarely experienced as a whole, except when viewed
from enough distance to see the (abstracted) skyline. The city as seen
from the street is a series of specific locales. Throughout this chapter I
have listed various archetypal urban locations that Eisner uses: stoops,
doorways, drain grates, windows, alleys, and so on. Eisner's city is a city
of fragments because that is how his characters perceive the urban
landscape. His characters feel modernity not as an overall totalizing
force but as a series of details and occurrences that have personal bear-
ing on their lives.

The city architecture impinges on the people who inhabit it, uncom-
fortably shoving them up against each other like characters on a comics
page. Will Eisner sees the city as a prison, but mostly he sees that prison
as being created by other people. In *The Name of the Game,* marriage
is a trap that constrains multiple generations of the Arnheim family.
In *Family Matter,* mute patriarch Ben is confined to a wheelchair by a
stroke, leaving him to be tortured by his family who air their grievances
in front of him. "Mortal Combat" tells a story of a couple whose chance
at romantic happiness is destroyed by an overbearing parent. There is
no escaping other people in the city, and so relationships make Eisner's
characters into jailors.

The emphasis in Eisner then is not on the city itself but on the personal lived experience of the city. The city can retreat to the background, providing a backdrop for his characters. It can be reduced to lived fragments or to abstract outlines. The city is rarely far away, however. The urban environment cannot be separated from these characters lives because they bear its indelible marks, just as melodrama is inconceivable without the shaping provided by modernity.

Works Cited
Comics

Eisner, Will. *A Contract with God*. Princeton, WI: Kitchen Sink, 1985.
Eisner, Will. *A Life Force*. Princeton, WI: Kitchen Sink, 1995.
Eisner, Will. "Bring in Sand Saref." In: *The Spirit*. January 15, 1950.
Eisner, Will. *Dropsie Avenue*. New York: DC Comics, 2000.
Eisner, Will. *Family Matter*. Princeton, WI: Kitchen Sink, 1998.
Eisner, Will. "Gerhard Shnobble." In: *The Spirit*. October 6, 1946.
Eisner, Will. "Life Below." In: *The Spirit*. February 22, 1948.
Eisner, Will. "Meet P'Gell." In: *The Spirit*. October 6, 1946.
Eisner, Will. *New York: Life in the Big City*. New York: Norton, 2006.
Eisner, Will. "Sand Saref." In: *The Spirit*. January 8, 1950.
Eisner, Will. *The Dreamer*. Princeton, WI: Kitchen Sink, 1986.
Eisner, Will. *The Name of the Game*. New York: DC Comics, 2002.
Eisner, Will. *To the Heart of the Storm*. Princeton, WI: Kitchen Sink, 1991.
Eisner, Will. "Visitor." In: *The Spirit*. February 13, 1949.
Eisner, Will. "Wild Rice." In: *The Spirit*. April 4, 1948.

Secondary Literature

Brewster, Ben and Lea Jacobs. *Theatre to Cinema: Stage Pictorialism and the Early Feature Film*. Oxford: Oxford University Press, 1997.
Brooks, Peter. *The Melodramatic Imagination: Balzac, Henry James, Melodrama, and the Mode of Excess*. New Haven, CT: Yale University Press, 1995.
Brownstein, Charles. *Eisner/Miller*. Milwaukie, OR: Dark Horse Comics, 2005.
Eisner, Will. *Comics and Sequential Art*. New York: Norton, 2008.
Eisner, Will. *Graphic Storytelling and Visual Narrative*. New York: Norton, 2008.
Gledhill, Christine. "Historicizing Melodrama." In: *Home Is Where the Heart Is: Studies in Melodrama and the Woman's Film*. London: BFI Publishing, 1987. 14–39.
Singer, Ben. *Melodrama and Modernity: Early Sensational Cinema and Its Contexts*. New York: Columbia University Press, 2001.
Stebbins, Genevieve. *The Delsarte System of Expression*. New York: Edgar Warner, 1886.

Notes

1 *To the Heart of the Storm* (Eisner 1991) depicts a fictionalized version of his father, the theater-set painter.
2 The popular success of Delsarte's method led to widespread dissemination by scurrilous teachers with limited understanding of his original principles, and

so much of American popular theater was probably influenced by bastardized, caricatured versions of "Delsarte."

3 For more details on melodrama, see Brooks (1995), Singer (2001) and Gledhill (1987).

4 We tend to misremember *The Spirit* as being more innovative than it probably was, partly because of Eisner's own guidance. In his more theoretical works, *Comics and Sequential Art* and *Graphic Storytelling and Visual Narrative*, written later in his career, Eisner emphasizes his more formally innovative Spirit stories such as "Gerhard Schnobble" (*The Spirit*, October 6, 1946). This gives a false sense that *The Spirit* was this innovative through most of its run, but closer perusal of a larger number of Spirit stories shows that for the most part Eisner's panels stay well within the frame borders. Most of Eisner's Spirit stories are well-wrought examples of the comics practices of the day; only rarely do they become experimental.

12

"A Fiction That We Must Inhabit" — Sense Production in Urban Spaces according to Alan Moore and Eddie Campbell's *From Hell*

BJÖRN QUIRING

INCE THE VERY BEGINNING OF architectural theory, it has been emphasized that the city is not only a place where people convene to live and trade, but also a place which commemorates a more or less glorified past. Temples, palaces, archives, and museums are all thoroughly urban institutions, and they are all considered storage houses of former times. Architecture deals not only with the ordering of space, but also with the preservation of time, just as history writing is often represented by its practitioners as the erection of undying monuments to great men and great nations (McEwen 2003: 82). Vitruvius, as its first theoretician, occasionally describes architecture as a sort of historiography, supposed to 'signify [*significare*] the customs of ancient times and to impress them on the mind' (Vitruvius 1981: 82–3; see also McEwen 2003: 81). The city is depicted as a mnemonic device, built to imprint a somewhat mythical past onto the psyche of a populace. It is only logical that some of the architectural vocabulary used by Vitruvius (e.g. *ordinatio, dispositio, eurythmia*) is borrowed from rhetoric (McEwen 2003: 79) and that in his texts knowledge and corporeality tend to blend into each other.[1] As a result, architecture is generally taken to be a discipline actively unifying the material and the spiritual. Urban architecture, according to this conception, functions as a basis for social engineering in that it makes tangible a perpetual cosmic hierarchy to which men must submit themselves. An integral part of this scheme is the representation of foundational myths and histories on the walls of significant public buildings; these renderings, in fact, seem to be the first stories told by a combination of images and texts. Representative pre-Vitruvian examples can be found everywhere, for example, the reliefs on Mesopotamian palace and temple walls, frequently depicting Marduk, the founder of Babylon, slaying the female demon Tiamat (King 1899: 101). When she is killed, he builds heaven and earth using her dead body as raw material, which makes him the world's primal architect (Wyatt 2001: 63–5). This mythical depiction of foundational violence[2] already hints at the fact that the city as mnemonic device has a somewhat sinister side: It commemorates that its urban law and order was established by acts beyond the law, namely violent seizures of power and acts of domination. The city still bears the scars; it thus provides the scene that produces or perpetuates unpleasant mythical memories. These myths of order are one of the primary devices by which political and imperial power "makes sense" of the world and gives a teleological direction to events. Sense is, in the words of Jörn Rüsen, a synthesis of the past and the future, "of experience and expectation" (Rüsen 2006: 41). In sketching out the past, the embodied foundational myth also implies where time is going. It mediates between the past, the present, and the future — and it fictionalizes them all to a certain degree, by integrating them into itself (McEwen 2003: 304). Insofar as urban space relies on these representations, it is neither quite real nor entirely fictitious; it is a montage of both, which counts on the city-dweller qua spectator/reader to synthesize mythical past, concrete present, and uncertain future into a meaningful whole (Boyer 1994: 175).

Since the city functions as a machine for the production of memory, it is no wonder that other mnemonic devices have often imitated its form. For example, the antique and medieval "theaters of memory" that were indispensable components of the ancient *ars memoriae* often took the form of a real or imaginary city.[3] Acting as venerable precursors of the modern "mind map," these memory theaters were mental spaces which served as storage rooms for perceptions, plans, and memories: All the facts the memory artist wanted to remember were emblematized as imaginary objects, signs, or persons, then combined and strategically deposited at certain locations of the theater so they all could be unified in a single (if very complex) conception and thus easily retrieved by memory, should the need arise (Yates 1999: 12). It was advised that the emblems and signs should either be very beautiful or very ugly and violent in order to heighten their memorability. Consequently, somebody schooled in the arts of memory gradually constructed a whole imaginary city in his head, with neatly laid out streets connecting houses that contained all the knowledge this person had ever acquired in the form of emotionally pregnant signs and memorable images. For example, if such a person was asked when Rome was founded, he would mentally enter the city, walk past Philosophy Lane and the Street of Poetry to the House of History, go to the Rome Room, walk to the cupboard all the way to the left and find in the uppermost shelf a blood-spattered spade with the number 753 on it. And by that, he would remember that Rome was founded in 753 B.C. (and perhaps that its foundation cost the life of Remus). It is easily noticed that this imaginary city of memory is nothing but an enormous metaphor by which complex information is drawn together, condensed, and allegorically structured. In the process, the progression of time is spatialized; the art of memory condenses the flow of experience into semantically highly charged and ordered spaces.

Subsequently, especially during the Renaissance, the claim was made that these mental spaces in fact mirrored the true order of the universe, hidden from us while we are mortal and subject to time. Indeed, one of the fundamental models for these mnemonic constructions was the Heavenly City of Jerusalem in which all that is redeemed and worthy would be assembled at the end of time and ordered according to its true station (Haverkamp 1996). A fair number of the ideal cities and utopias which permeate the history of literature and philosophy are derived from this basic metaphor in one way or another. Indeed, large parts of modern intellectual and political history can be characterized as disconcerted efforts to literalize it, that is, to build a new Jerusalem not only in the mind, but in a bodily, tangible form. Frances Yates supposes, for example, that the origins of Freemasonry are to be found in this context, so that Freemasonic rituals and their political ambitions have to be considered as degenerations of *ars memoriae* practices (Yates 1999: 278). Be that as it may, it is obvious that empirical cities always left something to be desired in comparison with such high ideals. The foundational violence on which they were built is a somewhat shaky ground, since it is shot through and threatened by competing forms of violence that might inaugurate alternative myths and histories. As a result, the city is not only a potential location for the eternal order of things, but also for indomitable chaos, a repository of fragmented histories, which, in their synchronicity, produce an overload of competing, disseminating senses and sense perceptions. Hence, the best the city can offer is a failed, uncertain metonymy of universal order, a wilderness of incompatible signs complemented by the promise of their ordering.

This unreconciled state of affairs has always haunted modernity (see Boyer 1994). Even the comic strip, as an inherently modern and urban medium, inherits the same tension working on the notion of spatialized time. The comic is a juxtaposition of incompatible, mass-produced signs in which entangled images and texts both disturb and complement each other. Of course, there are other influences on the comic form that are just as important. But it is the engagement with this troublesome heritage that has turned some comics into important cultural contributions; foremost among them are the works of Winsor McCay and Alan Moore. That Alan Moore's comics have been generally acclaimed as groundbreaking is to a large extent ascribable to the fact that he really "works through" the relation of the comic to the embattled urban theater of memory. This quality can already be discerned by observing some of the formal features of his comics: Moore is insistently establishing linkages between seemingly independent aspects of the narrative by visual and verbal echo effects, such as recurring motives and patterns, metaphors, puns, and other structural devices. The goal of these framing and condensing operations always seems to be the implication of an elusive conceptual as well as imaginative unity underlying all heterogeneities.

This is not a purely formal feature, however. In fact, the most important underlying topic of nearly all his comics is the building of the mnemonic heavenly city. This becomes quite obvious in his more didactical efforts, such as *Promethea* (Moore, Williams, and Gray 2000–5), which centers on a regenerative New Age apocalypse in New York and organizes itself according to the structure of the kabbalistic Tree of Life, that is, basically another version of the theater of memory (see e.g. Kaplan 1997: 21). If *Promethea* doesn't rank with Moore's most successful works, it's mainly due to the fact that an important dialectical ingredient is missing in it: The comic reads like an illustrated treatise most of the time, because the main protagonists are largely busy proclaiming the same kabbalistic wisdom that is also borne out by all aspects of the comic itself. The result is a pretty univocal, redundantly masterful affair. However, in most cases, Moore's approach to salvation is a somewhat more subtle business. His scenarios, to put it schematically, tend to thematize one-man conspiracies that strive for a utopian renewal and reordering of society. Self-appointed saviors try to establish the millennial city and to order the dissociated signs by the use of violence. Even though they're often the main protagonists, Moore puts these messianic figures together with the sense they make in an increasingly ambivalent light. This ambivalence is still somewhat underdeveloped in *V for Vendetta* (1982–8) (Moore and Lloyd 1990), in which a fascist state in Great Britain is brought down by a wise, rich, tasteful, and quite sovereign anarchist who gallantly hands power back to the people. When Moore started to work for DC, the story lines got more dialectical. You could call his *Swamp Thing* (1983–7) (Moore *et al.* 1998–2002) the most pronounced (if hardly the most articulate) Hegelian in mainstream comic strips, heroically defending the mutual interdependence of good and evil, nature and culture, city and country. But it is only in Moore's first masterwork, *Watchmen* (1986–7) (Moore and Gibbons 1987) that ambiguity really starts to bloom. Again, the basic scenario concerns a millennial conspiracy, namely the attempt of the ex-superhero Ozymandias aka Adrian Veidt to stop all wars and particularly the tensions between America and Russia by staging a fake alien attack on New York, costing the lives of several million people. This peculiar sort of supreme global city planning aims to effect a Hobbesian reconciliation of mankind through fear. However, the project ends in ambivalences: Veidt isn't explicitly condemned, but he is clearly an unsympathetic figure, shady at best. The comic hints at the fact that the reconciliation he achieves is volatile, and the price to be paid for it much too high (see e.g. Moore and Gibbons 1987: 27). Veidt's effort at sense-making fails, as do the somewhat less ambitious enterprises by the other masked heroes of *Watchmen* to bring about justice. The new, unified sense dissociates as soon as it is produced, the need for closure remains frustrated and the eternal city elusive. That doesn't mean it is altogether absent, however; it seems clearly to be at work in the enormous number of condensing devices that Moore uses in this comic. They seem to relate all the panels to all the other panels as if each mirrored some facet of the other in a crystalline and timeless structure. One of the most pronounced articulations of this conjuncture is the formal tour de force of the fifth chapter, "Fearful Symmetry," in which the first panel mirrors the last, the second the next-to-last, and so on. However, the specificity of its urban setting never really enters into these combinations: The New York of *Watchmen* seems largely devoid of landmarks and history. There's no Empire State Building to be found, no Central Park, no Town Hall, no Metropolitan Museum, not even the Statue of Liberty, just a Moloch of rather uniform Manhattan skyscrapers and rather uniform Brooklyn flats. Only the regular grid of the New York streets seems to be mirrored in the regular grid of *Watchmen*'s panels: A largely undecorated stage on which Veidt's Manhattan Project plays itself out.

In Moore's next magnum opus, *From Hell* (1988–98) (Moore and Campbell 2006), the cityscape of London is used a lot more memorably. This new variation on the urban salvation theme is the bleakest, but it might also be considered the most complex. Inspired by the psycho-geographical writings of Iain Sinclair, the London of *From Hell* abounds in landmarks incarnating its sinister, violent history. The comic relies heavily on historical source material, as its extensive, but not very solid bibliography makes clear. The main source of the story is Stephen Knight's discredited and sensationalist book about the Whitechapel murders, *Jack the Ripper, The Final Solution.* Knight's theory is also the plot of *From Hell* in outline, so they both can be sketched simultaneously: In 1884, Queen Victoria's slightly retarded grandson, Albert, meets a nice Catholic shopgirl, gets her pregnant, and secretly marries her. When Victoria finds out about this impossible liaison, the couple is separated, and the shopgirl is locked away in an asylum to be brainwashed by the Queen's personal physician, the Freemason Dr. William Gull. A friend of the shopgirl, the prostitute Marie Kelly, learns about the affair, and when she falls into dire straits, she along with three girlfriends attempts to blackmail a friend of Albert. In order to get rid of this permanent threat to the crown, Victoria has the four women systematically butchered, once more enlisting the help of her personal physician, the very cultivated Gull. These four killings (plus one accidental killing in case of mistaken identity) remain unsolved and subsequently become known as the Jack the Ripper murders. Soon afterwards, Gull goes mad and dies in a lunatic asylum. All Moore adds to this basic conspiratorial story line is an ambivalence. His version of the tale leaves open the possibility that Marie Kelly escapes and Gull kills the wrong woman. He also provides the plot twist that the investigating police inspector, Frederick Abberline, finally finds out the whole nasty story, but that there's nothing he can do about it, since the Queen is the supreme power in the country, backed by corrupt, Freemasonic police commissioners. As Moore has emphatically pointed out, he doesn't assume that Knight's conspiracy plot is true or even probable, he just considers it good story material (Moore and Campbell 2006: Appendix 1: 1). That is to say, it makes a good starting point for another, even more subtle game of millennial condensations, involving another questionable case of violent utopianism. Moore uses the killings as the base metaphor from which another theater of memory may be constructed. However, that doesn't mean that the comic would strive to become an accurate depiction of Victorian London; Moore focuses on hierarchical constellations of the curiously sinister and the noteworthy, but the reader learns little about Victorian politics in his pages, and even less about Victorian industry or trade. As can be gleaned from the fascinating appendices of *From Hell*, Moore isn't all that much concerned with accurate reconstructions of actual or even probable events. Instead, he endeavors to construct a memorial map involving all the known facts, persons, and circumstances of the case and relating them to one another in as many ways as feasibly possible. (For example, the supposition that the inspector investigating the Ripper case and the Ripper's prime target accidentally meet and fall in love has no historical probability whatsoever, but such a linkage allows Moore to condense the story even further.) This tightly-woven net of relationships even incorporates its own meta-level by including the numerous eccentrics who have written on the Ripper murders and indeed Moore himself, who briefly appears in the last chapter (Moore and Campbell 2006: Appendix 2: 16). In addition to that, Moore keeps relating the killings to the great utopian system-builders and visionaries who were living in London at one time or another: William Blake, William Morris, William Butler Yeats, Aleister Crowley; even Oscar Wilde and Robert Louis Stevenson make cameo appearances in *From Hell.*

In the center of these agglomerations, the main protagonist of *From Hell* is posited, that is, the murderous (and characteristically overdetermined) William Gull, complemented by his supposed last victim, Marie Kelly and Inspector Abberline. Gull's actions are ambivalent in more ways than one. Officially, he is just following orders; he murders the four women in order to perpetuate the power of the royal household, that is, to affirm the law, not to found or to break it. Consequently, from time to time Freemasonic policemen appear on the crime scenes who are clandestine accomplices of Gull. However, Gull does more than just execute the Queen's commands; he is also depicted as another visionary unifier and builder of heavenly cities. Thus, he enacts the killings as elaborate ritual sacrifices, echoing and repeating the foundational violence of London town. His accomplice, Netley, is told that the powers that comprise the city have been 'empowered by suffering' since the times of the druids (Moore and Campbell 2006: Chapter 4: 27). In a history lesson by Gull, which takes up the whole of the fourth chapter, the city itself is described as a map of the violent acts that have shaped it. Moore finds a striking metaphor for this in the circumstance that mortar often used to be mixed with some small amount of blood in the olden days (Moore and Campbell 2006: 31). So the buildings of London themselves incarnate as well as commemorate the mythical violence they're built on. In this context, Gull pays particular attention to the seventeenth-century churches of Nicholas Hawksmoor with their solemn proportions, vaguely phallic bell towers, and threateningly looming keystones. Hawksmoor's temples serve Gull as well as Moore as exemplary monuments eternalizing the terror of primeval bloodshed (Moore and Campbell 2006: 13). Moore also states that, according to his sources, Hawksmoor was "obsessed" with Vitruvius who is therefore liberally quoted in *From Hell* (see Moore and Campbell 2006: 13; Moore and Campbell 2006: Appendix 1: 3). Gull considers his task to be on a par with Hawksmoor's as well as Vitruvius'. (In this context, Moore occasionally hints at the fact that the British Empire of the nineteenth century liked to describe itself as the worthy successor of the Ancient Roman Empire (Young 2001: 33). For Gull, the murder series isn't just an unusual form of law enforcement, it is also a needful type of sacrifical city-planning, a stab at architectural design combined with social engineering. Summarizing, he describes the killings as reaffirmations of male power over the female; indeed, the female is to be used as the raw material for the building of a male-dominated city full of phallic symbols. It is only fitting that, during the last murder, the foundation myth of Marduk slaying Tiamat pops up in Gull's visions (Moore and Campbell 2006: 19). Gull produces sense by means of violence: The murdered women signify the supremacy of the male in so far as they make it visible, demonstrate its power by their significant mutilations. The most striking example is Gull's repeated disemboweling and extrusion of the slain women's uterus, apparently because it is a symbol of generative power. When Gull thus suppresses creative competition, his actions seem also directed against the fact of sexual and political division itself, the ambiguous, diffused, even schizophrenic side of sexuality as well as of the commonwealth of which especially the Victorian prostitute was an emblem (Walkowitz 2001: 21). It is only appropriate that he rationalizes his acts with phrases culled from Vitruvius and the treasury of Freemasonry, which designate the unified body of Man as God's architecture and the Freemasons as the builders of the "temple of civilization" encompassing its past and its future (Moore and Campbell 2006: 14–15). Of course, he takes these juxtaposed metaphors unusually literally; his violent acts aim to enforce a link between the abstract and the concrete, thus spiritualizing and eternalizing raw matter (Moore and Campbell 2006: 23). By these means, Gull establishes a hell on earth, if one defines hell as the place where law becomes indistinguishable from foundational violence and both seem to coincide with the whole of reality (Arendt 2000: 128; Agamben 1998: 171).

However, one might object to this classification of Gull as yet another specimen in Moore's long lineage of visionary utopians. After all, Gull avowedly doesn't want to inaugurate a golden future, but to reaffirm the hold of a mythical past. As he himself puts it: "Our grand symbolic magic, chaining womankind, thus must often be reinforced, carved deeper yet in History's flesh, enduring 'til the Earth's demise . . ." (Moore and Campbell 2006: 25). Gull sees the perpetual city both as a kingdom and as a corporate male body brought into being by infinite, interrelated, symmetrically arranged series of imperious bloody acts. By killing, he strives to keep the mythical history of London alive and palpable, thus expressing the order of time within the order of space. Yet there's a side to Gull's work that escapes him. Even though the murders are supposed to reinforce timeless truths, they effectively only manage to prefigure and inaugurate a sinister future. In the words of Moore: "The suggestion that the 1880s embody the essence of the twentieth century, along with the attendant notion that the Whitechapel murders embody the essence of the 1880s, is central to *From Hell*" (Moore and Campbell 2006: Appendix 1: 14). Consequently, the twentieth century comes across as a rather ugly epoch. Moore sketches it as the age of bio-politics, where the physician installs himself as the new secret sovereign (Foucault 2003) and where the sensationalist media exploiting violence for their own purposes become ever more powerful in his wake (see e.g. Moore and Campbell 2006: 13–14, 37–40). However, the most striking glimpses of the hideous twentieth century are mainly architectural ones, revealed to Gull in visions after his killings. A rather imposing example is the vision that appears before him after the killing of Kate Eddowes in Mitre Square, that is, a view of Mitre Square as it looked in the 1980s. It is notable that the high-rise seems to be growing from Gull's loins (Moore and Campbell 2006: Chapter 8: 40).Yet one wonders if this is really the sort of urban landscape that he had in mind when he was blathering about his projected renewal of divine architecture.

In fact, Gull's reaffirmation of urban memory by way of a sacrificial renaissance seems to effect a dialectical backlash resulting in an even deeper forgetfulness and splintering of foundational violence (Haverkamp 1996: 13). This is made more explicit in a vision Gull has after the murder of the woman supposed to be Marie Kelly. It is the vision of an 80s office interior, which gives even Gull the creeps (Moore and Campbell 2006: 20). He complains to the office workers walking around blissfully unaware of him: "You are the sum of all preceding you, yet seem indifferent to yourselves. A culture grown disinterested, even in its own abysmal wounds . . . You frighten me . . . This disaffection. This is armageddon" (Moore and Campbell 2006: 22). It would seem that the sacrifices Gull has made only serve to inaugurate a world of

Figure 12.1. *From Hell.* Part 8, 40. © Alan Moore and Eddie Campbell.

clean, clinical timelessness and deep repression on the one hand and even bloodier messes to support this repression on the other. The nineteenth century both decays and hardens into the twentieth. The same tension dominates the style in which Eddie Campbell draws throughout the book. The panels are obviously inspired by the pictorial style of the epoch; they look a lot like the realistic commercial engravings and woodcuts one would find in a Victorian newspaper. However, often the images either seem to harden into the clean, straight lines of technical drawings, as seen in the office scene, or to dissolve into messy smudges and gestural doodles, bordering on abstract expressionism (Moore and Campbell 2006). Often, the cross-hatching seems to get out of control, it stops following the contours of the cityscape and just accumulates independently, contradicting all laws of perspective and flattening the page in the process (e.g. Moore and Campbell 2006, chap. 3: 2, 10, 16, chap. 11: 10; see Figure 12.2 below). It almost looks as if devices of twentieth-century art were both energizing and traumatizing nineteenth-century illustrations. Plus, a sort of proto-Cubism and proto-Dadaism is implied by the multiplication of newspaper illustrations, sketches, maps, diagrams, posters, letters, photographs, paintings, calendars, advertisements, police files, engravings, and calling cards all crowding into the image space and oversaturating it (e.g. Moore and Campbell 2006, chap. 4: 19, chap. 6: 16, chap. 9: 25, chap. 13: 15). It is by these pictorial and topographical overloading devices that the depiction of urbanity in the comic really seems to come into its own. A diverging multiplicity of images and voices manifests itself in *From Hell*, but it seems to escape Gull and his project of rebuilding God's eternal temple of destiny within space and time. Thus, all that remains of his Jerusalem is a steady accumulation of obsolescent and overdetermined ruins. The city is so radically temporalized and diffused that its manifest destiny cannot help but become untraceable. Its story can only be told incompletely, and its sense must remain doubtful and needy of belated interpretation. Moore himself points out that "insignificant pieces of debris make up the corporeal mass of the largely mythic being that we call Jack the Ripper, and are deserving of comment" (Moore and Campbell 2006: Appendix 1: 23).

Gull, in his turn, endeavors to give the one true, unified sense back to the whole urban assemblage, this "literature of stone" (Moore and Campbell 2006: chap. 4: 9) of which he claims to have "penetrated [the] metaphors, laid bare its structure and thus come at last upon its

Figure 12.2. *From Hell.* **Part 3, 10. © Alan Moore and Eddie Campbell.**

meaning" (Moore and Campbell 2006: chap. 4: 9). It's this absolute certainty of the confirmed paranoiac which separates him from Moore himself. Otherwise, their mission statements and working methods are remarkably similar to each other. Both try to condensate contingency into a theater of memory in order to make sense of the world. Both obsessively establish connections and correspondences in the process, linking up the physical and spiritual. And both describe their work as an arrangement in the three dimensions of space as well as in the fourth dimension of time (Moore 2003: 30–2). One might even say that Moore also subjects his characters to a certain degree of mortification by turning them into emblems of their times; Moore himself hints at the fact that a degree of exploitation is involved in his own treatment of Marie Kelly and her companions (Moore and Campbell 2006: chap. 9: 2). He even draws the uneasy reader into this unholy alliance by forcing her or him to identify with Gull to a certain extent, for example by depicting the murder of "Kelly" and a considerable number of other proceedings from Gull's perspective (see Moore and Campbell 2006, especially chap. 2 and 10, and Appendix 1: 35). However, Moore also makes visible all those ambiguities and disseminations that Gull insistently ignores in his undertakings. Most importantly, it never seems to occur to Gull that his ritualistic reaffirmation of univocal male dominance is flawed from the start insofar as it has been inaugurated and legitimized by a female sovereign. In the center of Gull's supposedly misogynistic killer machine sits Queen Victoria herself to whose status as supreme ruler Gull never seems to have any objections. Accordingly, the sense Gull wants to eternalize is already scattered to the winds and his endeavor only serves to make it even more volatile and ambivalent. He doesn't reinvigorate the old law but its sadly parodic mimicry, which will subsequently inaugurate a society of spectacle. Moore depicts Gull as a meandering power of positing that is just as overdetermined as *From Hell* and as London itself. In that sense, Gull could even be seen as an emblem of the city as well as the comic, as the location of both disorder and order and the zone where both can no longer be distinguished. This is made most explicit in Gull's last vision, when he lies dying in the lunatic asylum. In this final vision, he metamorphoses into the Zeitgeist that is running through London: "Below the skin of history are London's veins that pulse and glisten with significance. That course with energy and meaning. And I am that meaning. And I am that energy" (Moore and Campbell 2006: chap. 14: 10). However, as Gull reaches his final apotheosis, all his senses begin to fail; the unifying vision that he has striven for through his life must exactly coincide with his own death, since the perception of totality can't be the perception of any conceivable subject (Moore and Campbell 2006: chap. 14: 23–5).

All that remains after his passing are scattered individuals searching their way in a wilderness of scattered signs, which all refer to each other circularly without any last term or any determinable hierarchy. In the words of Alan Moore himself, the city as well as the Ripper case "hold meaning and shape, but no solution" (Moore and Campbell 2006: Appendix 2: 16). In the search for a definite sense, map and territory, the sacred and profane, interpretation and creation, fiction and reality, all have mingled and started to mirror each other. It is enough to make the investigating Inspector Abberline "wonder how much of the world is true" (Moore and Campbell 2006: Epilogue: 9). Moore seconds his creation: "History, unendingly revised and reinterpreted, is seen upon examination as merely a different class of fiction . . . Still, it is a fiction that we must inhabit" (Moore 2003: 310). This state of affairs allows all self-declared masters to go on dreaming of omnipotence, but it also renders all their endeavors ultimately futile.

From Hell is an account which resists closure and thus opens onto the modern city. Its form mirrors the overdetermined and slippery sense production of urban spaces. In the process, Moore's comic becomes an allegory of its own production, the narrative process drawing the city into itself. It might be contended that Moore has found a somewhat dubious emblem for this elusiveness of sense in the elusiveness of Marie

Kelly — and an even more dubious emblem for the stubborn urge to make sense in the violent Dr. Gull. In any event, the inexorably increasing self-referentiality of Moore's comics is obvious enough. And there's a price to be paid for this development: His works become echo chambers in which history's violent compulsion to repeat reverberates with little hope of salvation. After all, a frustrated need for closure always has been inherent in the serial logic of comic books. In *Watchmen*, this is pointed out by the doomed black boy who has been reading the pirate comics at the newsstand through most of the series. Shortly before Adrian Veidt drops his bomb, the doomed newsvendor complains that the boy's been reading "that junk over and over." His reluctant customer replies with the memorable words: "Cause they don't make sense, man! That's why I gotta read 'em over" (Moore and Gibbons 1987: 23).

Works Cited
Comics

Moore, Alan and Campbell, Eddie. *From Hell: Being a Melodrama in 16 Parts.* Marietta, GA: Top Shelf, 2006.

Moore, Alan and Gibbons, Dave. *Watchmen.* New York: DC Comics, 1987.

Moore, Alan and Lloyd, David. *V For Vendetta.* New York: DC Comics (Imprint: Vertigo), 1990.

Moore, Alan, Williams III, J.H. and Gray, Mick. *Promethea 1–5.* New York: DC Comics (Imprint: America's Best Comics), 2000–5.

Moore, Alan *et al. Swamp Thing 1–5.* New York: DC Comics (Imprint: Vertigo), 1998–2002.

Secondary Literature

Agamben, Giorgio. *Homo Sacer: Sovereign Power and Bare Life.* Palo Alto, CA: Stanford University Press, 1998.

Arendt, Hannah. "Total Domination." In: *The Portable Hannah Arendt.* London and New York: Penguin, 2000.

Benjamin, Walter. "Zur Kritik der Gewalt." In: *Angelus Novus.* Frankfurt am Main: Suhrkamp, 1988.

Boyer, M. Christine. *The City of Collective Memory.* Cambridge, MA and London: MIT Press, 1994.

Foucault, Michel. "Society Must Be Defended." In: *Lectures at the Collège de France 1975–1976.* New York: Picador, 2003.

Haverkamp, Anselm. "Ghost Machine or Embedded Intelligence." In: *ANY Magazine* 15 (1996).

Kaplan, Aryeh. *Sefer Yetzirah: The Book of Creation in Theory and Practice.* Boston, MA: Red Wheel, 1997.

King, Leonard William. *Babylonian Religion and Mythology.* London: Kegan Paul/Trench, 1899.

McEwen, Indra Kagis. *Vitruvius: Writing the Body of Architecture.* Cambridge, MA and London: MIT Press, 2003.

Moore, Alan. *Writing for Comics.* Urbana, IL: Avatar, 2003.

Moore, Alan. *Voice of the Fire.* Marietta, GA: Top Shelf, 2003.

Rüsen, Jörn. "Sense of History, What Does It Mean?" In: Jörn Rüsen (ed.), *Meaning and Representation in History.* New York and Oxford: Berghahn, 2006.

Vitruvius. *Zehn Bücher über Architektur.* Darmstadt: Wissenschaftliche Buchgesellschaft, 1981.

Walkowitz, Judith R. *City of Dreadful Delight: Narratives of Sexual Danger in Late-Victorian London.* Chicago, IL: University of Chicago Press, 2001.

Wyatt, Nicolas. *Space and Time in the Religious Life of the Near East.* Sheffield: Sheffield Academic Press, 2001.

Yates, Frances. *Gedächtnis und Erinnern. Mnemonik von Aristoteles bis Shakespeare.* Berlin: Akademie Verlag, 1999.

Young, Robert J.C. *Postcolonialism: An Historical Introduction.* Oxford and Malden: Blackwell, 2001.

Notes

1 "... encyclicos enim disciplina uti corpus unum ex his membris est composita" (Vitruvius 1981: 30).

2 The term "foundational violence" derives from Walter Benjamin's *Critique of Violence* (see Benjamin 1988: 42–66).

3 See, for example, Quintilian's remarks on the topic, quoted in Yates (1999: 28).

13

The Ordinary Urban: *100 Bullets* and the Clichés of Mass Culture

JÖRN AHRENS

Introduction

When the first issue of Brian Azzarello and Eduardo Risso's comic series *100 Bullets* hit the market in August 1999, it quickly became the most popular title among the crime fiction being published by DC Comics' independent imprint, Vertigo. Writer Brian Azzarello convinces with an enigmatic as well as elliptical storyline, while artist Eduardo Risso finds a unique visual language to convey the narrative, using unusual perspective, camera angles and montage as well as heavy shading, contrasts, and speed for diegesis and panel arrangement.

Interestingly, the flagship of comic art criticism in the U.S.A., *The Comics Journal*, received it somewhat coolly, as demonstrated by a 2001 short review by Kent Worcester. His text starts with a strong normative judgment about *100 Bullets*, which he believes is "obviously a cut above the norm but hew[s] closely to familiar, pulp-derived conventions" (Worcester 2001). In Worcester's view, *100 Bullets* is "yet another comic whose horizons are defined by the introspect's holy trinity of comics, porn, and noir." He urges that "the idea that the world presented in this comic has anything to do with urban America circa 1990–2000 is laughable" (Worcester 2001). Hence, what is interesting about this review is the idea of what appreciable comics should be that lurks behind it. Evidently, Worcester does not appreciate the ostensibly genre-bound, pop-culture storytelling that *100 Bullets* produces. Calling it "pulp-derived," he gives in to a distinction between good and bad mass media. Following Worcester, one crucial characteristic of a comic that is of cultural relevance seems to be its documentary quality, or at least its appeal to realism. Regarding *100 Bullets*, he complains that "its 'realism' is as phony as a two-dollar steak sandwich." Worcester goes on to offer the reader his credo of realism, which demands that the focus should be on "ordinary" people: "It took eleven issues before readers were introduced to an 'ordinary' lead character, a married waitress." Ironically, when Worcester celebrates the staging of the "ordinary" as a merit in this medium, his clear-cut distinction between the broad field of mainstream comics (including those "a cut above the norm") and the predictably limited rest — which were of cultural and academic relevance, since their quality was above the norm — sharply rejects the ordinary (as being vulgar) in the aesthetic and narrative form of comics themselves. And this dimension of the "ordinary" in comics — in terms of aesthetics and subject — emerges directly from the medium's relatedness to an aesthetics of the ordinary instead of traditional art. What Worcester is doing here is therefore reiterating the common cultural idiosyncrasy against that which is seen to be trivial and kitschy. This chapter will argue instead that a comic like *100 Bullets* is able to unfold quite ambitious content in narrative and graphics due to its use of cliché and a trivialized style.

100 Bullets plays with all the conventions in style and narrative of diverse genres and graphic approaches to create an aesthetic based on exaggeration (Duttmann 2007). It not only radicalizes the ordinary as a foundation of the medium of comics, it also uncovers the meta-level of the ordinary itself in the context of cultural production and social imagination. In this sense, aesthetic and narrative exaggeration as practiced in *100 Bullets* can be seen as a radicalization of cultural patterns understood as techniques of contemporary symbolic representation. As such, social imagologies[1] are formed when depictions have been invented that find access to the collective imagination of society while also transcending social experiences, realities, and agreements. The story that underlies the series quickly confuses its readers when it represses relevant information or when it foregrounds narratives that are not central to the story. The mysterious Agent Graves hands out attaché cases to seemingly ordinary people whose lives have been blighted in various ways. Inside the attaché cases, these people find clear evidence about who is responsible for their calamities, together with an untraceable gun and 100 bullets. Only after a number of issues does writer Brian Azzarello reveal that Graves turns over his attaché cases to carefully chosen people. The story then twists to take on elements of the thriller and of conspiracy narratives, and eventually Graves turns out to be an insurgent who is leading his own private war against the clandestine de facto rulers of the U.S.A.: an organization called the Trust which consists of 13 rich and influential families. As its private police, this quasi-government maintains a group of professional killers called the Minutemen — modeled on the historical Minutemen in the eighteenth century and the North American War of Independence. For some reason, the Minutemen were to be executed by the Trust some time ago, but were instead only brainwashed and given new identities as ordinary people. Now, Agent Graves reactivates them one by one, making them soldiers in his war against the Trust. Azzarello presents a highly elliptical and intricate story that traces the war and the fate of its protagonists on both sides of the front line. The author takes his readers on a journey throughout the U.S., especially its big cities, but also to its countryside and to Mexico.

100 Bullets' Urban Super Ego

The city is almost always present in *100 Bullets*; nevertheless, it is for the most part not staged with great extravagance, but only indicated by a few details of urban scenery or cityscape silhouettes. In contrast to many comics that take place in an urban environment, artist Eduardo Risso does not depict the city as scenery in every panel. Were he to do so, the city landscape would quickly become ubiquitous to the reader and with such an overwhelming presence, the distinctive atmosphere of Risso's urban setting would be lost. The city would become no more than a background to the protagonists' actions instead of creating a realistic and vivid atmosphere. Such an approach could be called a false documentary style if it intended to present a fictional story in a documentary-like aesthetic. As a result, the city would become redundant, rigid and boring, its particularity consumed by the omnipresence of its depiction. Risso's style, in contrast, uses the clear depiction of the city in a precisely calculated way. Risso is a master of creating what Thierry Groensteen calls the "hyperframe" (Groensteen 2007) — the composition of the page as a mega-panel in itself. Risso's approach is

Figure 13.1. **Brian Azzarello and Eduardo Risso.** *100 Bullets* **Vol. 6: "Six Feet under the Gun."** New York: DC Comics, 2003, 26 (panels 1–3). © DC Comics.

often to work with clear and intense establishing shots, which introduce a certain scene and establish the atmosphere that will determine the sequences that follow them. In Figure 13.1, Mr. Shepherd and Agent Graves are clearly walking through downtown Chicago towards Lake Michigan, while shadowy skyscrapers loom behind them. However, in the subsequent smaller panels, Risso gives no background at all. Instead, he completely focuses on his characters, whom he shoots from various angles — first, he chooses a high angle and, in this panel, the two men are depicted not as walking through Chicago but as if they were crossing an empty space. Although the figures are small and should appear vulnerable, they draw all the reader's attention. The third panel changes into a low-angle close up, also cutting Shepherd's face and using heavy shading, which gives character to the figures who seem to be physically close to the viewer now. A panel at the end of the page completes the framework by reintroducing the city of Chicago graphically. Risso's full graphic concentration on his characters contributes to a dissolution of the city in *100 Bullets*, dissolving it into topographical voids that represent their protagonists in empty space which is, nevertheless, held together structurally by the hyperframe depicting the city architecture itself. Risso changes the perspective on his protagonists in almost every panel, which almost makes them seem to move physically, while at the same time his heavy use of shadows keeps the figures apart from the reader emotionally and makes identification impossible. The series is fully aware of the need for abstraction rather than to cultivate a fetishist depiction of realistic detail. Any detail given by Risso obeys two principles: First, it has a certain function within the narrative, providing information necessary to understand the present situation or a later point in the story. Second, it contributes to the aesthetics of the surroundings.

Yet the characters, too, fulfill distinctively defined roles concerning behavior and appearance, which makes them strange hybrids of schematized personas and multifaceted personalities. *100 Bullets* quickly develops a broad range of protagonists, some more prominent than others, who are all well established and, unless removed from the story by death, can reappear at any time. Over the course of the series, the main protagonists in particular reveal remarkably complex personalities, even if they do remain highly schematized, if not stereotyped.[2] This might be a specific characteristic of mass culture and the urban topography from which it once emerged. The anonymity formed by the emergence of cities, together with the increasing mechanization and automatization of society, leisure and the means of production, leads to a particular view of the urban masses. Siegfried Kracauer, for example, speaks of the "ornament of the masses," when he analyzes modern mass society. By this term he focuses the loss of personality in the modern urban individual — his featureless and mechanized nature (Kracauer 1992).[3] According to such a negative image of mass culture, the characters in *100 Bullets* can be defined as voids that are lent shape by their location in a specific genre, narrative, aesthetic, or setting. A personhood that emerges from a void that is defining its core structure can be called a mass-media character. The significance of such a character is to contain distinct cultural symbolization processes from which an individual signature can emerge. Through such ambiguity in their personalities, *100 Bullets* presents each character as a unique persona with complex psychology who, for all that, still functions quite lucidly as a stereotyped mass-culture creature. Thus, the Minutemen represent a commendable quality of mass culture, which is to cultivate cliché as personality without, however, affecting the effectiveness of each in his own right. The irony is that — in a comment on the clichés of mass culture — the Minutemen are given clichés as personalities when they are truly themselves, whereas they appear as classic full characters when living in their brainwashed state. Losing one's identity means gaining a decent social identity, while becoming oneself is the equivalent of freezing into clichés.

Most intriguing with regard to the Minutemen is their metamorphosis from any ordinary man's existence into a Minuteman: They do not transform into someone genuinely other, but simply into their original selves. Before their retransformation, the Minutemen are ice-cream men, drug addicts, private detectives or gas station attendants. They are ordinary people and belong to the huge community of city dwellers who are establishing the modern urban topography. It is mostly this emphasis on the ordinary that connects the story's aesthetically ordinary narrative to mass-culture cliché. Yet, such emphasis is eccentrically overdrawn by both its narrative and aesthetic. *100 Bullets* implies that mass-culture reality always suggests a connection between ordinary people and an aesthetics of the ordinary, even of the vulgar. Ordinary life can only be transcended by cliché-bound concepts; by the Minutemen for example becoming iconographic super-criminals. The ordinary as aesthetic concept is the opposite of the sublime, and mass culture, too, is by definition anti-sublime. Its formal instruments reduce any aesthetic or narrative form to its bare essentials. Within an extremely standardized medium like comics, this specialty becomes especially obvious. This anti-sublime phenomenon has to be seen within the social context of the modern individual's urban existence. With the rise of urban-centered societies in the early twentieth century, modern subjectivity as well as the struggle for uniqueness increased. This is a development which cannot be reversed. In this light, the ambiguous personalities of the Minutemen also connect to modern techniques and practices of sameness. They are unable to join their two alternate modes of existence by any means, always forgetting about the one while occupying themselves with the other. This reflects the dichotomy of modern individuals between distinctiveness and uniformity; those who become extraordinary lose their individuality and have to conform to the modes of a stereotyped anti-existence. Some literary scholars unfold the thesis that the representation of the city in literature either electrifies or suppresses and abolishes the individual (Meckseper and Schraut 1983). In the city, the meaning of existence becomes opaque, and the city's very dynamics are erratic and undirected, simply a rhythmic back and forth. The cultural representation of the city reflects a crisis in the production of meaning that characterizes modern urban culture and eventually results in an existential threat to the individual.

It was Georg Simmel who first outlined the contours of a new "type of metropolitan individuality" (Simmel 2008: 905). The crucial effect of the urban topographies emerging in the early twentieth century, he says in a 1903 essay, is an increase of neural agility that results from the quick and incessant variation of inner impressions: "Man is a being of difference" (Simmel 2008: 905). With this sentence Simmel expresses that in the modern city the ability to distinguish between contingent impressions, impulses, experiences and occurrences becomes essential. This is of importance because that city, as a life-world, is dominated by mass culture, technology, and speed. Thus, the modern self tends intellectually and habitually to be defined by speed and by its distinctiveness. Difference as personality produces a personal need and indeed expectation to become complete and cohesive as an individual. This ability to not only distinguish oneself from others but also to dominate the other at the level of discourse and symbolization is integral to the emergence of the modern self as a cohesive phenomenon within a fragmented and hybrid society, communicating as it does the vulnerability of the individual.

In this sense, the modern self is far from being defined by the freedom to pursue happiness or even lust. Instead, Fredric Jameson correctly speaks of the glorification of modern individuality: "Modern people are individuals and that which is unfree in the others appears to be their obvious lack of individuality" (Jameson 2007: 59). Thus, freedom is restricted to the freedom of the self, detached from any social or cultural terms. Individuality is defined with reference to the amount of control exerted by the self — in the sense of both external mastery and inner self-restraint. This very kind of ambivalence is at least in part bound to certain modes and practices of violence. Only those who successfully master the techniques of self-restraint may enter a state of social orgiasm as social freedom. This condition is clearly related to an aesthetics and practice of violence that functions as a benefit to these individuals' master control as modern selves. According to Michel Maffesoli, this state represents one of the fundamental structures of sociality. Following Maffesoli, orgiasm naturally operates against a background of violence. Even if violence was ritualized and even if orgiasm sought to domesticate violence, it still remains an absolute term which, Maffesoli says, should be better realized as such in a realistic way (Maffesoli 1986: 113). It is at this point of the shaping of the modern self that one finds the phenomenon of the Urban Super Ego, a term by which the modern self is defined as being realized through a process of rough self-regulation and overdrawn adoption of the cultural norms of violence.

The combination of self-control on the one hand and violent action on the other is representative of the figure of the self within modernity, as Norbert Elias and Michel Foucault have pointed out. They define becoming a self as an act of subtle violence that minimizes individual affection and therefore facilitates interdependent structures of cultural practices. Such practices, then, have been related to an increase of the individual's control of its effects as well as to the emergence of social and cultural discourses. The self itself is hostage to a cultural realm that is re-pacified by such practices and characters like the Minutemen. As super egos they represent an individual yearning to overthrow such regimentation. Hence, the natural habitat of such ambiguous selves is the modern city with its emphasis on artificiality. Since modern culture is a culture of artificiality, best seen in the realms of mass culture and mass production, the accentuation of such artificiality as the very pattern of modern culture is found precisely in such radically stylized characters as are presented in *100 Bullets*. In the present state of late modernity the Urban Super Ego represents a certain imagology that radicalizes what society and culture might anticipate and schematizes in lucid ruthlessness what the present self would be like if its program were taken seriously — this would be the rise of anarchy, violence, and solipsism. Again, the aesthetic and narrative technique of exaggeration not only connects to the ordinary and vulgar but eventually becomes identical with it. That which is rejected as being ordinary and vulgar inherits modes of a radical representation of cultural reality. Cliché, especially in the context of mass culture, must not be seen simply as an underesteemed aesthetic; it is also a way of transmitting unspoken truths about cultural and social affairs. The metropolis serves as the natural habitat of such selves as the Urban Super Ego, since the metropolis is the one social realm in which twentieth-century modernity reveals its cultural significance on a global scale.

To control the city as the genuine realm of modern society is a major concern of almost any comic book superhero (Klock 2002). What these characters articulate on the level of socialization is a constant yearning to govern the city and its people completely. If the classic comic book superheroes are part of a mythic narrative of the modern city and its struggle for order and justice, then *100 Bullets'* Minutemen function as a pastiche of this motif by omitting the costumes. Instead, *100 Bullets* insists on presenting a contemporary version of superheroes. As such it transfers the idea of the superhero into a cultural realm in which he adapts to the mass-cultural iconography of ordinary crime, violence and absolute autonomy. This is only possible within the absolutely artificial environment of the modern metropolis as metaphor, which hints ubiquitously at the artificial production of culture in general and of any specific cultural item. However, the Minutemen share with the superhero the momentum of metamorphosis. They become indeed an Urban Super Ego, and it is this habitus of complete self-awareness and autonomy that identifies them in the same way as a classic superhero's costume would. What distinguishes them from superheroes, however, is that the Minutemen cannot ever disrobe. Once they become super egos, they are forced to remain as such, forever detached from their former individuality.

The metamorphosis into Minutemen is irreversible, and their iden- tity as Urban Super Egos is absolute. As such, the Minutemen, who are the real main characters in *100 Bullets*, can be understood as timeless representations of urban anomie. The phenomenon of social erosion and rupture is iconographically entitled by Azzarello and Risso. This is made patently clear by the wide range of social backgrounds from which the Minutemen are reactivated to take on their symbolical as well as physical unity and underlined by their dress code as elegant vigilantes. They de-transcendentalize the superhero from the higher spheres of justice into those of ordinary life, vulgarity, and crime. It is this aspect of the ordinary that gives the Minutemen their distinctiveness with regard to the usual superhero. As such, the exaggerated graphical style of *100 Bullets* undermines its superficial depictions, since the graphics clearly intend to transform the documentation of ordinary life into the documentation of ordinary imaginations, as an exaggeration of modern urbanity's clichés.

The City as Habitual Presence

Not only does *100 Bullets* stress the meaning of the urban self; inevitably the series also addresses the modern American cityscape. In this regard, it can be seen as a paradigmatic depiction of modern urban topography.

The series' settings are spread across the whole of the U.S., city after city — New York, Miami, Chicago, New Orleans, Los Angeles, Boston, Atlantic City. In this perspective, the depiction of the cities in *100 Bullets* cannot be separated from the distinct personas that walk them. All these existing cities ultimately merge into one grand and imaginative mega-city that can no longer be distinguished from its diverse and original sources. And this mega-city defines the whole society it contains as an environment deeply shaped by urban living conditions, social norms and cultural values. Even if each city depicted in the progressing story is remarkably easy to identify by its landmarks and certain details of daily life, the city as a constant background always remains the same — except for some very special and distinctive places like New York's Washington Square. This location serves as background for what *100 Bullets* is famous for: the amalgamation of the story's dominant narrative with a discrete side story. Risso depicts Washington Square in winter, which is contrary to its popular iconography and renders it bleak and miserable.

Risso's composition of the sequence pans from a conversation between Mr. Shepherd and Benito Medici, the son of the most influential member of the Trust, to a struggle between rival drug dealers arguing about which of them has the power to run Washington Square, which finally results in a shooting. Black trees, a landscape covered in snow, and foggy

Figure 13.2. **Brian Azzarello and Eduardo Risso: *100 Bullets* Vol. 4: "A Foregone Tomorrow." New York: DC Comics, 2002, 16 (panel 6). © DC Comics.**

air represent almost nothing of what the place has been known for in popular culture since it was cleaned up during the 1980s and 1990s. Although the familiar Washington Square Arch is shown prominently in various panels, the place appears sinister, in contrast to its family-park image. While the war fought by the drug dealers serves to underline the theme of Shepherd and Benito's discussion, Washington Square acts as a third kind of protagonist. The place is clearly identifiable, yet it also illustrates the universal city life and atmosphere that pervades the whole narrative of *100 Bullets*. In sequences like this one, it becomes clear that the city as a constant presence plays an essential role in *100 Bullets*. In his analysis of the modern city, Klaus Scherpe calls the city in general a Foucauldian heterotopia: "The city is both the construction site of social conditions and also the stage of the imaginary ties which are connected to these conditions" (Scherpe 1988: 131). This means that any tale that takes the modern city as its stage is a tale not only about its individual protagonists, it is also about the city as the natural habitat of man in modernity. This does not mean that such narratives and their aesthetics necessarily have to adopt a documentary-like style; they may also show different viewpoints of or about the city which are of cultural impact for artificial life-worlds. "The modern world is the structured world par excellence. However, it is also . . . a world which is ruled by phantasmagorias" (Scherpe 1988: 148). A comic like *100 Bullets* strikingly shows that these two aspects are inseparable.

The city itself appears as a powerful influence that frames and structures the lives of its inhabitants and especially those of the characters in *100 Bullets*. Even though rural scenes do occasionally appear in the series, the city clearly functions as its identifying location, subsuming all the differences between its various incarnations into a universal, unified setting. According to psychologist Alexander Mitscherlich, two experiences are made possible by the metropolis: "It is an environment that both forces its people to partake in community and also gives and guarantees individual freedom" (Mitscherlich 1965: 120). Simmel adds the observation that the freedom of man is "not necessarily reflected in his emotional life as a state of well-being" (Simmel 2008: 912). Freedom and emotion are thus clearly distinctive, and the formation of the modern self — autonomous though it may be — gives no guarantee of a social structure which benefits its members. On the contrary, as discussed above, the modern self is bound to habits of violence that usually do not produce well-being but pain, and the urban environment — as physical as well as iconic topography — constantly reflects this aspect of the modern, urban self. It is in this context that the modern cityscape, as presented by *100 Bullets*, serves as an icon of the monistic city, which is itself the genuine realm of globalized culture. Just as Mitscherlich points out, the Minutemen are forced into a community that will never set them free and that is bound to the urban culture of artificiality, speed and violence; still, they are thus also granted an exceptional freedom from their social environment. This freedom is not without parameters — it finds its limits in the joint needs and interests of the group. Although the city loses its power as a social environment over such individuals, they are still far from enjoying absolute power. Such power is inhibited by the community and by a form of mega-power which, in *100 Bullets*, is embodied by the Trust. Even though modern city planners are afraid of the "uncontrolled and vital city" and therefore always aim to provide the maximum possible control (Hasse 2000: 30), the anomic self as a super ego, in the form of the Minutemen, shows that distinct rules and structures guide even the actions of those freed from such management.

Against this background, the graphic narrative in *100 Bullets* plays with a certain awareness of the constant presence of the city in story and meta-frame. Although the city at large orchestrates the comic's atmosphere, it may in fact be realized as a variety of cities from which it has been composed. Throughout the series, nevertheless, it remains one city as cultural icon and as imagology. Thus, as the icon of the paradigmatic mega-city it permanently mirrors the habitus of a life-world that focuses on urbanity. Urbanity, here, it is not just graphically depicted, but its representation is also inspired by the various imaginations and phantasmagorias that are eventually adapted in the comic. *100 Bullets* demonstrates precisely this drive towards a unification of the urban world and thus mirrors the formation of one consistent self by mass culture. The idea of the city, like the modern self, emerges from its people's behavior and ideas. The city itself is the synthesis of its various inhabitants; the universal city, through the habits of urban modernity, is as diverse as any individual city, since it is a product of the particular experiences of individuals and social groups (Löw 2001: 260). This means, as Hasse points out, that the physical realm of the city exists alongside the idea of the city. Both are interwoven but also separated into distinct realms and cultural topographies. In *100 Bullets*, a city emerges that is not the one experienced physically. Naturally, a comic like this cannot therefore be called documentary-like in the sense of Kent Worcester. Nevertheless, this comic book city shapes the idea of the real city that remains with the reader, by furnishing a set of culturally informed and formative images of the city. This iconography may not be real in the material sense, although it becomes part of the reader's perception of reality.

Concluding the "Ordinary" Bullets

The guiding principle of contemporary culture is accessibility and ubiquity. In the age of globalized mass culture, the real signature of culture is not only the possibility of its technical reproduction, but also the technical and standardized production of any of its artifacts. This results from the significant changes culture has undergone since the process of urbanization at the turn of the twentieth century altered the social structure of industrialized societies. By degrees, high culture, with its efforts for distinction and exclusion as well as education, has been pushed to the sidelines. In contrast, mass culture is accessible to everybody. As a result, it has often lowered existing aesthetic standards when it foregrounds the ordinary, even the vulgar, and serves mass audiences instead of an elite public. It is the medium of comics that has shown this most precisely. Traditionally, the "ordinary" has been a pro-grammatic discourse in the arts that intends to depict the dimensions of "real life" in culture and society. But within the mass-cultural realm it changes into a set of formal aesthetical practices — as they are used by Azzarello and Risso. As such mass-culture aesthetics and narratives stress the connection between the ordinary as a depiction of daily life and its aesthetic dimension, because it is often bound to forms of cliché, trivia and the vulgar. The modern self, widely shaped by meaning and cultural symbolizations communicated through mass-culture products, is entirely tied to this relationship between ordinary life and vulgar aesthetics. In the course mass culture's gradual rise to dominance in the Western hemisphere, the shaping of meaning as symbolic form has been increasingly derived from mass culture, whereas the influence of high culture has significantly dropped. Thus, the "ordinary" itself obtains the status of a technique of the self and, thus, it also permits imagological realms to transcend the chains of the self towards the implementation of an absolute Urban Super Ego. A comic like *100 Bullets* serves this yearning in two ways: First it provides a fantastic realm in which the super ego might become true. Second, it also represents the contours of this particular self, connected to modernity and urbanity.

An essential feature of this change is that strategies of cultural representation have emerged that, although far from avant-garde art, assess rather than simply authenticate what they depict. Such strategies do broadly cultivate imagination, even if only in the form of cliché and stereotype. About a century after the emergence of mass culture, *100 Bullets* gives proof of such representational strategies that do reach beyond authentication. It undermines the claim for pure authenticity, which it possibly claims to represent, by adopting the stylistics of colportage in its narrative and aesthetic. It has to be seen as an attempt to confront its cultural environment with an aesthetic of colportage, used as an influential tool of cultural sense-making. What a comic like *100 Bullets* is doing, as one representative of a mass culture, both aptly and successfully, is to establish the ordinary or even the vulgar as a decisive cultural code of abstraction. This comic combines a trivial and stereotyped narrative with cartoonish graphics, but nevertheless manages to transmit subtle elements of imaginative and material culture which eventually intermingle with and shape the reader's experience of social reality. The allegation that a comic like *100 Bullets* is mainstream, and therefore culturally irrelevant, is more than ineffective, since today mainstream-culture products define the very standard of cultural reflection and representation. As such, the mainstream cultural artifact stands as the symbolic form of the contemporary. By conjoining the self, violence, and urbanity, *100 Bullets* also finds its own historical and medial meta-representation that explicitly reflects its own ambiguities. In *100 Bullets*, the city serves as a constant protagonist and catalyst of cultural reflection — it is in a series like this that the art of mass culture finds its true expression.

Works Cited

Düttmann, Alexander Garcìa. *Philosophy of Exaggeration.* New York and London: Continuum, 2007.

Groensteen, Thierry. *The System of Comics.* Jackson, MS: University of Mississippi Press, 2007.

Hasse, Volker. *Die Wunden der Stadt. Für eine neue Ästhetik der Städte.* Wien: Passagen, 2000.

Jameson, Fredric: *Mythen der Moderne.* Berlin: Kadmos, 2007.

Klock, Geoff: *How to Read Superhero Comics and Why.* New York and London: Continuum, 2002.

Kracauer, Siegried. *Der verbotene Blick. Beobachtungen, Analysen, Kritiken.* Leipzig: Reclam, 1992.

Löw, Martina: *Raumsoziologie.* Frankfurt am Main: Suhrkamp, 2001.

Maffesoli, Michel: *Der Schatten des Dionysos. Zu einer Soziologie des Orgasmus.* Frankfurt am Main: Syndikat, 1986.

Meckseper, Cord and Schraut, Elisabeth (eds.), *Die Stadt in der Literatur.* Göttingen: Vandenhoeck & Ruprecht, 1983.

Mitscherlich, Alexander. *Die Unwirtlichkeit unserer Städte. Anstiftung zum Unfrieden.* Frankfurt am Main: Suhrkamp, 1965.

Scherpe, Klaus R. "Nonstop nach Nowhere City?" In: *Die Unwirklichkeit der Städte. Großstadtdarstellungen zwischen Moderne und Postmoderne.* Reinbek bei Hamburg: Rowohlt, 1988. 129–52.

Simmel, Georg. "Die Großstädte und das Geistesleben." In: *Philosophische Kultur.* Frankfurt am Main: Zweitausendeins, 2008. 905–16.

Worcester, Kent: "Thrown to the Wolves: *100 Bullets.*" In: *The Comics Journal* (2001). Available online at: http://www.tcj.com/3_online/w_review_bullets. html (accessed June 30, 2008).

Notes

1   I use the term "imagology" to address cultural and social imaginations that shape the perception of reality.

2   For example Lono, the series' most cruel protagonist, appears to be not just the animal-like "Dog" alone, as his nickname suggests. Instead, Lono turns out to be an intelligent and also cultivated strategist. Similarly, Cole Burns is not only an insensitive killer but is driven by a clear understanding of loyalty and righteousness.

3   All quotes from German texts have been translated by the author.

V

The City-Comic as a Mode of Reflection

14

Seeing the City through a Frame: Marc-Antoine Mathieu's Acquefacques Comics

ANDRÉ SUHR

Comics and the City

When early "comics" appeared in newspapers for the first time, this coincided with the pinnacle of cultural modernity in the late nineteenth/ early twentieth century, a time which finds its paradigmatic locus within the modern city. The parallel evolution of the modern city and comics is not a purely spatiotemporal coincidence — newspapers and thus comics were in fact a medium primarily located in cities. Indeed this specific place of origin has deeply influenced comics' stories, aesthetics and structural appearance such that comics' visual rhetoric both emulates and informs the city's characteristic modes of perception.

The significant role of the city in comics' development is still very apparent in today's comics, maybe most obviously so in U.S.-superhero comics. Nearly every superhero is located in a specifically outlined city, a city with which he or she shares a close, although sometimes ambivalent relationship that is constitutive to his or her character — be it Spider-Man's or the Great Machine's New York, Superman's Metropolis, Madman's Snap City or Batman's Gotham City, and so forth.

The city of U.S.-superhero comics indeed often plays an integral role in their stories, but in most cases it ultimately remains a superficial element, the visual and narrative background of the unfolding plot. It rarely gets explicitly connected to the inner workings of comics' structure, to the way they work as a specific medium.

Thus despite the important role of the city in superhero comics, this representation conveys only a blurred mirror-image of the actual, constitutive part the city had in shaping comics' aesthetics. More complex realizations of this relation between comics and the city, however, do exist — for example, in the Acquefacques comics of Marc-Antoine Mathieu.

Acquefacques's Adventures in Comics and the City

With his Acquefacques comics Mathieu explicitly highlights the intricate link between the specifics of comics as a medium and the city as their place of origin. He lays bare the inner workings of comics as a medium to such an extent that the structural aspects of comics themselves become the story being told. This apparent interest in the specific formal characteristics of comics is certainly similar to the approach of Oubapo, a group of comic artists from France.[1] Yet Mathieu's comics cannot be reduced to being formal finger exercises. It is in fact quite significant that these stories always take place in an elaborately designed city. The mechanisms of perception exposed in the structural aspects of Mathieu's stories can be linked to the city of Modernity. And it is precisely this city that becomes recognizable in the panels of his comics.

Here is a short introduction to these (mostly) black-and-white stories, all of which rely on an unresolved ambivalence between dream and reality. The "hero," Julius Corentin Acquefacques,[2] works as a civil servant for the Ministry of Humor in a vast and chaotic city. All of his adventures feature very obvious self-referencing strategies regarding their medium, that is, comics. Each of them concentrates on some characteristic structural trait of comics, a specific meta-feature which becomes relevant within the actual story being told.

In his first adventure, *L'Origine* from 1990, Acquefacques starts to receive single pages of a comic book, pages the reader soon recognizes as pages of the very comic he/she is reading. Acquefacques realizes so too, feels the short lifespan of 42 pages rush past him, becomes the object of close scrutiny at the Ministry of Science and finally has to experience the last page of his story being burned by its author.

This forces Acquefacques to acknowledge the notion of a creative outside to his enclosed world of the comic: His world is not self-sufficient, it is created and consists of boxed pictures on pages. There is an "origin," a word (and a concept) up to then unknown in Acquefacques's world.

There actually is somebody — an author, godlike — with the power to write and draw his papery world in black and white and, eventually, even to undo it. Here, a first important meta-feature is addressed — the creative process from which fictional worlds like Acquefacques's originate.

His second adventure, *La Qu . . .* from 1991,[3] finds Acquefacques in the aftermath of this event, falling through limbo, into the coffee cup of his author, from which he reappears in his familiar reality, as if from a dream. He is then taken into custody by "Living-Space Control" for illegally using non-assigned living space by means of an opened drawer. As punishment for this offense he is sent on a mission outside the city, where he eventually encounters the up-to-then unknown four colors — an epistemological shock for his black-and-white world, which sends all of it back into the limbo the story began in. The contact with color shatters the foundations of his "reality," as "color" was not only unknown, but unthinkable before. A second meta-feature of comics is thus exposed — coloring.

In the third installment, *Le Processus* from 1993,[4] Acquefacques meets a doppelganger, on whom a scientific experiment is conducted. The effects of this experiment literally take the roof off of Acquefacques's world of dreams, which are presented as rooms that are in fact panels of the comic. So he starts to walk on the roofless walls of his dreams as if walking on the space between panels.

Again, his actions pose an epistemological attack on the founda-tions of his world leading to an implosion in which the page's orderly structure of panels is dissolved into a maelstrom. This is presented in frames on a die-cut paper spiral, which in fact materially links one page of the comic to the next. A vortex of panels dispels Acquefacques from his comic-world onto a photorealistic plane, from which he re-enters the pages of his story — only to be reclaimed by the maelstrom, which on the last page becomes a feedback loop once more leading back to the story's beginning, finally explaining his first encounter with the doppelganger.

By entering the space between panels Acquefacques encounters another founding principle of his world. The unsignified spaces between panels, on which he walks as if on top of a wall, are the grid normally holding his world, a grid that loses its hold in the all-consuming spiral of the process. Framing is the distinctive meta-feature on which *Le Processus* concentrates.

In his fourth adventure *Le Début de la Fin* from 1995 Acquefacques

Figure 14.1. *Le Processus*, 26. © 1993, Guy Delcourt Productions — Marc Antoine Mathieu.

realizes that something is wrong with himself as suddenly most of his daily life works the wrong way around. Again he meets a doppelganger, who started into the story from the other end of the book, namely from *La Fin du Début*. The book can be read from both ends and both directions of the story meet in the middle of the book through a mirror.[5] Here, Acquefacques is primarily confronted with another basic principle of his world and sequential art in general, namely the meta-feature of linearity (or in this instance, rather its paradoxical inversion).

The fifth adventure, *La 2.333ᵉ Dimension*, was finally published in 2004. It starts with two "Reality Enforcers" accidentally releasing a forbidden dream of Acquefacques. In this dream he loses a vanishing point, which affects the confined world of his comic once more. Its two-dimensionality starts to show. Acquefacques has to reinstate the three-dimensional illusion, which eventually allows the panels of his story to become stereoscopic, three-dimensional pictures to be viewed with a stereoscope that is sold along with the comic. It is the first time things work out: The dangerous dream, which triggered this inter-dimensional extravaganza, is collected by the "Reality Enforcers" and Acquefacques sleeps on as if nothing happened. In regard to the line of characteristic meta-features, *La 2.333ᵉ Dimension* exposes the two-dimensionality of comics as "flat" drawings on a page.

With these meta-features, Mathieu explicitly draws our attention to the structural aspects of comics, to their process of production, their linear structure, framing, inking, coloring, and so forth. In doing so, Mathieu also highlights the principal modes of perception inherent in comics: What kind of (fictional) "reality" is available to the characters of his stories? How can they perceive it? How do we as readers perceive the construction of this fictional universe in sequenced panels?

Mathieu's prominent focus on the formal construction of comics essentially indicates that comics are, after all, a very orderly, rational medium: Significant elements are deliberately put in frames, these frames are neatly put in sequence. Of course, this principle can be played with, just like Mathieu and others do — but in the end, the advanced, complex conundrums of the Acquefacques stories rely on the very basic structure of comics as pictures in sequential frames. This element of rational organization will prove essential in connecting Mathieu's comics with the modern city.

At first sight this may all seem like your typical 1980s/90s intellectual poststructuralist game-play (letting the material features of whatever medium emerge, looping or upending the story to fall back in on itself, etc.).[6] At second sight these self-referencing strategies connect quite seamlessly with the picture of the modern city presented in Mathieu's comics. In contrast to many efforts of Oubapo, "Mathieu is not simply interested in formalist experimentation for the sake of experimenta-tion" (Beaty 1997: 29).[7] When Mathieu himself talks about what he likes in the works of other comic artists, for example, "J'aime le travail des auteurs qui, au travers de mondes imaginaires, réussissent á faire émerger une réflexion, philosophique ou sociologique. Schuiten et Peeters nous amènent à réfléchir sur ce qu'est l'agora, la cite . . ."

(Mathieu 2002: 52), this is also true for his own work. His interests in formal structures, philosophical questions and sociological observations converge in one focal point: the topos of the modern city and its rational organization.[8]

Mathieu's Version of the City

What characterizes the city as the setting of these stories? Mathieu's city is an amalgamation of a surreal, at times even futuristic, vision and a city showing characteristics of modernist urbanism. There is literally nothing beyond this city and if characters and the story do ever leave the city, like Acquefacques does in *La Qu . . .*, they enter a nothingness of white, unmarked, unsignified space, emptier than a desert (Mathieu 1991: 35).

The living-space within the confines of the city delineated by Mathieu's comics is completely filled with buildings and design. It is artificial throughout, pure "culture." It does not present even a residual idea of a "natural" place, a space that has not been worked on. There is no sky to be seen anywhere, no plants, trees or animals, no effects of weather. It is all just the city, its buildings and its working inhabitants.

The paradigmatic dichotomy at work in this city then is not that of culture vs. nature or city vs. country. In the nature/culture opposition, nature may be strange or wild, but it is still something possessing a (different) logic in its own right. There is nothing like that outside of or opposed to Mathieu's city. Its fundamental principle is that of black and white: There is ink on the page or there simply is not.[9] There is something built/structured/drawn or there is plain nothing.

Mathieu's city is a densely built-up structure, horizontally and vertically, without free spaces, intermissions or openings. The buildings of the city fill panels and pages, from left to right and bottom to top (Mathieu 1990: 25; 1993: 12). This density of the city's built-up structure is paralleled by the masses of people inhabiting it. The whole city is always densely populated. The streets are filled with an amorphous mass of men in suits on their way to work (Mathieu 1990: 7 *et seq.*; 2000: 19), while the buildings seem to be divided into the smallest one-room apartments, which are often inhabited by more than one person. Due to the obvious lack of space, creative solutions are called for — as in the case of Acquefacques's neighbor, who is apparently living on the landing of their flight of stairs (Mathieu 1990: 5).

The design of the characters populating Mathieu's city and everything we get to know about them clearly marks them as versions of an archetypical bourgeois bureaucrat (Mathieu 1990: 10) — wearing suits, going to work, clocking on and off from their jobs in an office, surrounded by files on shelves (Mathieu 1990: 12). Practically everybody in this city seems to be working as civil servants, white-collar workers in different ministries, public offices and institutions. We visit the Ministry of Humor, where Acquefacques works (Mathieu 1990: 13, 15), and where workers are sometimes delivered to in truckloads like the human resources they obviously are (Mathieu 1995: 14). We get to see the Ministry of Science, where Acquefacques's peculiar role in the comic that is his world is explored (Mathieu 1990: 34). There is the office of "Living-Space Control," measuring Acquefacques's apartment to the last inch (Mathieu 1991: 9) and bringing him to the Ministry of Justice to be judged (Mathieu 1991: 13).

One of the most important offices in this world, of course, is the cadastral register we get to see in *Mémoire Morte*. Here, the built-up structure of an urban space is transferred to a two-dimensional map, laying the groundwork for a planned, rationalized city (Mathieu 2000: 16). In these cadastral maps the close connection between comics and the city finds a most striking illustration: The map's grid of streets and blocks closely resembles a comics page consisting of panels in their grid of blank space, thus stressing the analogy between comics and the city in their respective rational organization.

Another public institution of importance in this city alongside the ministry/office is the library/archive (Mathieu 1990: 28), which is often visited throughout the stories (Mathieu 1993: 31). Again, it is a place where everything is supposed to be neatly captured and catalogued, yet in fact these archives very soon show that the omnipresent quest for rationality is futile (Mathieu 2000: 43) — very often they appear a little messy, the archivists are unable to locate the object searched for. Or if they do, things get even more complicated from then on.

These institutions and archives convey a most frantic drive for rationality, exactness and punctuality. Punctuality seems to be very important, perhaps most strikingly represented by the central time clocks at Acquefacques's office (Mathieu 1995: 14) and his constant concern about being late or early. Rationality and exactness represent the efforts made to insure an orderly system of the city, which is always threatened by disorder. This in turn is mostly produced as a paradoxical effect of the city's own overzealous pursuit of rational organization.

The people or institutions of the city go so far in their pursuit of rationality as to invade dreams, like the "Reality Enforcers" in *La 2.333ᵉ Dimension* (Mathieu 2004: 10). They try to rationalize that which produces disturbing effects of irrationality in a world which has been rationalized to the extent of absurdity, becoming irrational in itself.

The citizens of this absurdly rationalized city become indistinguishable — an amorphous mass mostly devoid of individual features (Mathieu 1990: 34). In trying to cope with this situation, several characteristic effects occur. The densification of living-space produces a constant fight between the public and private sphere. Means of public transport, such as elevators, move right through private space such as apartments (Mathieu 1990: 22). Private space, the sphere of individuality, ceases to be. Even tiny apartments like Acquefacques's have to be shared by many people. Following an order from the Ministry, he sublets his wardrobe to one colleague (Mathieu 1993: 5), and his bed during the daytime to another who is working the night-shift (Mathieu 1995: 7). Under these conditions, identity becomes a precarious quality. This is most apparent in the (almost too conventionally employed) device of the doppelganger Acquefacques encounters in his adventures (Mathieu 1993: 8; 1995: 24–5). Though it is certainly not the primary topic of the Acquefacques comics, the loss of and search for identity are a part of the idea of the city inherent in the comics of Mathieu.[10]

The interaction between characters often seems cool and reserved. Acquefacques remains totally indifferent to the advances of his neighbor, who tries to impress him with jokes (Mathieu 1990: 5). In general, citizens behave rather disinterestedly to each other, and social values are quoted at an all-time low on the "value market" (Mathieu 1993: 16).

Looking at frames showing life in the streets, the citizens' indifference to each other sometimes even seems to carry an air of latent aggressiveness (Mathieu 1990: 8) — in their efforts to push their way through the crowd, in their contorted faces, strained from the effort.

Weber and Simmel's City — The City of Modernity

The city thus portrayed in Mathieu's comics, distorted as that portrait may be, is the city of Modernity. It is not today's shrinking city, not the urban sprawl of suburbanization, not the endless slums of mega-cities like Lagos or Mexico City. It is certainly a comics city — and at the same

Figure 14.2. *L'Origine, 7.* © 1990, Guy Delcourt Productions — Marc Antoine Mathieu.

time it bears striking similarities to the modern city Max Weber and Georg Simmel described sociologically at the beginning of the twentieth century.[11] The prominent features of their ideas of the city are recognizably the same characteristics the city in Mathieu's comics possesses.

Weber and Simmel see the European city as the breeding ground for rationality, capitalism and bureaucracy — the main currents working together in Western Modernity. Weber finds the primary cause for this general shift towards rationality in a specific Protestant work ethic especially prevalent in the modern city. Simmel adds another reason for the strong inclination cities and their inhabitants show towards reason and rationality, a reason more directly founded within the specific conditions of life in the city. Its citizens are practically unable to process the sheer amount of different stimuli city-life confronts them with. The constant level of impressions from people, crowds, traffic, shops, media, and so forth, produces an increased functioning of the nervous system, which carries the danger of an informational overload. A preservative, a kind of filter is called for and Simmel finds this filter in human reason. Reason and rationality help the inhabitants of the city to separate the important from the insignificant in order to reduce the level of input they have to process.

If the informational overload produced by the city is one motivation for a turn towards rationality, another force helps this process along: the market or monetized economy. According to both Weber and Simmel this economical system is closely connected to the space of the city. It favors a decidedly calculating approach to the world in general. So the rise of a calculating rationality is simultaneously propelled by the city's aesthetic condition, as a place abundant with impressions and stimuli, and its economic condition, as a marketplace.

Simmel points out the effects of rationality, which can be found at work on different levels of city life. On the official level one finds a thriving body of public administration regulating as many aspects of life as possible. On the private level, one finds peoples' interactions to be mainly distanced and reserved. Simmel describes quite convincingly how a certain indifference, a coldness with occasional touches of outright aggression, is characteristic of modern city life — a mechanism to keep others at a convenient distance.

Rationality thus allows the complex system of the city to work. Without rational planning, without regulations, control and punctuality the system would break down. And without rationality appearing as indifference, the city's inhabitants would be unable to cope with each other's proximity and their fundamental differences as persons. This continuous proximity of others blurs the difference between public and private space. Private space for personal recreation and individual activity becomes smaller and smaller, while public space becomes a domain of often involuntary intimacy.

How can one retain a sense of individuality in this situation? Simmel argues that rationality is a tool of stimulus relief and individual exemption from social constraints. This exemption produces an ambivalent experience of individuality in the city. On the one hand it liberates the individual to concentrate on him- or herself, because they cannot and do not have to care about others anymore; on the other hand this very liberation may produce loneliness and isolation. In an atmosphere of general indifference it gets harder and harder to be recognized as an individual. So, according to Simmel, individuality in the modern city becomes a staged production of superficial effects. With apparent nostalgic overtones, he sees his idea of an integral persona on the decline.

Despite the brevity of this paraphrase of Simmel's and Weber's theories of the modern city, the central arguments do provide obvious parallels to the main features of the city as Mathieu portrays it in his comics. The conglomeration of buildings and people, the complexity and density of stimuli within the city, the importance of rationality, the indifference of citizens to each other, the conflict of public and private, the problems of being an individual within the city — it is all there. That is not necessarily to say that Mathieu deliberately set out to merely illustrate Simmel's and Weber's ideas of the city. But he certainly participates in the same discourse — working it from a different angle, but coming to very similar conclusions. Yet one significant difference stands out. Looking back at the city of Modernity from the end of the twentieth century, Mathieu's comics show the ambivalence of rationality in much more clarity than Simmel was able to. While Simmel only entertained doubts about the ambivalent nature of the city's need for rationality, Mathieu's comics actually illustrate a general aporia of Modernity. They portray a kind of inverted rationality, which produces the irrationality it originally set out to control.

Framing the City

Despite the difference in historical perspective, the concern for rational organization, which the Acquefacques stories show in both form and content, provides a significant link to the city of Modernity. On a formal level, the basic structures and subsequent modes of perception at work within comics show a strong similarity to the city and certain modes of perception it produces. Mathieu's use of meta-fictional strategies points us to the fact that comics are constituted of sequenced pictures in frames. When one walks through a city, frames feature prominently in many views of it. Windows, openings, doorways, street entrances — they all frame our view, putting things into the picture and others out of it, just as comics' frames do. The perception of a city is defined by abrupt changes of perspective. You walk down a street, you look into another one branching off it, then you are past it. Passing a shop, you look into its framed window. A line of view, a door, a window opens, a new scene comes into view, then it is gone. Connecting these very diverse impressions from a walk through the city to a coherent idea can be very similar to making sense of a comic's sequenced panels. At night, the illuminated windows of an apartment block show scenes and situations in a frame, fixed in the building's dark grid — just like panels on a comic's page. Mathieu explicitly points towards this similarity between comics' frames and the city's buildings and especially their windows in *Mémoire Morte* (Mathieu 2000: 8).

Along with this rather obvious analogy, the process of framing sequenced pictures can more specifically be linked to characteristic

Figure 14.3. *Mémoire Morte*, 8. © 1999, Guy Delcourt Productions — Marc Antoine Mathieu.

features of the city of Modernity. As was pointed out earlier, framing, as the organization of space-units on a page, is a reproduction of the organizational rationality at work in the modern city. It means putting things, namely pictures, onto a grid, just like the cadastral register does for the city. Its formal precision in framing and sequencing panels makes comics, in a certain way, a very rational medium.

Furthermore, putting together panels and frames can be seen as an active representation of the city's aforementioned need for a perceptional decision, which Simmel described. There is just too much to see and react to in the modern city, so to avoid an informational overload, one needs a filter letting through only the important stimuli. A decision needs to be made: what to see and what not to see. In the city, if we follow Simmel, reason and rationality do the trick. In comics, it is framing:

Figure 14.4.   ***La Qu . . .,*** **9. © 1991, Guy Delcourt Productions — Marc Antoine Mathieu.**

What gets into the picture, what does not?

To come back to that moment from *La Qu* . . . mentioned earlier, when the agents of "Living-Space Control" measure out Acquefacques's apartment: The white lines of the agents' measuring tape cutting through the room/the panel clearly resemble the blank spaces on a comic page between panels. The white space in between panels is the measuring tape of comics' "Living-Space Control," that is the artist — and Mathieu quite bluntly points out this analogy to us (Mathieu 1991: 9).

What makes Mathieu's comics such an intriguing read is their complexity, their way of interconnecting multiple levels of significance and meaning. Yes, they can be read as meditations on the formal constraints of comics. Yet at the same time they offer reflections on modes and possibilities of perception, on the construction of reality and the question of identity — all of these aspects of meaning are brought together in the depiction of an abstract, fantastic and yet familiar city.

Different media have been described as being best suited to represent the conditions of life in the city. Is it the modern novel? Or the movies? If that question really needs an answer (which, of course, it actually does not), the title has to go to comics. This answer is not only based on comics' historical origin. On a deeper, more structural level, Mathieu's Acquefacques comics make a good case for the idea that if there is one prime medium of the city of Modernity, it is comics.

Works Cited
Comics
Mathieu, Marc-Antoine. *La 2,333ᵉ dimension.* Tournai: Delcourt, 2004.
Mathieu, Marc-Antoine. *La Qu* . . . Tournai: Delcourt, 1991.
Mathieu, Marc-Antoine. *Le Début de la fin/La Fin du début.* Tournai: Delcourt, 1995.
Mathieu, Marc-Antoine. *Le Processus.* Tournai: Delcourt, 1993.
Mathieu, Marc-Antoine. *L'Origine.* Tournai: Delcourt, 1990.
Mathieu, Marc-Antoine. *Mémoire morte.* Tournai: Delcourt, 2000.

Secondary Literature
Beaty, Bart. "Comics and the Modern Moment (Introduction to the Oulipo feature)." In: *Drunken Boat*, No. 8. (2006). Available online at: http://www.drunkenboat.com/db8/oulipo/feature-QWRTYZoulipo/para/oubapo/beaty/comics.html (accessed December 1, 2008).
Beaty, Bart. "Euro-Comics for Beginners: The Compelling Experimentation of Marc-Antoine Mathieu." In: *Comics Journal*, No. 196. (June 1997). 29–34.
Kafka, Franz. *Das Schloss,* ed. Malcolm Pasley. Frankfurt am Main: S. Fischer Verlag, 1982.
Kafka, Franz. *Der Prozeß,* ed. Jürgen Born. Frankfurt am Main: S. Fischer Verlag, 1990.

Leinen, Frank. "Spurensuche im Labyrinth. Marc-Antoine Mathieus Bandes dessinées zu Julius Corentin Acquefacques als experimentelle Metafiktion." In: Frank Leinen and Guido Rings (eds.), *Bilderwelten — Textwelten — Comicwelten. Romanistische Begegnungen mit der Neunten Kunst.* München: Martin Meidenbauer, 2007. 229–63.

Mathieu, Marc-Antoine. "Interview." In: *Dossier Schuiten — invité Mathieu: Les Dossiers de la Bande Dessinée,* No. 14. Paris: DBD, 2002. 51–6.

Morrison, Grant. "Interview." In: Dan Phillips. *Inside the Mind of Grant Morrison* (February 2, 2009). Available online at: http://uk.comics.ign.com/ articles/950/950703p1.html?RSSwhen2009-02-03_145000&RSSid=950703 (accessed February 23, 2009).

Musil, Robert. *Der Mann ohne Eigenschaften,* ed. Adolf Frisé, 2 Vols. Reinbek bei Hamburg: Rowohlt, 1986.

Oubapo. *Oupus 1.* Paris: L'Association. 1997.

Oubapo-America. A Website Exploring Oubapo: The Workshop for Potential Comics. http://www.tomhart.net/oubapo (accessed December 1, 2008).

Schmitz-Emans, Monika. "Mittelachsen. Symmetrien. Asymmetrien." In: Kurt Röttgers (ed.), *Mitte. Philosophische, medientheoretische und ästhetische Konzepte.* Essen: Die Blaue Eule, 2006. 166–89.

Simmel, Georg. "Die Großstädte und das Geistesleben." In: *Brücke und Tür,* ed. Michael Landmann and Margarete Susmann. Stuttgart: K.F. Köhler, 1957. 227–42.

Waugh, Patricia. *Practising Postmodernism/Reading Modernism.* London and New York: Edward Arnold, 1992.

Weber, Max. *Die protestantische Ethik und der Geist des Kapitalismus,* ed. Dirk Kaesler. München: C.H. Beck, 2006.

Notes

1 Oubapo ("Ouvroir de la Bande Dessinée Potentielle," which translates into English as "Workshop for Potential Comics") was inspired by its literary predecessor Oulipo ("Ouvroir de Littérature Potentielle"). Oubapo was established in 1992 as an ongoing project by critic Thierry Groensteen and several members of L'Association, the French comics publishing cooperative. The starting point for the group is the idea of formal constraints or principles constitutive for comics. In their works (collected in *Oupus* 1–4, published by L'Association) the Oubapo artists explicate these constraints.

　　Mathieu has been loosely associated with the group. In 2003 he took part in an event organized by Oubapo, which connected the simultaneous comic festivals in Lucerne (Switzerland) and Bastia (France/Corsica). Working within constraints set for the event, artists in both locations created comic strips, shared them over the internet, commented on them and reworked the strips of others. This resulted in an impressive body of hundreds of strips.

　　For Thierry Groensteen's preliminary list of constraints, see the first volume of *Oupus* (Oubapo 1997). An English summary of these constraints, translated by Matt Madden, can be found on the unofficial Oubapo-America website founded by Matt Madden, Tom Hart, and Jason Little: http:// www.tomhart.net/oubapo/constraints/groensteen/index.html (accessed December 1, 2008).

　　For an introduction to Oubapo and some comments on the Lucerne/

Bastia event see Bart Beaty's introductory article to the Oulipo feature in *Drunken Boat*, No. 8 (Beaty 2006).

2   "Acquefacques" is a phonetic palindrome. When pronounced in French, it sounds like "Akfak" — which is the sound of "Kafka" read backwards. It is an obvious reference to Franz Kafka, whose novels *Das Schloss* and *Der Prozess* describe machineries of an uncannily absurd and threatening bureaucracy quite similar to the vision of the Acquefacques comics.

3   The title "*La Qu . . .*" is the unfinished beginning of a mysterious word and hints at an unimaginable secret, a taboo on which the story rests. It is short for "la Quadrichromie," or four-color printing.

4   The title is another obvious reference to Kafka and his novel *Der Prozess*.

5   Monika Schmitz-Emans has highlighted the strategies of mirror-images and symmetry employed in *Le Début de la Fin* (Schmitz-Emans 2006).

6   These strategies let Frank Leinen conclude that Mathieu's comics are exceptional works of postmodern art (see Leinen 2007: 259). While Mathieu's aesthetic strategies can indeed be located within a postmodern context, the setting of his stories (the city) does, as I have tried to show, point back to modernism. This, however, is not necessarily a contradiction, but another indicator of the vital lines of continuity between modernism and postmodernism (see Waugh 1992).

7   Frank Leinen pinpoints the difference between Mathieu and the Oubapo artists. While the latter make an effort to work within the constraints set for their comics, Mathieu tries to free himself from these formal constraints. The constraints and formal principles of comics are still very apparent in his work, but they are in a state of being transgressed (see Leinen 2007: 229f.). Leinen's essay on Mathieu's Acquefacques comics offers a comprehensive study of their meta-fictional strategies.

8   Between 1995 and 2004 Mathieu published a few stand-alone titles not directly related to the Acquefacques series. *Mémoire Morte* from 2000 is worth mentioning because it features a very similar vision of the city, maybe even more prominently than the Acquefacques stories.

9   In a recent interview on his run on DC Comics' *Final Crisis*, Grant Morrison talks about this fundamental contrast of black and white in comics: "I was thinking, what is the basis of the comic book story? What actually is it? In the case of comic book stories, it's the war between white page and ink" (Morrison 2009). Different as *Final Crisis* and Mathieu's Acquefacques stories may appear, they certainly share a meta-perspective on the structural aspects of comics.

10 In regard to dealing with the question of identity, Frank Leinen compares Acquefacques's quest to another text dating back to modernism, namely Robert Musil's *Der Mann ohne Eigenschaften* (see Leinen 2007: 243f.).

11 My short introduction to Simmel's and Weber's views of the modern city refers to Georg Simmel's *Die Großstädte und das Geistesleben* (Simmel 1957) and Max Weber's *Die protestantische Ethik und der Geist des Kapitalismus* (Weber 2006).

15

Calisota or Bust: Duckburg vs. Entenhausen in the Comics of Carl Barks

ANDREAS PLATTHAUS

ET'S HAVE A LOOK AT a place that is called "Entenhausen" in German Disney comics — its original name of course is "Duckburg." The panel in Figure 15.1 was drawn in 1950. It is the splash for "The Magic Hourglass" (*Four Color Comics*, No. 291).It shows a megalopolis, not unlike Chicago with the river running through the city center and the skyscrapers being built close to the river banks. This is one of the few panels in which Carl Barks gives us a close look at downtown Duckburg, underlined by the words uttered by Huey, Dewey, and Louie: "A great view over our city." The balloon proves that we are looking at Duckburg and so we get a glimpse of the size of this city — in no way can it be a small town.

But how about a panel Barks drew exactly ten years later? Figure 15.2 shows its German version (*Micky Maus* 1961, No. 17)in which we see the city council of Duckburg and its mayor asking Donald Duck, who has become a blacksmith in this story, to melt a war memorial down into a plough. The storyline is of no importance — what matters for my argument is the dialogue: It tells about a battle which made "unser Dorf" famous in military history. "Unser Dorf" of course means "our village," a description no citizen of a metropolis would ever use for her hometown. We have a riddle to solve here: Duckburg seems to be a big city but sometimes it is spoken of in terms of a small town or even a village.

Figure15.1. **Duck_FC 291 © The Walt Disney Company**

Figure15.2. **Duck 40_52 © The Walt Disney Company**

In the original panel, shown in Figure 15.3, as Barks drew it in 1960 (*Walt Disney's Comics and Stories*, No. 239), no mention of "village" can be found. Only the transition text speaks of "the village smithy." Donald Duck's actual profession is described in ancient terminology, which doesn't represent the normal state of things in Duckburg. Barks started the story with a parody of a famous poem by Henry Wadsworth Longfellow: "Under the spreading chestnut tree / the Duckburg smithy stands! / The smith, a mighty duck is he, / with blisters on his hands!" This mockery is the reason for the use of the term "village smithy." To preserve this parody in the German translation a completely new reference has been chosen — a pastiche of the German poet Wilhelm Müller's lyric poem *Der Lindenbaum*. In both cases — with "unser Dorf" and Müller's poem — the translation doubtlessly has to take some liberties, and this is not the only example of this practice one can find in the German *Micky Maus* magazine, which published most of Barks's stories. To make them work in the foreign language they needed to be reshaped.

That might come as a surprise for any foreign language reader who knows how popular the German translations are and what praise they have received. The name of Erika Fuchs, who translated almost the whole body of work drawn by Barks, is famous in Germany, Austria, and Switzerland; she even received two literary prizes for the quality of her work. But the fact that she never gained an award for translation might explain the obvious paradox we are facing here. Because she was dealing with many of the best-known characters in comic history and with an author who is generally ranked one of the greatest in his field, one can see how some might be irritated about the fame that Erika Fuchs enjoys today.

In this chapter I will not try to analyze the accuracy of Fuchs's translations. Nor will I give further examples of the liberties she took. But the first panels I presented already should have given a slight impression of what I am interested in when I am looking at how Duckburg became Entenhausen. I will try to use the differences between the urbanistic concept articulated by Barks and the one found in Erika Fuchs's translations to make some remarks about urbanistic aesthetics in different comic cultures and about Barks's work in particular. The way Fuchs reshaped that work allows us to point out a specific blindness, which is very common in comics but not very well considered up to now. What is meant here are the graphic and narrative results of the task of presenting a plausible story to the reader — working in a media that doesn't even try to hide that it is fictional. This fact makes comics different from other

Figure15.3. **Duck_WDC-239_1 © The Walt Disney Company**

Figure15.4. **Duck 40_47 © EHAPA Verlag GmbH**

narrative forms: You might believe in a film when it mocks documentary style or you might take a novel for a non-fiction book, but you will never believe a comic shows us the real picture. One can't get anything much more fictitious than drawn stories. The world is not drawn. It is not photographed or described either, but we are used to acknowledging these forms of representations as more realistic ones — even if an artist like David Mazzucchelli has found brilliant ways to depict a place like Manhattan (see Karasik and Mazzucchelli 1994).

It is a little bit bizarre that there still exists no city map of Duckburg.[1] The home of Donald Duck and his family is without doubt one of the best-known cities in the world but we don't even know where Killmotor Hill, home of Scrooge McDuck's money bin, is located in terms of the town's topography. Is it near the harbor as some panels seem to suggest? Does it lie in the shadow of Old Demon Tooth, a mountain impossible to overlook? Are there several money bins, or was Killmotor Hill leveled in those stories that show us McDuck's building on flat ground? We don't know. And yet everything in Duckburg seems to stand at its proper place: Donald's house, which he changed at least 30 times if we just look at the comics drawn by Carl Barks, Grandma Duck's farm, which sometimes is situated close to the city and on other occasions far away, and the town hall, which varies in size and shape and style as often as it is depicted. Duckburg offers no fixing points beside its inhabitants, and that is already one of the aesthetic secrets of Barks.

Barks's use of buildings and landmarks is a metonymical one. He never filled his backgrounds with urbanistic detail, but preferred to add single elements that represent the whole city. The narrative principle of storytelling in comics consists of reader participation. It is she who fills the gaps — not just *between* the panels but even more *in* the panels. Few comic artists draw in a way that might be called realistic in terms of illusionistic perfection. Barks's work is the leading example of a style of graphic storytelling that minimizes the necessary effort to communicate a given amount of information to the reader. Even if he became famous for the accurate research he did and for his use of *National Geographic* magazine as the source for many of his adventure stories, he only gave optical hints about the settings. His mastery lies in the efficiency of his stories, and the way he depicted Duckburg allows us to observe this technique in particular. The metonymical use of elements which provoke the imagining of the city as a whole has its origin in animated cartoons, and Barks and most other comic book artists — NB: not the comic strip artists! — adopted it. Their output was too big and their wages too low for them to allow themselves any unnecessary work. Thus the only recurring element of the Duckburg skyline is the money bin, and even this famous icon of comic architecture wasn't introduced until 1951 (*Walt Disney's Comics and Stories*, No. 135), which means that Barks spent nine years of his comics career shaping a city that was not recognizable at all — and shouldn't be. Otherwise he would have been limited in his settings, repeating all the same backgrounds again and again, because at the beginning the Duck family rarely left their hometown. He could draw a simple house or a sidewalk and every reader would have conjured Duckburg with all its wonders before their inner eye — outside and inside the panel borders.

But metonymical use of single aspects of city life is not enough, or else every comics artist would have done it the same way. Barks had the incomparable advantage of drawing ducks instead of men, and though Donald Duck without any doubt is the best representation of an average guy, he will never be mistaken for anyone else because of his iconic appearance — beak and sailor suit. Every panel that shows him or one of his kin also has to show Duckburg. After being established as the home of the Ducks by Barks it wasn't necessary to add anything more specific to the city. Certainly several further aspects of Duckburg city life were added later — by Barks and by his successors. But that happened out of the sheer joy to work within a framework that didn't need to be widened and yet gave the artists the liberty to develop their particular version of Duckburg. The name was more than enough once it became known all over the world.

It is interesting to examine the way Barks let the Ducks speak about themselves. While Erika Fuchs tended to let them call themselves "Entenhausener" — Duckburgians — Barks almost never did that. In his dialogues the characters called themselves "Ducks." The name of the species became the name of the family and it became the name of the inhabitants of a city called after them. In deciding to keep the name "Donald Duck" in the German translations, Fuchs could also have stuck to the name of Duckburg. But she didn't. She chose the similar name of "Entenhausen," but did not let the Ducks call themselves "Enten." For her they should be regarded as humans. That concept radicalizes the specific aesthetic of Barks's comics. One never thinks of the strange look of these "people" who are walking around without pants, acting like normal citizens while they are so small that they can't reach the hip of humans or even the tabletop in their own home without standing on a chair. No other comic artist has ever drawn more unrealistically than Barks, but that is hardly mentioned. The simple reason for this lies in the fact that he never mentioned it himself in the comics. The Ducks are not small people; they are ducks. But Barks' characters act so self-conscious that we can't believe them to be different from the rest of their world. We simply don't trust our eyes.

So there is also no need to present Duckburg as a realistic city. Barks is an illusionist — not in terms of realism but as a kind of magician who deceives our eyes. Duckburg is a latent place that is seldom seen but always present. Erika Fuchs changed all that. By letting the Ducks speak about being "Entenhausener" — citizens of Entenhausen — all the time she put the city in the middle of the "saga," as German scholar Henner Löffler calls the body of Barks's stories (see Löffler 2004). But let us return to the Carl Barks who was born in 1901 in the state of Oregon and died there 99 years later. Although Barks himself didn't get around much, he made the Duck family travel all around the world and even into outer space. For more than 25 years, from 1942 till 1968, Barks wrote and drew Duck stories. Even when nobody knew his name he was already famous as "the good artist," because readers recognized his narrative and graphic skills. Barks was employed by the Disney studio in 1935 as an in-betweener, moving very quickly to the story department where he worked for the greater part on Donald Duck cartoons. His poor health made him quit the studio in 1942, but when Western Publishing was in need of artists to draw for the ever more popular Disney comic books they asked Barks to join the staff. The first script the publishing house sent him in 1943 was of such a low quality that Barks rewrote most of it. His editor was pleased by this effort; from then on he was his own author for a quarter-century, writing and drawing more than 600 stories, which are praised today as one of the great achievements in comic history.

Disney comics were new to Germany because during the Nazi era they had been prohibited. A few comic strips had been published in Switzerland during the late 30s, but the new format of the comic book was still almost unknown in all German-speaking countries. The Duck stories were published by Ehapa, the German branch of a Danish publishing house, that resided in Stuttgart, more than 300 kilometers away from where Erika Fuchs lived. Born in Rostock in 1906 she was only a few years younger than Barks, and she also died at a very old age, in 2005. Fuchs started translating Barks's comics in 1951, which means she was with *Micky Maus* magazine from its start. It also was her first job as a translator, when she was already 45 years old. Her children were grown up by then and she was looking for something to do while her husband ran a middle-sized factory in the little town of Schwarzenbach, Bavaria, very close to the Czechoslovakian border — in other words, at the end of the world, at least of the Western world.

Erika Fuchs was hired not because of her skills as a translator (as a debutant she had none) but because she was the only candidate who could provide a Ph.D. (NB: not in English but in art history). An academic background seemed crucial to the publisher because at that time and for many years after comic books in Germany were regarded as trivial or even trash. Many parents feared that their children would become illiterate when they got into comics, so a lady with a Ph.D. at the editorial board seemed the best way to prove the literary quality the Disney comics claimed to have. Consequently Erika Fuchs was never listed in the editorial of *Micky Maus* magazine as translator but as editor-in-chief, a job she never actually held. The only thing she ever edited were the texts in the balloons while all the real editing was performed in Denmark before the stories were sent to Fuchs for translation. Many of Barks's stories were edited heavily, for example, the beaks of the Ducks were shortened; single panels or whole sequences up to half a dozen pages were cut from some stories if they did not seem to fit into the magazine schedule. Erika Fuchs, then, had to fill the unavoidable logical gaps in the storyline without knowing what was missing in detail. This was one of the reasons why Erika Fuchs worked quite arbitrarily with the original balloon texts.

Another reason was her aim of guaranteeing the aforementioned literary quality into comics. She loved to use quotes from classical texts and therefore let the Ducks speak in a manner that might have been up to date in her own youth but was no longer so in the 50s or even later. But that didn't matter either, because it suited the pedagogical claim the publishing company had made. And it made Fuchs famous when parents were stunned to discover such allusions in the speech balloons of an art form that was considered to be of minor value, to say the least. So the word spread that there was an elderly lady turning American comic trash into pearls of German classics. And even better: Fuchs became a classic herself. And she behaved like one. The fascinating thing about her way of translating is that it repeats the habits of former times. Foreign language texts in the eighteenth or even the early nineteenth century were regarded as raw material by the translator whose job it was

to produce a German version that was understandable to the public —
not just in terms of language but also in terms of style. There is a famous
remark from Christoph Martin Wieland, the first German translator of
Shakespeare in this connection. When his version of *Hamlet* came out
in 1766 it lacked large parts because Wieland found them unsuitable
for his readers. When he omitted two complete "mock speeches" as he
called them from Act III, he added a footnote in explanation: "Here
two mock speeches of Hamlet have been left out, because the first is not
understandable to the translator and the second one is a dirty joke with
a double meaning" (Shakespeare 1993: 112).

Erika Fuchs worked in a similar way, even if she never explained
the reasons for her alterations in such a disarmingly frank manner as
Wieland's. Asked some 40 years later about some of her translation
errors from the beginning of her career she told me that she simply
hadn't enough reference material. She didn't know the Disney characters and so she shaped them after her own will. Sometimes she had
to work with nearly unreadable Xerox copies of stories that she had
to make sense of. And she worked on her translations all alone in
Schwarzenbach, because Stuttgart was much too far from her home.
That meant she lived in complete professional isolation in her small
town at the Czechoslovakian border.

This was not so different from the life that Barks led, however. After
resigning from the Disney studio which was located in Burbank near
Los Angeles, he moved to the Californian countryside. Most of his
early stories were drawn in Hemet, nowadays famous as the home of
Scientology. In the late 40s and early 50s, however, the city was still
rural. By coincidence author and translator shared the same situation
concerning their individual living and working conditions.

They also faced similar problems. Barks had to stick to strict rules concerning the way Disney characters had to be presented. He had to accept
some editing of his stories even in America, especially in the early 50s
when he was already an established comic book artist. After using more
and more realistically drawn people as sidekicks in his stories Barks was
told to give up all depictions of humans. So he had to get back to ducks
and dogs and chickens and any other talking animals. That was a blow to
his plans for establishing his own comic strip, which he was working on
at this time. It would have featured human characters, but without any
the chance to improve his skills in drawing human anatomy as he had
had during the years before when he had made Duckburg's population

so realistic, Barks had to abandon his ambitious plans and stick to Disney comics. Some of his narratives were also heavily edited, especially "Trick or Treat" from the year 1952 (*Donald Duck*, No. 26).

The editing of "Trick or Treat" is hard to understand because Barks didn't devise that particular story himself. He adapted the script of an animated cartoon of the same name that had been released in cinemas some months before. Barks just copied the opening sequence of this cartoon, which included a witch's ride on her broomstick over a cemetery. But cartoons and comics were regarded differently at Disney's: While cartoons had to please an audience comprising all generations, comic books were thought of as kids' stuff. Barks always said that what he had in mind when writing and drawing was a 12-year-old boy. Alone, he had more confidence in 12-year-olds than his editors. The 50s saw a massive public attack on comic books in America led by Frederic Wertham and resulting in the Comic Code of 1954. Western Publishing was very careful at that time and so the opening page of "Trick or Treat" had to be cut while earlier stories that had depicted cemeteries too — for example "The Old Castle's Secret" from 1947 (*Four Color Comics*, No. 189) or "The Sheriff of Bullet Valley" from 1948 (*Four Color Comics*, No. 199) had passed uncensored.

There are other parts of city life in Duckburg that Barks had to be cautious about using. Religion was one of them. For example, there are not many examples of churches in Duckburg, the most famous among them being the cathedral of Notre Duck, drawn by Barks in 1965 (*Uncle Scrooge*, No. 60). But that church was given the characteristics of a museum, without any hints of religious acts being performed in it. This is another example of Barks's mastery in establishing settings that are unusual in the context of Duckburg but that are so carefully worked out that no one would wonder about their sudden appearance and their vanishing afterwards, because not one of these places will ever be found again in later stories. Erika Fuchs found it necessary to add the information that the cathedral looks older than it is. And she changed the content of the balloon. The commentator — by the way a very unusual role not only in Barks's but in any other comic books — tells us that Notre Duck is nearly as big as the Stephansdom in Vienna, but less beautiful (*Micky Maus* 1967, No. 48). Fuchs didn't appreciate Barksian eclecticism. She did him wrong in this instance because Barks had accurately copied his cathedral from historical model drawings by the French architect Eugène Viollet-le-Duc.

Figure15.5. **Duck_US-60 © The Walt Disney Company**

The crucial point for the urbanistic aesthetics of Barks is the cred-
ibility of his city. Duckburg could stand every surprise its author would
think of, but one thing had to remain intact: the feeling that the Duck
family is living in an idealized American township. And that resulted in
the biggest problem for any foreign translator: How to keep the basic
American setting without alienating their own readership from the
world of Duckburg? The answer Erika Fuchs found was quite radical:
The dialogue and the names were cleaned of any trace of their American
origin. Her Entenhausen was populated with citizens with names that
Fuchs took from the telephone book of her hometown and most of the
hills and towns around the city of Entenhausen can easily be detected
on a map showing the surroundings of Schwarzenbach. In opposition
to Barks, Erika Fuchs had no metropolitan concept of urbanity because
she chose a small town as the model for Entenhausen while Barks had

Berkeley at least in mind — and that of course included the close by Los Angeles.

Barks and Fuchs only met once. In the summer of 1994 the American artist left his country for the first and last time. He toured Europe and visited Erika Fuchs in her house in Munich where she lived after retirement. But even at the age of almost 90 she was still translating Barks's stories that had not been printed in German yet, while Barks had just started to provide American Disney publisher Gladstone with some new scripts he had written. So the two seniors were quite active in their old age — still shaping the fate of Duckburg and Entenhausen. However, they didn't find access to each other easy, since they each were king and queen of their own domains — Barks reigning over an American-cultivated Duckburg, Fuchs over a Germanized Entenhausen.

In fact Duckburg is a true image of its time, depicting such short-termed phenomena as hippie culture, the Davy Crocket hysteria of the mid-50s and the triumph of the television set in private homes. But Duckburg also offers us glimpses of slums and the houses of the rich. All this is part of its city life. But we must not imagine Barks as an admirer of urbanistic living. In several stories he mocks the efforts of technical progress or even depicts the poverty in Shacktown, the slum of Duckburg (*Four Color Comics*, No. 367). A curious observer of social and technical developments, Barks was a conservative and urban life seemed especially ambivalent to him. In 1960 he drew "Monsterville" (*Four Color Comics*, No. 1184), a Gyro Gearloose tale that shows the great inventor modernizing the whole city of Duckburg only to find out that the citizens don't want an easy life without any challenges. At the end it is Gearloose, the mastermind of modernization himself, who leads his fellow Duckburgians to destroy all the new achievements in order to get back to the status quo. Duckburg, as Barks loves to show it, is a city with the typical features of an American town. Let's forget the gigantic statues of Cornelius Coot (*Walt Disney's Comics and Stories*, No. 138), the founding father of the community, and the bizarre effect they create in representing a pilgrim father-like founder figure of a city that is placed on the West Coast of America. Look at the skyline at the feet of these memorials instead, where a neoclassical town hall, some steeples and some larger buildings can be spotted while all the rest of Duckburg seems to consist of small houses. There is no trace of the skyscrapers we saw in Figure 15.1, nor even the river, not to mention the shoreline, which is part of so many stories drawn by Barks.

So there seems to be a lack of consistency in the presentation of Duckburg in Barks's comics: It doesn't even need Erika Fuchs to puzzle us. But, in fact, no reader was puzzled when the stories originally appeared. I've already mentioned that Barks had no interest in continuity. His characters have no remembrance of their own past — with the exception of only three stories in which the Ducks explicitly are looking back to their previous experiences (see *Walt Disney's Comics and* Stories, No. 62; *Uncle Scrooge*, Nos. 27 and 31) — and so they won't visit the same places again either. Barks, as we have already heard, just drew what he needed for his plots. If he wanted to tell a sea adventure, well hey presto: Duckburg lies on the shore. If he liked to tell a winter story he let snow fall in streets where normally palms would grow. Or he had Duckburg situated at the foot of a mountain chain — that Duckburg that we can see in Figure 15.6, lying in the plains, surrounded by nothing more than farmland. In a very witty moment from 1952, Barks mentioned the name of the state Duckburg is a part of: "Calisota" (*Four Color Comics*, No. 422), a mixture of California and Minnesota (Löffler 2004: 9). The first of these two states is famous for its warm climate, the second for its hard winters. Only this combination could explain the Duckburg experience of climatic extremes, but the name Calisota was dropped immediately: Barks never used it again. And Erika Fuchs didn't even try to translate it. The name of Entenhausen stands for city and state or country alike.

There is no doubt that Barks thought of Duckburg as an American city, while Erika Fuchs made it a German town. Both wanted to make the place acceptable for their readership. So an American freeway interchange shown by Barks (*Walt Disney's Comics and Stories*, No. 149) was shaped into a German one in which traffic signs mention cities like Frankfurt, Hamburg, Bonn, Basel, and Wien (the latter two were chosen as little nods to Austrian and Swiss readers) and obviously fictitious towns like Hogtown or Noplace became real German places (*Micky Maus* 1954, No. 2).While Barks makes fun, Erika Fuchs is quite serious and tries to be as realistic as possible. She has no sympathy for funny names or puns. It is as if she wanted to save Barks' work from its own creator's silliness.

One might also think that Barks and Fuchs are typical of the comic cultures they each stand for. The European tradition prefers realistic settings: Tintin lives in Brussels, Corto Maltese comes from Venice, and Adèle Blanc-Sec solves crimes in Paris. European artists love to let their characters act in surroundings that are familiar to their readers. You

Figure 15.7. **Duck_WDC-149_1 © The Walt Disney Company**

Figure 15.8. **Duck 22_51 © EHAPA Verlag GmbH**

can walk through London with Blake and Mortimer, travel to Budapest with Freddy Lombard, or go to Berlin with Lena Desrosières. When Jean Giraud alias Moebius once described the difference between European and American comics in terms of physiognomic aspects, he contrasted the bigger-than-life heads of the Franco-Belgian comic heroes like Asterix or Gaston with the small heads of muscle-packed American superheroes and declared this phenomenon as the necessary outcome of intelligent vs. stupid storytelling. He could have added another significant difference: While European comics seek to place the action in settings known from everyday experience, American ones prefer parallel worlds. There is no Metropolis or Gotham City or Central City in real life, even if New York City was the inspiration for all three of them.

Of course there are also European comic artists who abandon reality and flee to fantasy worlds, and likewise there are American artists who stick close to reality — and both groups contain some of the best in their respective fields. Just think of the storyline of *The Incal* illustrated by Moebius or the *Donjon* series by Lewis Trondheim and Joann Sfar. From America let us mention Art Spiegelman and Jason Lutes with their history-based comic books or Adrian Tomine and Daniel Clowes with their contemporary everyday stories. But the mainstream in America is superhero stuff and these stories long for backgrounds from the big cities — not from real ones but from those that remind us of the most familiar places in America without claiming to be identical with them. That is a very smart concept because it allows such urbanistic extravaganzas as the art deco architecture of Gotham City or the overwhelming buildings of Metropolis: The bigger the city, the greater the heroes. And vice versa: Just think of places like Coconino County in *Krazy Kat* or Dogpatch in *Li'l Abner*.

Most American comics' plots have big cities for settings, however. This is, in some respects, still a consequence of the birth of the comic, which took place in the weekend supplements of the large papers of the East Coast. In the early twentieth century most comic strip artists lived in New York, and the same was true 30 years later when the comic book started to rise. The shops of Eisner and Iger or Siegel and Shuster were located in Manhattan and therefore were the settings of their stories, even if the cities had different names. These stories were written for city folk, not for farmers from the Midwest. Exceptions like *Gasoline Alley* or the later *Peanuts* and *Calvin & Hobbes* discovered the romantic appeal of a Midwestern pastoral in which pumpkin fields and woodlands were places of sentimental remembrance of a world passed. That is the explanation for the success of Walt Disney's work, too.

In his cartoons from the late 20s and from the 30s, Disney idealized a rural America, which he knew from his childhood in Marceline, Missouri. Barnyards and livestock were the reservoir he took his ideas from for the early *Mickey Mouse* cartoons. And this country setting was adopted for the comic strips by Floyd Gottfredson, who started to draw *Mickey Mouse* in 1930, and by Al Taliaferro, who worked on *Donald Duck* from 1936. There is neither a Duckburg nor any other identifiable city at all in Taliaferro's strips: He drew whatever he needed for his gag sequences: harbors, mountains, shops, parks. That's what Barks took over from him, but Barks developed a much more refined way of story setting. With the introduction of Duckburg he gained a focus for his work, which before had consisted of nothing more than Taliaferro's dailies blown up to ten or even more pages. Even if Duckburg never seems to stay the same, it keeps its name, and so it allows the reader to find at least something continuous in Barks's stories. Thus he could be true to the Disney tradition of characters without a memory while providing them with a cultural background — an urban one. This is the reason for the popularity of Barks's work all over the world: His stories don't rely on simple puns or slapstick but on wit and context. Barks transformed the Disney tradition from country life into city life. Taliaferro never found it necessary to tell where his stories took place and he chose either a farm or a village or the city as settings — it didn't matter. But it mattered to Barks, and that's why Duckburg stands at the center of all the stories told by him.

Barks didn't use the city as a spectacular playground for his characters and he only made fun of the city a few times. For example, Barks once drew a skyscraper, called the Limpire State Building, which ducked under the borders of a splash panel (*Donald Duck*, No. 60). Of course it never appeared again, and Erika Fuchs couldn't find a German equivalent for the name Limpire State Building because in the 50s there were no famous German skyscrapers that could be mocked. So the name was just whitened out (*Micky Maus* 1959, No. 31). In other cases Fuchs translated American names into German ones, but while Barks loved to make up his own names, Fuchs chose real cities or landscapes. For this reason the region of Fichtelgebirge where she lived while she worked as a translator became the home ground of the German Donald Duck who then was Germanified.

Figure15.9. **Duck_TitanicAnts-60 © The Walt Disney Company**

However, the way Barks tells us about Duckburg is so consistent that it leaves no room for interpretation while Erika Fuchs's translations create voids — voids that result from the impossibility of shaping the world of Duckburg into that of Entenhausen without losing something. In some cases panels that document the metropolitan look of Duckburg, like the one in "Land beneath the Ground" (*Micky Maus* 1959, No. 31) were edited out of the German comic books. The choice might have been coincidental, but it is interesting that only this panel, with its San Francisco-like setting, seemed superfluous to the editors. What we lose is the feeling of taking part in an American saga. The German version can't substitute every aspect with a fitting transformation, so we have to explain the contradictory elements of the texts and the pictures ourselves.

That makes the world of Entenhausen richer, at least for interpretation, than the world of Duckburg. But it is also the origin of misunderstandings like the one we started with. While Barks had a clear urbanistic concept that he was true to, Fuchs involuntarily went back to Barks's predecessors who had no idea of the narrative value of a convincing setting. But perfection isn't everything. Carl Barks will be remembered as one of the greatest storytellers of the twentieth century, as a man who gave us his vision of America, and as an artist who came close to perfection. Erika Fuchs will be remembered as a woman who gave us things to think about — as a result of her struggle to reshape this American pastoral into a German one: an impossible task, but one that offers us countless possibilities for reflection.

Works Cited

Karasik, Paul and Mazzucchelli, David. *Paul Auster's City of Glass: A Graphic Mystery*. New York: Avon Books, 1994.

Löffler, Henner. *Wie Enten hausen. Die Ducks von A bis Z*. München: C.H. Beck, 2004.

Shakespeare, William: *Hamlet, Prinz von Dänemark*, trans. and ed. Christoph Martin Wieland, Hans Radspieler, and Johanna Radspielder, Zürich: Haffmanns, 1993.

Wollina, Jürgen and Pfeiler, Christian. "Der Stadtplan von Entenhausen." In: *Donald Duck — Sonderheft 55*. Göttingen 2008.

Note

1 There is actually a map of Entenhausen, which was published only recently by two German scholars (see Wollina and Pfeiler 2008).

16

Enki Bilal's *Woman Trap*: Reflections on Authorship under the Shifting Boundaries between Order and Terror in the City

THOMAS BECKER

L ES HUMANOÏDES ASSOCIÉS, FOUNDED IN 1975 as one of the first independent comic publishers in Paris, claims to have published the first graphic novels in France, translating titles by Will Eisner and Art Spiegelman (Groensteen 2006: 75). Indeed, Will Eisner's *A Contract with God* was first distributed in France by this publisher in the late 1970s. In 1980 Les Humanoïdes Associés published the first part of Enki Bilal's *Nikopol Trilogy, La Foire aux Immortels* (*The Carnival of Immortals*), followed by *La Femme Piège* (*The Woman Trap*) in 1986 and *Froid Equateur* (*Cold Equator*) in 1992. The first two parts of this trilogy are some of the earliest graphic novels that create a complex narration by using a symbolic structure of colors.

The *Nikopol Trilogy* has often been considered as one of the typical science fictions of the pessimistic 1980s, which counter the 1960s promise of the democratic evolution and technological progress in Western societies. The art historian Otto Karl Werckmeister calls the vision of Bilal's trilogy a critique of the citadel culture because cities in the Western world are shown as powerful centers defending their standards of health and security systems against immigrants at high military costs (Werckmeister 1989: 17). I will argue here that this is only the intention of the first part of the trilogy. If we are aware of the coloring that is implied in the complex narration in the *Woman Trap*, then another political message will appear. The author considers his paradoxical position on criticizing the future citadel culture in Western cities like Paris, London, Berlin, and New York as an apocalyptic view that denies any critical autonomy of art production.

Woman Trap starts with the mourning of Jill Bioskop for the loss of her boyfriend John, a victim of a terrorist attack. Jill is a young journalist in the London of 2025. She owns a mysterious typewriter that she thinks is able to send her reports about the desolate situation of the contemporary citadel culture to the cities of the past — that is, to our time. After a breakdown — as a result of an overdose of drugs she took in order to forget the death of John — a former boyfriend suggests she go to Berlin to write some reports about the city. Whereas London corresponds well to the theory of Werckmeister as a citadel culture, Berlin with its Wall is shown as a new kind of normalized culture able to defend the city without visible borders.

Between the first and the second parts of the trilogy, Bilal in fact visited Berlin. He produced a volume with fictional drawings of this city to express his vision of a new kind of power in the normalized culture of communication. Werckmeister thinks that Bilal saw Berlin as a realized citadel of freedom, protecting itself with its Wall against unwanted enemies, immigrants, and lower classes that exist outside it. But in Bilal's vision, the Berlin Wall is not a real frontier because the checkpoints seem to represent a performance for tourists in both sides of the city and the soldiers do not try to avoid communication between East and West. In one of the drawings, we find a person with an umbrella and sunglasses sitting on the Wall in which missiles are stuck in both directions. In the later *Woman Trap*, the fictional Parisian newspaper *La Libération* describes these missiles in the city buildings as the invention of an artist. Thus, the missiles represent a spectacle in this picture and not a document of a former conflict.

Berlin with its Wall is not seen as a living ruin of an ancient capital but as the avant-garde of a new kind of citadel culture that has transformed its former frontier into a spectacle to entertain tourists and to let them know what the field of power in Western society will be like in the future. In the background of the man sitting on the Wall, there are two military jets heading to the defense of the border in a very distant area, something that would never occur to the city dwellers in their everyday

Figure 16.1. **Otto K. Werckmeister.** *Zitadellenkultur. Die schöne Kunst des Untergangs in der Kultur der achtziger Jahre,* **München/Wien: Carl Hanser, 1989, title page.**

life. The stripes on the man's pants do not signify pajamas but are rather an allusion to the clothing of a prisoner. Although it is not raining, the man on the Wall has an umbrella in his hand and although there is no sun, the man is wearing sunglasses because he must be prepared for all kinds of weather since it seems to be his job to represent the past history of the citadel culture during the day. He is an actor and his function is to remind his audience of the ancient status of the citadel as a kind of spectacle for tourists. The person therefore represents the prisoner of the ancient citadel culture of Stalinism, as a primitive form of power that once needed visible walls to lock up its people. While the Stalinist citadel tried to avoid the borderless stream of communication, the new power of controlling culture works within and not against it. Disturbances are no longer seen as an absolute opposition to the communication that have to be avoided; they can instead be used by the communication systems as material for dramatizations able to reproduce the desire for entertainment. Hence, communication and disturbances have to be synchronized by the power of a new citadel culture into a spectacle of over-communication. This power no longer completely excludes unwanted elements and conflicts with a visible wall, but produces the want to communicate for the sake of communication by using otherness as material for dramatizing entertainments. The fall of the Wall in the real political world did not counteract the up-to-dateness of Bilal's vision. Although Bilal saw the fall of the Wall as a very desirable event, he nevertheless considered the representation of the event by the mass media a grotesque "surmedialisation" (Bilal 1994: 16), overcharging our sense of the reality and its political conflicts.

In *Woman Trap* Jill has an interview with a 14-year-old immigrant in Berlin. Unfortunately this interview does not exist in the English version of the comic, although these pages are constitutive for the construction of its political message. The effect of a "soft" but enduring exclusion by over-communication is shown in the mentality of this young Shiite in 2025: "Yes," the pubescent boy boasts in the interview, "I'm born in Berlin . . . Yes, I have a lot of sisters and brothers. My parents are dead. Of course, I've fought a lot, even killed some men. I have raped someone, so what. It's all normal. And yes, sometimes I dream of a sunny country with camels. I won't stay here anyway . . ." (In the original French version this appears on the second of the last four pages, imitating the layout of the Parisian newspaper *Libération* Jill sends her reports to.) This autobiography is of course a fake, which reproduces the logic of over-communication by exaggerating the social otherness of the young Shiite in order for it to be perceived by the mass media. But there is also the premonition that this myth of an authentic subjectivity will come true. When the young immigrant grows up he realizes that he was nothing but a ghost representing the synchronizing power of over-communication. This power needs such exaggerated and dramatized discourses for entertainment. Later on, the grown-up guy will have an even stronger desire of over-communication by realizing this projection of his otherness.

The criminal trusts dominating the future world with drugs are a metaphor for the desire of over-communication in the trilogy, keeping people dependent on dramatized disturbances. The new world order will not need a wall in order to control unwanted invaders and conflicts any longer because the normalized mass media establishes the map of the frontiers in the mind of the city dwellers by euphemizing any conflict as a dramatic performance. This transforms the public space into an apolitical world of spectacles. The control of the cities now is by an invisible power able to deny the distinction between disturbance and communication within the stream of communication. There is a relevant metaphor that was invented by Claude Lévi-Strauss in order to understand the problem of racism produced by over-communication in the interplay between cultures (Lévi-Strauss 1987: 43–50), although I use this metaphor in a wider sense than the famous French anthropologist: If two trains pass each other in different directions, none of the passengers in the different trains can see each other. But, if they move in the same direction for a while, there is a lot of information about the passengers in the other train to be gained. Thus, a controlling power has to synchronize again and again the speeds between the different streams of information in the city in order to produce sense, which makes forgetting the violence behind such synchronization possible. The other possibility for keeping the stream of communication irreversible is to avoid any synchronization, as if the two trains in the above example were moving in two completely different directions, denying any possibility of information exchange between two different streams of culture. This other force is represented by the violent attack of terrorists in *Woman Trap*. In the situation immediately before the attack of the terrorists, the terrorists do not speak. There is no one speaking apart from John in a phone box. The only message Jill finds after the attack is a message in her dead boyfriend John's hand. It is a note about her success in sending reports written on her typewriter to the past.

Since the extreme positions of normalizing power and terrorist attacks reflect each other in their desire to dramatize reports in the mass media, Jill feels guilty about John's death and decides to stop writing about the systematic slaughter in the cities. From this point on, the discourse in the block text appears as white letters typed on black background. Several pages later we see how these black blocks are transformed into simple signals of a transmission as a result of Jill's second drug overdose, while her typewriter is seen as an apparatus that is out of order. The black block texts, with the white letters typed on a black background, therefore seem to be nothing other than the transmission of her reports via her mysterious typewriter, so that she can only be seen as the narrator of the black blocks. But how can this typewritten report be her narrating voice if she decided to stop writing at the beginning of the story, after the death of John?

Some days before Jill flies from London to Berlin, the comic shows us how Jeff, another friend and journalist, wakes her up from a deep coma as a result of the first overdose she took in order to forget the death of John. We can see how she nevertheless reports in the black boxes the story as if she were observing herself. Obviously the synchronism of pictures and her typed reports represented by black block texts in the comic are an expression of her memory's brainstorming under the influence of drugs. Moreover, after having been woken up by Nikopol and Horus from the dreams of her second breakdown later on in Berlin the black block texts completely disappear. This synchronism of a stream of pictures and typed words, which starts in the story after the decision of Jill to stop writing, is a metaphor for the shifting boundaries between the terrorists and the normalized communication. In the comic, these terrorists belong to criminal trusts dealing with drugs. Iconoclasm or stopping writing about the attacks are acts of illusionary resistance against the normalizing communication. After Jill has told us about the death of her boyfriend John, he appears again. Convinced of his death, Jill cannot therefore be the only narrator of this panel. According to Gerard Genette's theory of narration, the black block texts represent an internal focalization up until this panel: Jill describes what she sees. But in this panel the picture and the typed discourse in the block text are two different points of view in one panel. Since this appearance of John

Figure 16.2. **Enki Bilal. *The Nikopol Trilogy,* Hollywood and New York: Humanoids/ DC 2004, 82.**

would be a counter-sense in the linear narration of Jill, her voice in the black block texts is not synchronized any longer with her perspective to see things. The picture corresponds to another narrating point of view. A distracted reader of comics certainly does not become aware of this double perspective and the end of the linearity in Jill's narration. The second voice remains only implicit. Who might be the second voice in this panel?

In a later sequence of the comic, shortly before Jill's second breakdown, in Berlin, German police are shooting at John who is bleeding white blood. It is white like the color of the paper in the gutter, which is the main medium for a comic's author to maintain the reader's projection. John must be understood as a figure that is more than a simple figure of the narration when he disturbs the logic of linear storytelling. In the theory of the novel it is debated (see Kindt and Müller 2006) whether there is such a thing as the implied author invented by the American theoretician Wayne Booth (Booth 1961: 74, 151). An implied author is the author who is seen by the reader as a second self in his mind because of a certain style in the text: Is the author old, a man or a woman, and so forth? However, in a graphic novel, where stories are told not only with words but also with pictures, there is the interplay between an implied and a more explicit auctorial perspective of narration

Figure 16.3.   **Enki Bilal. *The Nikopol Trilogy,* Hollywood and New York: Humanoids/ DC 2004, 115.**

analogous to the interplay between pictures and words. Therefore I want to adapt a concept of the German theoretician, Wolfgang Iser, that of the author's implicit reader, so that the pictorial representation of a figure as an explicit and undefined person can function as a metonymy for the interplay between an implicit and explicit auctorial narration. Although the figure of John is represented pictorially, every part of his skin, including his face, is hidden by clothes and a mask, which make him mysterious. His face remains undefined and implicit so that the reader can project a second self in spite of his explicit pictorial representation. However, an attentive reader is able to understand that the counter-sense of John's resurrection and the appearance of his white blood are implicit commentaries by the auctorial perspective on the explicit representation of figures in the story.

If we want to understand this ambivalent narrative status as an incitation to an active readership we need more than a semiotic analysis of the representation. Only the paradoxical and ambivalent situation of a modern urban culture could establish the graphic novel as an art form beyond the large-scale production of mainstream comics. This is a paradoxical situation because the mass market is the condition of every avant-garde with strong differences from the mainstream, as Pierre Bourdieu points out in his social theory about art production (Bourdieu 1996: 47–87, 141–60). Without the heteronymous mass market working for profit there could be no freedom for experiments in small-scale production. Only a mass market produces a virtual public where the author is no longer obliged to legitimate the field of power by art production. This is the democratic potential of every mass market but not the reality because profit favors redundant symbolic forms in order to maintain its reproduction.

Scott McCloud argues that the so called "gutter" in comics produces signification (McCloud 1994: 60–5) because it is needed in order to combine at least two pictures into one meaning. We have the first picture as a signifier and the following as the signified of the first. Otherwise we could not speak of the one meaning of two pictures. Indeed, for this function of closure we need the gutter. But I do not agree with McCloud that the gutter has the sole function of combining pictures in the mind of the reader. In semiotics we discern between the paradigm and the syntagm.[1] Whereas the syntagm is nothing but the closure in a linear sequence of a comic, as McCloud describes, the paradigmatic function of signs can stress the single sign as a representation outside of the combination in a sequence. According to Ferdinand de Saussure, every sign is pregnant with a backyard of associations beyond the sense that the sign produces in combination with other signs. The single sign is a knot of associations that are different from the main meaning of a sign established by the logical sequence of the story. Therefore, in the emphasizing of a single sign against the linear sequence lies the potential to produce new meanings beyond the logic of a story. When the synchronism of pictures and typed discourse breaks off in *Woman Trap* (see Figure 16.2), an active reader gets especially involved with the story because one single panel is emphasized against the allegedly irreversible and logical story narrated by Jill. The formal practice of emphasizing a single panel against a sequence makes a story reversible, as Roland Barthes would have described it (Barthes 1981: 37–8).

In comics every panel has the potential of a two-way signification, that is, to be a sign motivated by a linear story and a sign outside of the closure in order to produce a polyvalent meaning against the logic of the story. This is a genuine symbolic value of the comic itself. A film can of course stress the paradigmatic function, but it cannot give to the beholder the possibility of going back in the story. In contrast, the reading of a comic is never fully determined by linear time, meaning its undetermined readership can favor the paradigmatic function within the sequence of pictures far more. The emphasizing of a single panel in a stream of pictures is a genuine urban perception first established by the social conditions in New York at the end of the nineteenth century. The closure of panels (the syntagmatic function) existed in the European caricature as well, especially in the work of Rodolphe Töpffer and Wilhelm Busch. But only the mass market of newspapers in a city of immigrants like New York at the end of the nineteenth century created the paradigmatic cognition of pictures in a sequence of panels because the comic was used as a means of increasing distribution. Analogous to the catchword in the headline, a single picture could function as a "catch-picture" against the devaluation of all pictures by mass production and distribution.

Indeed, the mass market always has the tendency to devaluate the uniqueness of a single picture by bringing things closer to the distracted reader. Long before the established market in New York, this condition can be found in Wilhelm Busch's *Bildergeschichten* in Germany as well.[2] But the melting pot of New York, with its polyphony of different immigrant languages, has always favored the perception of great tension between a single picture and the devaluating stream of images. The catch-picture was necessary in order to produce information analogous to a written headline when a common language did not exist. This is not the return of the uniqueness of academic art: a singled picture in the comic still remains integrated in a devaluating sequence of other pictures. This situation produced an urban gaze/habitus with both a distracted and examining perception by favoring a field of comic production in which the first indications of the differences between mass-market and small-scale production are visible (for example, George Herriman). This potential of a two-way signification of a panel corresponds therefore to the paradoxical habitus of a "distracted examiner," as Walter Benjamin described the mode of cognition of the modern urban public (Benjamin 1968: 241).

According to Bourdieu the autonomy of authorship in small-scale production is not a personal autonomy or a personal self-determination (Bourdieu 1996: 214–77). Authorship is created by the relationship of a specific social market, which is marked by the competition for new symbolic forms, claiming a higher value than the economic market dominated by the fight for profit. The competition between the producers in the small-scale market is more determined by the fight for inventions and the search of new ways to understand the symbolic possibility of their specific art or media. Bilal belongs to the style of the *couleur directe*, which can be seen to be in direct competition to the *ligne claire* invented by Hergé with *Tintin*. Colors having a metaphorical meaning and the refusal of a simple linear story distinguish the *couleur directe*, from the *ligne claire*.

When Nikopol has a nightmare sent to him by the god Horus the whole panel is shown like a picture from a blue-colored screen. While the picture is here shown as a representation in the brain of Nikopol, it nevertheless tells us a story that happens at the same time as a real event seen by the eyes of the god Horus. The blue color is an implicit commentary on authors involved in a meaningful communication of a linear narration with voices synchronized to a single point of view. The title *Woman Trap* seems to be a simple metaphor for the modern myth of the emancipated woman as a cool, man-killing vamp in the city on one level. But the cool colors of Jill here — white skin and blue hair, blue lips, blue eyes, blue tears — are metaphors. As I have argued above, the blue color can be seen as a voice/gaze, which is synchronized to one single cognition whereas the white is a metaphor for a projection by the active reader against the normalized meaning of a simple linear

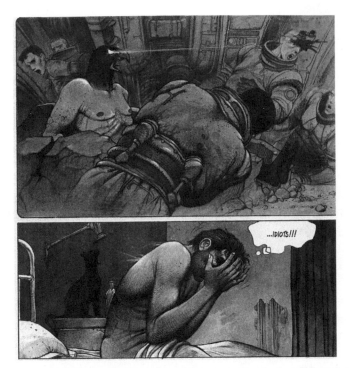

Figure 16.4.   **Enki Bilal.** *The Nikopol Trilogy,* **Hollywood and New York: Humanoids/
DC 2004, 76.**

narration. Jill stands on both sides, like her mysterious lover John: As
a creation of the author she is the woman next to the author but at
the same time she is a projection of the distracted reading of science
fiction, which corresponds to a normalized sense of Jill as an attractive
erotic vamp. Hence, Jill is not a trap because she kills men but because
she is nothing other than the male cliché of a trap for the distracted
reader.[3] All the murders that the female protagonist Jill commits in the
story are not real but fictions committed under the influence of drugs.
The murders happen when John seems to be killed by the attack of
terrorists, since she is still in love with his creator. She kills every other
man trying to have sex with her — with one exception that confirms this
logic. When she meets the Yugoslavian journalist Ivan Vabek in Berlin
she finds that he is the only man she desires after the death of John. As
everybody knows, Bilal was born in Belgrade. As an explicit figure of the
narration, Vabek is only one journalist among others, but he is also an
implicit allusion to Bilal himself.

According to Umberto Eco, the possibility of different levels and a polyvalent code system constitute a main element of what he calls an "open work" one that integrates the reader as an active person to restructure the art work — although I am very hesitant to use the academic label "art work." However, Eco's concept of an open work can be transformed into an "open art production." This way a sociological point of view will avoid the academic formalism of a pure semiotic analysis that does not consider the differences between the normalized mass market and small-scale production as constitutive for symbolic innovations. According to Bourdieu, polyphonic open art production is far less likely in the mass market than in the smale-scale one. Therefore, the author is not dead, like Roland Barthes once proclaimed (Barthes 1994: 493), but he is rather an effect of a field position. Autonomy really exists but as an effect of a social field; however, the belief in an autonomous author as a genius, as an uncreated creator rather threatens this autonomy. "God is dead," Bourdieu says, "but the uncreated creator has taken his place" (Bourdieu 1996: 189). Bilal's concept of narration is quite aware of these two different theories of authorship. On the one hand the implicit commentary of an auctorial perspective occurs by disturbing Jill's linear narration in her stream of consciousness, as I have argued above. But on the other hand there is a moment when the auctorial narrator gets transformed into a sovereign god of the story, that is, into an "uncreated creator" starting up the normalized linear story again. During Jill's second breakdown, John goes to her room in the Berlin Hotel where he meets Horus and Nikopol. The black block texts have disappeared because Jill is senseless and her typewriter destroyed; her narrating voice thus disappears as well. Nikopol is now the narrator of the block texts with black letters on white paper confirming the powerful status of John as the creator who is respected even by the god Horus as the most powerful person in the room. Just as John speaks for the first time after his alleged death, he gives his secret away: "Wrong dosage you little fool," he says to Jill and gives her the right dose in order to wake her up and to start her story again by putting two other pills on the table with the remark: "For another story." With these words he finally gives away that John has become a narrator who keeps the trilogy going on in order to establish the belief in a sovereign authorship.

This narrator can function as a powerful *deus ex machina* and corresponds to the belief in the uncreated creator replacing God, a drug of over-communication that a mass market in the modern city always requires. This drug is the belief in an authorship able to keep on making sense. As a condition of critique, the modern authorship of comics has to acknowledge its double and ambivalent status in apocalyptic science fiction about the urban culture. This double status is symbolized in the *Woman Trap* by John's ambivalent involvement with Jill. With her white and blue body, Jill represents the erotic trap of the mass market and a Trojan horse against it at the same time. A critical authorship has to work with its power of producing meaning against the normalized sequential narration. This reflection of Bilal's position as an effect of his ambivalent social status is clearly distinguishable from the apocalyptic mass-market science fictions about the future of Western cities.

Works cited

Barthes, Roland. "La mort de l'auteur." In: *Œuvres complètes*, Vol. 2, 1966–1973. Paris: Seuil, 1994. 491–5.

Barthes, Roland. "Theory of Text." In: Robert Young (ed.), *Untying the Text: A Postructuralist Reader.* London: Routledge. 1981.

Benjamin, Walter. "The Work of Art in the Time of Mechanical Reproduction." In: Hannah Arendt (ed.), *Illuminations.* New York: Pantheon Books, 1968. 217–51.

Bilal, Enki. "Enki Bilal en 6 chapitres" [Interview with O. Maltret and A. Ledoux]. In: *Sapristi* 29 (Winter 1994). 8–43.

Booth, Wayne. *The Rhetoric of Fiction.* Chicago, IL: University of Chicago Press, 1961.

Bourdieu, Pierre. *The Rules of Art: Genesis and Structure of the Literary Field.* Palo Alto, CA: Stanford University Press, 1996.

Eco, Umberto. *The Open Work.* Cambridge, MA: Harvard University Press, 1989.

Groensteen, Thierry. *Un objet culturel non identifié.* Paris: L'An 2, 2006.

Iser, Wolfgang. *Der implizite Leser. Kommunikationsformen des Romans von Bunyan bis Beckett.* München: Wilhelm Fink, 1972.

Kindt, Tom and Müller, Hans-Harald. *The Implied Author. Concept and Controversy.* New York and Berlin: De Gruyter, 2006.

Le Duc, Dominique. "Femmes en Images et Images de Femmes: L'Heroine de la *Femme Piège* d'Enki Bilal." In: Charles Forsdick *et al.* (eds.), *The Francophone Bande Dessinée.* Amsterdam and New York: Rodopi, 2005. 149–58.

Lévi-Strauss, Claude. *Race et Histoire.* Paris: Gallimard, 1987.

McCloud, Scott. *Understanding Comics. The Invisible Art.* New York: HarperPerennial, 1994.

Werckmeister, Otto K. *Zitadellenkultur. Die Schöne Kunst des Untergangs in der Kultur der achtziger Jahre.* Wien and München: Hanser, 1989.

Notes

1   The terms paradigm and syntagm are better known as part of the linguistic theory of Roman Jakobson. Saussure used instead the distinction between associative and syntagmatic function. Later, Lacan, for example, preferred Saussure's model to Jakobson's because the term associative indicates in a better way that a knot of meanings will be unconsciously implied in every word we use.

2   Rodolphe Töpffer published his first book *Monsieur Jabot* in 1831. The first *Bildergeschichten* of Wilhelm Bush were published in 1854; his book *Max und Moritz*, the model for the later *Katzenjammer Kids* of Rudolph Dirks, found its first success in the mass market in 1868.

3   The analysis of the heroine in *Woman Trap* as an ambivalent representation between a femme fatale and a victim of male desires (see Le Duc 2005: 152) seems to be the only obvious normalized level of the narration.